EXPLORING IMAGINARY WORLDS

From *The Brothers Karamazov* to *Star Trek* to *Twin Peaks*, this collection explores a variety of different imaginary worlds both historic and contemporary.

Featuring contributions from an interdisciplinary and international group of scholars, each essay looks at a particular imaginary world in-depth, and world-building issues associated with that world. Together, the essays explore the relationship between the worlds and the media in which they appear as they examine imaginary worlds in literature, television, film, computer games, and theatre, with many existing across multiple media simultaneously. The book argues that the media incarnation of a world affects world structure and poses unique obstacles to the act of world-building. The worlds discussed include Nazar, Barsetshire, Skotopogonievsk, the Vorkosigan Universe, Grover's Corners, Gormenghast, Collinsport, Daventry, Dune, the *Death Gate Cycle* universe, Twin Peaks, and the *Star Trek* galaxy.

A follow-up to Mark J. P. Wolf's field-defining book *Building Imaginary Worlds*, this collection will be of critical interest to students and scholars of popular culture, subcreation studies, transmedia studies, literature, and beyond.

Mark J. P. Wolf is Professor in the Communication Department at Concordia University, Wisconsin. His 23 books include *The Video Game Theory Reader 1* and *2* (2003, 2008), *The Video Game Explosion* (2007), *Myst & Riven: The World of the D'ni* (2011), *Before the Crash: An Anthology of Early Video Game History* (2012), *Encyclopedia of Video Games* (2012), *Building Imaginary Worlds* (2012), *The Routledge Companion to Video Game Studies* (2014), *LEGO Studies* (2014), *Video Games Around the World* (2015), *Revisiting Imaginary Worlds* (2016), *Video Games FAQ* (2017), *The World of Mister Rogers' Neighborhood* (2017), *The Routledge Companion to Imaginary Worlds* (2018), and *The Routledge Companion to Media Technology and Obsolescence* (2018), which won the SCMS 2020 award for Best Edited Collection.

EXPLORING IMAGINARY WORLDS

Essays on Media, Structure, and Subcreation

Edited by Mark J. P. Wolf

Routledge
Taylor & Francis Group

NEW YORK AND LONDON

First published 2021
by Routledge
52 Vanderbilt Avenue, New York, NY 10017

and by Routledge
2 Park Square, Milton Park, Abingdon, Oxon, OX14 4RN

Routledge is an imprint of the Taylor & Francis Group, an informa business

Library of Congress Cataloging-in-Publication Data
A catalog record for this title has been requested

ISBN: 978-0-367-19730-8 (hbk)
ISBN: 978-0-429-24291-5 (ebk)

Typeset in Bembo
by codeMantra

A. M. D. G.

CONTENTS

CONTRIBUTORS

Scott Adams was born in Miami, Florida, and is now living in Platteville, Wisconsin. Scott was the first person known to create the first commercial adventure-style game for personal computers with his first game, *Adventureland* (1978). His company, Adventure International, released games for many major computer platforms throughout the 1980s. Adams worked as a senior programmer for AVISTA in Platteville until 2016. Scott founded Clopas, the "PLAY the game! LIVE the adventure! CREATE your story!" company in 2017, with his wife of 30 years, Roxanne. Scott and Team Clopas are currently working on *Adventureland XL*, a Conversational Adventure™ game, in celebration of the original's 40th anniversary, with a holiday 2019 release. [scott.adams@ clopas.net]

Lily Alexander, PhD, has taught in New York since 2003, including at NYU and Hunter College, CUNY. She has a Master's degree in Drama and Film, and a dual doctorate in Anthropology and Comparative Cultural Studies. Her research interests include symbolic anthropology, semiotics of culture, creative algorithms, and evolution of consciousness. She has taught world mythology, history and theory of narrative media, comparative literature, genre studies, science fiction, comedy, story structure, screenwriting, interactive storytelling, and world-building. She has presented at 40+ conferences, including the MIT *Media in Transition* series and the forum *Cognitive Futures*. She wrote for the History Channel, henryjenkins.org, *The Journal of Narrative Theory*, *Cinema Journal*, and *Cinema Art*. Her publications also appeared in Italy, France, the Netherlands, Canada, Russia, and Israel. She contributed to book collections *Filmbuilding* (2001), *Revisiting Imaginary Worlds* (2017), and *The Routledge Companion to Imaginary Worlds* (2017). Lily Alexander authored a book set, *Fictional Worlds:*

Traditions in Narrative and the Age of Visual Culture (2013/2014). Her website is: storytellingonscreen.com. [lily.alexander@hunter.cuny.edu]

Helen Conrad O'Briain was born in Wheeling, West Virginia, but has lived most of her adult life in Dublin where she is adjunct Professor of Old English and Old Norse at Trinity College. She has published on Augustinian theology in early insular Latin literature, the Middle English "Breton" Lais, and Trinity Vergil incunabula, as well as on the works of M. R. James, Dorothy Sayers, and Phyllis McGinley. She is the author, with Laura Cleaver, of the forthcoming catalog of Trinity and Chester Beatty Psalter manuscripts. [conrado@tcd.ie]

Christopher Hanson is an Associate Professor in the English Department at Syracuse University, where he teaches courses in games studies, digital media, television, and film. His book *Game Time: Understanding Temporality in Video Games* was published by Indiana University Press in spring 2018 and his next book project is on game designer Roberta Williams. He previously worked for a number of years in video game and software development. His work has appeared in the *Quarterly Review of Film and Video*, *Film Quarterly*, the *Routledge Companion to Video Game Studies* (2014), and *LEGO Studies: Examining the Building Blocks of a Transmedial Phenomenon* (2014). [cphanson@syr.edu]

Jennifer Harwood-Smith has a PhD from Trinity College Dublin, and is researching world-building in science fiction. She has contributed two chapters to *Battlestar Galactica: Mission Accomplished or Mission Frakked Up?*, "I Frak, Therefore I Am", and "Dreamers in the Night". She has also co-authored "'Doing it in style': The Narrative Rules of Time Travel in the *Back to the Future Trilogy*" with Frank Ludlow, published in *The Worlds of Back to the Future: Critical Essays on the Films*. Her essay "Fractured Cities: The Twinning of Tolkien's Minas Tirith and Minas Morgul with Fritz Lang's *Metropolis*" has been published in *J.R.R. Tolkien: The Forest and the City*. She is the 2006 winner of the James White Award and has published fiction in *Interzone* and with Ether Books. [harwoodj@tcd.ie]

Andrew Higgins is a Tolkien scholar who specializes in exploring the role of language invention in fiction. His thesis "The Genesis of Tolkien's Mythology" (which he is currently preparing for publication) explored the interrelated nature of myth and language in Tolkien's earliest work. He is also the co-editor with Dr. Dimitra Fimi of *A Secret Vice: Tolkien on Invented Languages* (HarperCollins, 2016). Recently he has had papers published in *A Wilderness of Dragons: Essays in Honour or Verlyn Flieger* (Gabbro Head Press, 2018) and *Sub-creating Arda* (Walking Tree Publishers, 2019). He has also taught an online course on language invention for Signum University/Mythgard Institute and is a Trustee of Signum University and the UK Tolkien Society. He is also Director of Fundraising at Glyndebourne Opera in East Sussex England. [asthiggins@me.com]

Matt Hills is Professor of Film & TV Studies at Aberystwyth University. He is the author of *Fan Cultures* (2002) and *Triumph of a Time Lord* (2010) among other titles. His work has been published in the *Journal of Fandom Studies*, *International Journal of Cultural Studies*, *Science Fiction Film and Television*, *Participations: The Journal of Audience & Reception Studies*, and the *Journal of Transformative Works and Cultures*. His latest book is the edited collection *New Dimensions of Doctor Who* (2013), and he's currently working on a new monograph, *Sherlock — Detecting Quality Television*. [mjh35@aber.ac.uk]

Edward James is Emeritus Professor of Medieval History at University College Dublin, working on early medieval European history. A long-term SF fan, he began writing about science fiction in the 1980s, and for fourteen years was editor of *Foundation: The International Review of Science Fiction*. He has won many of the awards in the field, including the Eaton Award (for *Science Fiction in the Twentieth Century*), the Pilgrim Award, the Hugo Award (for *The Cambridge Companion to Science Fiction*, co-edited with Farah Mendlesohn), the BSFA Award for Non-Fiction (for his website on Science Fiction and Fantasy Writers in the Great War), and most recently the IAFA's Distinguished Scholarship Award. His most recent book is on Lois McMaster Bujold. [edwardfjames@gmail.com]

Kara Kennedy is a PhD candidate in English at the University of Canterbury studying the representation of women in Frank Herbert's *Dune* series. She has published on the significant role that names play in the world-building in *Dune*. She also researches in the field of Digital Humanities and is looking to analyze 20th-century science fiction in new ways through digital technology. [dunescholar@gmail.com]

Lars Konzack is an Associate Professor at The Royal School of Library and Information Science in Denmark. He has an MA degree in information science and a PhD degree in Multimedia. He is working with subjects such as ludology, game analysis and design, geek culture, and subcreation. He has, among others things, published "Computer Game Criticism: A Method for Computer Game Analysis" (2002), "Rhetorics of Computer and Video Game Research" (2007), "Video Games in Europe" (2007), and "Philosophical Game Design" (2008). [mtw296@iva.ku.dk]

Edward O'Hare is a PhD student at Trinity College Dublin. After studying for a Degree in Philosophy, he completed anMPhil in Popular Literature in 2009. Since 2012 he has been working on a thesis on Antarctic Gothic

Literature, focusing on the Polar Fictions of writers including Edgar Allan Poe, Jules Verne, H. P. Lovecraft, and John W. Campbell Jr. A regular contributor to *The Irish Journal of Gothic and Horror Studies*, he has published articles and reviews on a range of subjects. His research interests include Victorian Gothic Fiction, Imaginary Voyage Narratives, Ghost Stories and other Supernatural Fiction, the Weird Tale, British and American Horror and Science-Fiction of the 1950s, 60s, and 70s, and Cult Cinema and Television of the past and present. [ohareer@tcd.ie]

William Proctor is a lecturer at the University of Sunderland, UK, where he teaches in Film, Media, and Cultural Studies. His PhD thesis examines the reboot phenomenon in comics and film and was published by New York University Press in 2015. William has published articles and book chapters on *The Walking Dead*, Batman, and the fan reaction to the Lucasfilm takeover by Disney alongside a number of articles on the reboot phenomenon. His next pursuit is an audience research project focusing on fantasy fans in collaboration with Martin Barker and an edited collection which explores the impact of Nordic Noir. [billyproctor@hotmail.co.uk]

Mark J. P. Wolf is a Professor in the Communication Department at Concordia University Wisconsin. His books include *Abstracting Reality: Art, Communication, and Cognition in the Digital Age* (2000), *The Medium of the Video Game* (2001), *Virtual Morality: Morals, Ethics, and New Media* (2003), *The Video Game Theory Reader* (2003), *The Video Game Explosion: A History from PONG to PlayStation and Beyond* (2007), *The Video Game Theory Reader 2* (2008), *Myst and Riven: The World of the D'ni* (2011), *Before the Crash: Early Video Game History* (2012), *Encyclopedia of Video Games: The Culture, Technology, and Art of Gaming* (two-volume First Edition, 2012; three-volume Second Edition, forthcoming), *Building Imaginary Worlds: The Theory and History of Subcreation* (2012), *The Routledge Companion to Video Game Studies* (2014), *LEGO Studies: Examining the Building Blocks of a Transmedial Phenomenon* (2014), *Video Games Around the World* (2015), the four-volume *Video Games and Gaming Cultures* (2016), *Revisiting Imaginary Worlds: A Subcreation Studies Anthology* (2017), *Video Games FAQ* (2017), *The World of Mister Rogers' Neighborhood* (2017), *The Routledge Companion to Imaginary Worlds* (2017), *The Routledge Companion to Media History and Obsolescence* (2018), *101 Enigmatic Puzzles: Fractal Mazes, Quantum Chess, Anagram Sudoku, and More* (2020), *World-Builders on World-Building: An Exploration of Subcreation* (2020), and two novels for which he is looking for a publisher. He is also founder and co-editor of the Landmark Video Game book series from the University of Michigan Press and the founder of the Video Game Studies Scholarly Interest Group within the Society of Cinema and Media Studies. He has been invited to speak in North America, South America, Europe, Asia, and *Second Life*; has had work published in journals including *Compar(a)ison*,

Convergence, Film Quarterly, Games and Culture, New Review of Film and Television Studies, Projections, Religions, and *The Velvet Light Trap*; is on the advisory boards of Videotopia, the International Arcade Museum Library, and the *International Journal of Gaming and Computer-Mediated Simulations*; and is on several editorial boards including those of *Games and Culture* and *The Journal of E-media Studies.* He lives in Wisconsin with his wife Diane and his sons Michael, Christian, and Francis. [mark.wolf@cuw.edu]

FOREWORD

The original world-building, according to some of the most ancient texts that are still available to us today, is said to have taken place long ago when God spoke everything into existence.

It seems that this Creator was not wanting to just create a sterile puppet world that would only follow a preset program. There must have been a much deeper plan at work, since along with the Universe, He also created humans, and more importantly, as the ancient texts report, He made the latter in His own Image.

A very odd turn of phrase indeed. Many may take that to mean this Creator is an anthropomorphic being that exists in a state similar to our own and his shape is that which mankind owes its physical appearance.

There seems to be many issues with that idea. Perhaps instead it meant giving humans something very special. A piece of Himself in their very nature, so they could then truly reflect His ultimate Image.

If so, that piece may be Free Will with its very important offshoot of Creativity. Ultimately, though He was in overall control, His creation could do things as they desired within the reality He had created for them.

The articles in this treatise all have an underlying theme. They all look at the works of people creating worlds that did not previously exist, but even more interesting is they all look at works that were originally created for the entertainment of others.

The importance of the latter shows the very deep-seated desire that exists in people to not only be entertained but also for many the desire to create things that have never existed before, even if that creation itself is only imaginary with just tenuous roots in our reality.

Mankind has an innate drive to both create and to also be entertained by new creations. Speaking from my own experiences, nothing brings more joy to a world creator than seeing others also enjoy that creation. One without the other is useless. A creator wants an audience and audiences need creators. Perhaps that's why Humankind is even here?

Let's go ahead now and look at some of the more notable world-builders and their creations, along with how they touched the diverse audiences that interacted with them.

Scott Adams

December 16, 2019

Scott Adams is author of the Scott Adams series of adventure games and co-founder of Adventure International and Clopas LLC. Born in Miami, Florida, and now living in Platteville, Wisconsin, Adams was the first person known to create an adventure-style game for personal computers with his first game, Adventureland. His company, Adventure International, released games for many major computer platforms throughout the 1980s. Adams worked as a senior programmer for AVISTA in Platteville until 2016. Scott founded Clopas, the "PLAY the game! LIVE the adventure! CREATE your story!" company in 2017, with his wife of 30 years, Roxanne. Scott and Team Clopas are currently working on *Adventureland XL, a Conversational Adventure*™ game, in celebration of the original's 40th anniversary, aiming for a holiday release 2019. Adams's works include the classic Adventure game series of 14 games: *Adventure #1 — Adventureland* (1978), *Adventure #2 — Pirate Adventure* (1979), *Adventure #3 — Secret Mission* (1979), *Adventure #4 — Voodoo Castle* (1979), *Adventure #5 — The Count* (1979), *Adventure #6 — Strange Odyssey* (1979), *Adventure #7 — Mystery Fun House* (1979), *Adventure #8 — Pyramid of Doom* (1979), *Adventure #9 — Ghost Town* (1980), *Adventure #10 — Savage Island, Part I* (1980), *Adventure #11 — Savage Island, Part II* (1981), *Adventure #12 — Golden Voyage* (1981), *Adventure #13 — Sorcerer of Claymorgue Castle* (1984), and *Adventure #14 — Return to Pirate's Isle* (1984), as well as *Return To Pirate Island 2* (2001), *The Inheritance* (2013), and *Escape the Gloomer* (2018), a game set in the Redwall Universe of Brian Jacques.

ACKNOWLEDGMENTS

An anthology like this is only possible because of all the people who enjoy writing and reading about imaginary worlds, and I am grateful to see this interdisciplinary area of study increasing in academia over the years. I would like to thank video game designer Scott Adams for his Foreword, and for all the work he has done to advance world-building in text adventure games. A hearty thanks go to all the contributors, Lily Alexander, Helen Conrad-O'Briain, Christopher Hanson, Andrew Higgins, Jennifer Harwood-Smith, Matt Hills, Edward James, Kara Kennedy, Lars Konzack, Edward O'Hare, and William Proctor for their participation and great essays, and for the on-line conversations we have had regarding imaginary worlds. I am also grateful for the enthusiasm and encouragement of Erica Wetter at Routledge, and the anonymous book proposal reviewers for their thoughtful and thorough reviews. Thanks also to my wife Diane and my sons Michael, Christian, and Francis, who put up with me during the time while I was working on this book. And, as always, thanks be to God, the Creator of all subcreators.

INTRODUCTION

Mark J. P. Wolf

I find it amusing, and secretly pleasing, that I have so many fans who are interested in the history. I'm not sure if they would so eagerly study real history, you know? In school perhaps they're bored with all the Henrys in English history, but they'll gladly follow the Targaryen dynasty.

—George R. R. Martin[1]

It is probably true that there are fans in a number of fandoms — those of the worlds of Tolkien, *Star Wars*, *Star Trek*, and others — who know the histories of their favorite imaginary worlds better than that of the real-world country they live in. Of course, one of the major differences between the history of a secondary world versus the history of the Primary World is that the former is always finite, and thus there exists the possibility of knowing it all; a mastery that is simply not possible when it comes to real-world history. The bigger the world, the greater the challenge, perhaps, but an imaginary world is always finite, despite all the gaps and missing pieces that allow fans to endlessly speculate and extrapolate a world. Rather than create a feeling of being unfinished, gaps and missing pieces invite participation and speculation, examination of a world's many details, and many return visits.

Our ability to explore an imaginary world varies greatly from author to author, medium to medium, and world to world. Some authors, particularly in the area of literature, see the world in which their story is set as merely the background for it; we are given only as much of the background world as is needed to advance the story, and no more. Indeed, this kind of narrative–centric outlook is even often taught to authors, who are told to keep moving the story along, like a horse with blinders being driven at full gallop. Others are more leisurely and give their readers a little time to look around and experience their worlds, building more of it than what is strictly needed just for the story. Some, like Austin Tappan Wright, enjoy world-building so much that their worlds are arguably just as important as the stories set in them, which, of course, are often inseparable, as it should be. In fact, Wright so enjoyed world-building that his original draft of *Islandia* (1942) was around 2,300 pages or so when he died in 1931, not including another 135,000-word document about the world's history, and more appendices as well. It was Wright's widow who transcribed her husband's novel, cutting it down by about a third of its length, before finally getting it published 11 years after his death. Plenty of fantasy and science fiction authors have included appendices, glossaries, timelines, maps, and so forth with their novels, enriching the experience of the visitors who wish to visit them.

The medium used to represent a world also has a great impact on the visitor's experience. In audiovisual media, we often get to see a wealth of detail, some only tantalizing glimpses of wide and distant vistas that only hint at all the things that lay beyond the scope of the story being told; paths untrodden and places unseen which give rise to speculation as to what we may find there if we are ever allowed to return for further exploration. Some fans, unwilling to wait or frustrated at the limits of their visits, turn to fan fiction, exploring the potential offered by a world. Interactive media, like video games or virtual reality, go one step further than film and television, by allowing the audience to navigate the world themselves, often not without goals, challenges, obstacles, and nemeses. These vicarious experiences may explain why video games have displaced more traditional media like film and television, though they both have certainly continued to flourish as well.

Finally, some worlds are made with exploration in mind, regardless of the media in which they appear; plenty of world data detail is available, in every imaginable form, narrative and nonnarrative, through word, image, sound, object, and interaction, and every kind of object and experience one can offer (and often sell) to an audience. Naturally, it is these kinds of worlds, going beyond the stories set in them, which are most enjoyably and fruitfully explored, and are thus the kind to be examined in detail in an anthology like this one.

As a follow-up to my book *Revisiting Imaginary Worlds* (itself a follow-up to *Building Imaginary Worlds*), *Exploring Imaginary Worlds* is not only the exploration of imaginary worlds in general, but also the exploration of particular, individual worlds, a different one for each essay in this collection. Nazar, Barsetshire, Skotoprigonyevsk, the Vorkosigan universe, Grover's Corners, Gormenghast, Collinsport, Daventry, Arrakis, Chelestra, Twin Peaks, and the Star Trek universe are a wide range of locales, but they all share one thing in common; they began in someone's imagination and grew from there. Together, these essays explore the relationship between these worlds and the media in which they appear. Some are made entirely of words, while others are designed to appear in audiovisual form, whether on stage, movie screen, television screen, computer monitor (with interactivity), or across multiple media venues simultaneously. Different media incarnations also affect world structures, posing different obstacles to further world-building of the world due to the varying requirement of different media venues, and the capabilities of different time periods during which the world-building occurred.

The essays present in this collection are each about a particular imaginary world, ranging in time from Ludvig Holberg's novel of 1741 to the *Star Trek* of 2019. After the Introduction, which examines what it means to explore an imaginary worlds, and the various pleasures and lessons it can provide, we have 15 essays arranged in 3 sections, each with a different focus. The first section, "Worlds of Words", looks at the earliest form of world experiences, literary worlds, which arose out of books, each written by authors who had to rely on words alone for the building of their worlds. The worlds examined here include Nazar, the world of Ludvig Holberg's *Niels Klim's Underground Travels* (1741) which is the subject of Lars Konzack's essay. This is followed by Helen Conrad O'Briain's study of Barsetshire, the imaginary British county which was invented by Anthony Trollope, and has been added to by other authors over the next hundred years or so, placing it among the early transauthorial worlds. Next, Lily Alexander looks at what she refers to as the "Journeyworld" of Dostoevsky's *The Brothers Karamazov* (1880), the symbolic, mythological world through which the characters travel. Finally, Edward James looks at the creation of the Vorkosigan Universe in the novels of Lois McMaster Bujold, who has continued adding planets to her world over her long career.

The second section, "Worlds across Media", expands out to worlds which are depicted in audiovisual form; my own essay looks at world-building on the theatrical stage and particularly in Thornton Wilder's *Our Town* (1938), examining the difficulties of world-building on the stage and how Wilder succeeds in producing an immersive world. Edward O'Hare's essay on Mervin Peake's *Gormenghast* examines its world, which has been adapted into various media, relating it to the themes of tradition and disintegration, and the desire to escape from history. Next, Andrew Higgins writes about the television series *Dark Shadows* (1966–1971) which was remade as a feature film of the same name in 2012, and the Gothic world-building taking place in it. The last essay of the section is on Daventry, a video game world from the *King's Quest* series of computer games (1980–2016), which Christopher Hanson examines.

The third section, "Transmedia Worlds", begins with Kara Kennedy's examination of the impact of the social sciences on world-building in Frank Herbert's Dune universe, followed by Jennifer Harwood-Smith's take on the topic of balance and interconnectivity in the worlds of Margaret Weis and Tracy Hickman's *The Death Gate Cycle*. The last two essays examine the recent extension of two long-running television franchises, which began on television and spread to other media; Matt Hills explores the continuation of David Lynch and Mark Frost's *Twin Peaks* franchise, after a hiatus of nearly a quarter century, while William Proctor looks at the problems faced by the new reboot of *Star Trek*, and their solutions and repositioning of the franchise and the perils of pre-quelization. Finally, the Appendix, "On Measuring and Comparing Imaginary Worlds", is a reflection on the attempt to compare subcreated worlds with each other, how one might go about doing it, the problems encountered, and what may be possible.

Of course, the essays presented here have many overlapping concerns and together they provide the reader an exploration of world-building examples that extend over several hundred years, and through multiple media incarnations, including literature, plays, movies, television shows, video games, comics, trading cards, and more. Together, the essays demonstrate a wide yet related range of approaches and concerns found within Subcreation Studies, providing the reader analyses of worlds and the world-building used to create them. As their contributor biographies reveal, the distinguished set of contributors whose work is collected here come from interdisciplinary backgrounds which include the theory, history, and practice of world-building, the variety of which further enriches the explorations found in this volume.

While these essays may function like travelogues, introducing the worlds they survey, they naturally cannot convey more than a glimpse of the worlds they discuss, so they should be seen as invitations encouraging readers to make their own excursions into these worlds, perhaps enjoying them from a new perspective if they are already familiar with them, or enjoying them entirely as first-time visitors. Either way, it is hoped that these essays will not only aid readers in the exploration of imaginary worlds, but will perhaps even inspire them to explore other worlds, or even the *potential* of imaginary worlds, through attempts at building their own.

Note

1 As quoted in Gilmore, M., "George R. R. Martin: The Rolling Stone Interview", *Rolling Stone*, April 23, 2014, available at https://www.rollingstone.com/culture/culture-news/george-r-r-martin-the-rolling-stone-interview-242487/.

Worlds of Words

1

THE JOURNEY OF NIELS KLIM TO THE WORLD UNDERGROUND BY LUDVIG HOLBERG

Subcreation and Social Criticism

Lars Konzack

Ludvig Holberg (1684–1754) is the father of both Danish and Norwegian liter-ature. Inspired by Jonathan Swift's *Gulliver's Travels* (1726), Holberg, sometimes referred to as Lewis Holberg, wrote *The Journey of Niels Klim to the World Un-derground* (original Latin: *Nicolai Klimii Iter Subterraneum*) concerning a journey into the Hollow Earth, published in 1741, and a second edition in 1745 adding the Apologetic Preface as the noteworthy change. While Ludvig Holberg, as playwright, wrote in Danish, he wrote *The Journey of Niels Klim to the World Underground* in Latin and published it in Leipzig in order to reach a larger audi-ence and avoid reprisals in Denmark. *The Journey of Niels Klim to the World Un-derground* was Ludvig Holberg's breakthrough novel among the scholarly public of 18th-century Europe.

It is a strange work in the sense that apart from being a traveler's tale, science fiction, and contemporary satire, it is a work of high style and light comedy at the same time. It is the story of Niels Klim, returning to his native Bergen in Norway after ten years of study at the University of Copenhagen in Denmark. One must keep in mind that Denmark-Norway was a dual Monarchy at the time. Inside the Hollow Earth, Klim meets the sentient and philosophical trees from the planet Nazar orbiting around a sun in the middle of the Earth. Hol-berg reveals a utopian society of sentient trees as well as many different sentient minor tree societies. Eventually, the government exiles Klim to the inner rim of the Earth's crust. Here he meets a sentient monkey society, becomes a slave, and ends up as a conqueror and a malevolent tyrant before returning to his home in Norway. His journey there and back again took 12 years.

What makes Hoberg's *The Journey of Niels Klim to the World Underground* interesting or even remarkable? How does it relate other literary genres like satire, utopian fiction, fantasy, and science fiction? What themes and content makes it distinct and why is it mostly unknown to the public?

Summary

The novel has autobiographical inclinations because the author, Ludvig Holberg, just like Niels Klim, grew up in Bergen and came to Denmark to study at the University of Copenhagen. However, the similarities stop there. In the year 1664, Klim examines a cave in a mountain. With a rope around his waist, he is slowly descending into the unknown until the rope breaks (Figure 1.1).

Klim falls, but suddenly comes to a halt. He does not crash down on the planet Nazar orbiting the sun at the center of the Earth. Instead, he finds himself floating between Earth's crust and the planet. The gravitational forces catch Klim and he finds himself orbiting the planet. A griffin attacks him and after a fight, they plunge down onto the planet Nazar. He ends up in the land of Potu (Utop(ia) backwards). Attacked by an ox, he climbs up a tree, which to his surprise, is able to speak and even move around. They are sentient tree-like beings with faces right below the braches and with up to six arms. Klim is taken into custody accused attempted rape of the mayor's wife. It becomes apparent that it has been a misunderstanding and Klim is sentenced to learn the native language.

Potu is the land of reason, a realm of sentient and very sensible trees, and comes closest to a perfect state in the eyes of Holberg. It is also the part of the novel with the most coherent subcreation, introducing the reader to how the Potuan society and the planet Nazar work. The subcreation of Nazar presents a

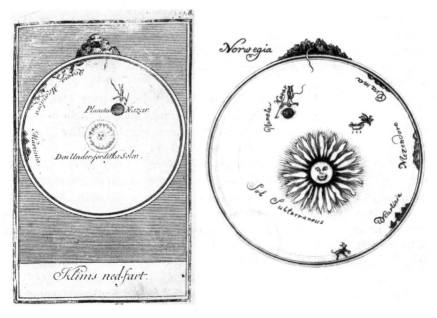

FIGURE 1.1 Map of the underground world.

planet with one language of which the reader only gets a small sample of words and phrases, geographical knowledge, education, the laws of Potu, and the Potuans' relationship to religion.

The planet is scarcely 600 miles all around the globe. The roads have milestones with clear markings of distances. We also learn that there are different kinds of tree inhabitants on the planet such as oak, lime, poplar, thorn, and pine trees.

Before his banishment, Klim comes to be the messenger for the King and Queen and is later asked to visit the whole planet because he has the ability move much faster than the trees. Although, they also think he is too hasty and he gets the nickname "Skabba" that means "overhasty". The Potuans' value measured consideration rather than rushed decisions and project making. Klim visits 27 provinces of different species of sentient trees, turning his explorations into a book. The book becomes popular and Klim hopes to advance in society. Following his success, he becomes ambitious and proposes that women should become second-class citizens. The Potuans reject his suggestion and exile him from Nazar to the firmament, the underside of the Earth's interior.

Klim arrives at the City of Martinia, the habitants of which are intelligent monkeys. Again, he learns the native language. Contrary to the Potuans, the Martinians are quick-witted and superficial. They view him as dimwitted and sluggish and name him "Kakidoran" meaning "slow" or "hebetated". Nevertheless, Klim becomes an instant success when he introduces the French fashion of wigs. Now a respectable nobleman, Klim lives in luxury among High Society. His luck, however, changes after a couple of years when the president's wife falls in love with him. He rejects her and she accuses him of trying to seduce her. In order to save his life Klim pleads guilty and subsequently sentenced to become a galley slave on a trading voyage to the Mezendorian islands.

On this journey as a galley slave, he encounters Music-land in which everyone is a musical instrument and then arrives shortly at Pyglossia, where the Pyglossians disgustingly communicate by breaking wind. During this voyage, Klim come across a range of other peculiar beings and wondrous civilizations.

Following a disastrous shipwreck, Klim ends up among a savage human tribe named Quama (the only savages mentioned in the entire book) and turns them into his army. He introduces guns and gunpowder into the underworld and sets out to conquer the entire firmament, and in the course of this empire building, he marries a deceased emperors' daughter and becomes a tyrannical ruler. During his campaign he rejects the offer of marrying an emperor's daughter, a beautiful lioness, because he is already married. Finally, the people rebel against him and he flees into a cavern and returns to Norway where he originally came from.

Niels Klim has been away for 12 years. An old friend of Klim's listens to his story and advises him not to go public with his adventures in the wake of religious persecution. He therefore decides to keep quiet about his exploits and settles down as a custodian, marries a merchant's daughter, Magdalena, and has three sons, Christian, Jesper, and Caspar. His friend later publishes Klim's manuscript posthumously.

The Question of Genre

The question of the genre of *The Journey of Niels Klim to the World Underground* has been a matter of debate. There is a long tradition of fictional travel narratives going back to at the very least *The Tale of the Shipwrecked Sailor* (The Middle Kingdom, 2000–1500 BC) and *The Odyssey* (8th century BC). Lucian of Samosata's *True History* (125 AD), *The Book of Sir John Mandeville* (1357), Margaret Cavendish's *The Description of a New World, Called The Blazing-World* (1666), and Jonathan Swift's *Gulliver's Travels* (1726) are noteworthy examples of this genre. Often these stories present a glimpse into a world of wonder but also a world of satire and social criticism. In many cases, this kind of social criticism is necessary because it is unwise and even dangerous to criticize a contemporary power structure directly. Holberg was aware of this long tradition and knew as playwright how satire happened to be useful as social criticism, too (Paludan, 1878).

Peter Fitting recognizes three genres in the work of Ludvig Holberg: (1) utopia, (2) satire, and (3) fantasy (Fitting, 1996, 2018). Potu is of course Holberg's utopia. Here, Holberg introduces the reader to a world in which men and women are equal and the laws of the land are rational. The satire begins when Niels Klim leaves Potu and journeys to the Nazar provinces and continues on the firmament up until Klim becomes a galley slave. It then turns into almost entirely fantasy when Klim fights his way from galley slave to become a conqueror and sinister tyrant.

It is, however, possible to comprehend the entire novel as the genre of fantasy fiction. From this perspective, the novel is a fictional chronicle complete with an epic travel adventure, strange lands, a map of the fantasy world, fragments of fictional history books, and fantasy races with their own languages like the tree-people of Nazar, the Monkey-people of Martinia, and many others. Particularly, the tree-people causes a modern fantasy reader to think of Tolkien's Ents and it has even been suggested that Tolkien was in fact inspired by *The Journey of Niels Klim to the World Underground* (McNelis, 2006). Surely, Holberg found inspiration for some of his races in Plinius (Paludan, 1878). The entrance to the fantasy world is also an often-used trope in fantasy fiction.

Klim falls through a hole like Alice does in Lewis Carroll's fantasy novel *Alice's Adventures in Wonderland* (1865), although she fell through a smaller hole. C. S. Lewis in his fantasy novel *The Lion, the Witch, and the Wardrobe* (1950) likewise uses this trope of suddenly entering a fantasy world through a passage when Peter, Susan, Edmund, and Lucy walk into a wardrobe and reach the world of Narnia. This is different from other books like *The Hobbit* (1937) and *The Lord of The Rings* (1955) by J. R. R. Tolkien, where the subcreation is not only just a backdrop for a visit to a fantasy world, but also exists in its entirety and totality as fully fledged as possible. The problem with visiting a fantasy world and returning to the Primary World is that the people from the Primary World do not necessarily believe the returning visitor's account of the experienced events. This applies to Lucy returning from Narnia as well as Niels Klim, risking religious persecution if he goes public with his story. Tzvetan Todorov terms an accepted supernatural world as "the Marvelous", while uncertainty of the supernatural world is termed "the Fantastic-Marvelous" (Todorov, 1975). Within this terminology, *The Journey of Niels Klim to the World Underground* is reckoned as Fantastic-Marvelous. Even so, the Marvelous and the Fantastic-Marvelous are both considered instances of fantasy fiction.

Furthermore, *The Journey of Niels Klim to the World Underground* presents magic and references to myth and folklore. In the introduction, we are being told that in Norway many superstitious people believe in fairies and supernatural spirits coming from under the mountains. Fittingly, Norwegian folklore is bursting with mountain dwellers like trolls and goblins who spellbind and enthrall humans, replacing human babies with changelings (Holbek and Piø, 1967). In addition, a Finnish shaman portrayed in the Apologetic Preface to *The Journey of Niels Klim to the World Underground* practices witchcraft to turn himself into an eagle. When Klim enters the fantasy world, he encounters a griffin — a classical mythical creature. Even so, it is unclear if the fantasy races are magical beings. The fantasy world, it seems, does not really use magic at all. There are no wizards or magical items. The shaman appeared in Norway (the normal world), not in the Nazar or the firmament. This gives one the impression that Holberg is playing wittingly with our prejudices.

The lack of magic in the fantasy world leaves us with another option that Holberg's novel could be considered science fiction. Depending on one's perspective, science fiction began when Hugo Gernsback coined the term in 1926, or when Jules Verne published *Journey to the Center of the Earth* (1864), or when Mary Shelley Published *Frankenstein: A Modern Prometheus* (1818). Works before that are often considered proto-science fiction, although scholars do not agree and some accept any work of fiction with science fiction tropes to be more-or-less science fiction regardless of age. Accordingly, *The Journey of Niels Klim to the World Underground* is either proto-science fiction or plain science fiction. If we accept Holberg's novel as science fiction, then it is one of the first science fiction novels in history along with Johannes Kepler's *Somnium* (1634), Cyrano de Bergerac's *Comical History of the States and Empires of the Moon* (1656), Jonathan Swift's *Gulliver's Travels* (1726), and Voltaire's *Micromégas* (1752) (Kincaid, 2011; de Sousa, 2015; Keen, 2015; Roberts, 2016).

From a science fiction perspective, the novel is a fictional exploration of the Hollow Earth theory and describes a voyage to another planet and the inner rim of Earth. The sentient beings from the planet Nazar and the firmament are alien life forms, each with their own civilization. The main character, Niels Klim, is a graduated academic in Theology and Philosophy from the University of Copenhagen and even though this is a digression from the typical scientist or engineer in modern science fiction, he still has an academic background. His academic curiosity makes him wonder about the mysterious phenomenon of a mountain chasm that seems to breathe. This means that scientific exploration prompts the journey into the abyss. In addition, his intelligence makes him able to learn new languages and write books. Another digression from modern science fiction is that Klim tumbles down into the abyss rather than building a machine or other scientific means of travel. From a modern science fiction perspective, it appears to be lazy storytelling, though bear in mind Holberg did not have any ambition of creating a modern science fiction story.

Another well-known trope in science fiction is the invention of new technology. The canals in Potu have self-moving boats with quiet machine-propelled oars. Holberg writes:

> There are also seas and rivers which bear vessels, whose oars seem to be moved by a kind of magic impulse, for they are not worked by the labour of the arm, but by machines like our clockwork. The nature of this device I cannot explain, as being not well versed in mechanics; and besides these trees contrive everything with such subtlety, that no mortal without the eyes of Argus or the power of divination can arrive at the secret.
> *(Holberg, 2004 (original: 1741/1745), p. 48)*

This would, of course, not be science fiction in the world of today, since boat and ship technology have moved far beyond what Klim describes. Nevertheless, it was science fiction back in the 18th century. The mechanical boat is a way to present the Potuans as a highly sophisticated race, but it does not become a central artifact of the story and as such, it is merely a prop (Lewis, 1966; Wolfe, 2011). Then again, the technology is described as if it seems to be some kind of magic, no mortal may grasp its secret, and the power of divination is needed to understand it. Do these descriptions indicate wizardry rather than technology? Now, it is unclear how this vessel actually functions but the important thing is that it works like a clockwork and therefore probably some kind of automaton or mechanical device (Fitting, 2017). The technology is so advanced that Klim fails to fully realize its nature. As Arthur C. Clarke once stated, "Any sufficiently advanced technology is indistinguishable from magic" (Clarke, 1984, p. 36). In this sense, this technology is not wizardry, but to Klim it almost seems like magic and accordingly, he applies supernatural metaphors in order to fathom these underworld wonders.

Another technology in *The Journey of Niels Klim to the World Underground* is guns and gunpowder. This technology has the opposite quality. While it was, and still is, a fairly common technology in Europe where Klim comes from, it is a weird and almost magical technology to the inhabitants of the firmament. Subsequently, it is not science fiction to Klim, Holberg, or the reader, yet the introduction of guns and gunpowder is like science fiction to the underworld. Such a what-if-scenario is also used in Mark Twain's *A Connecticut Yankee in King Arthur's Court* (1889) in which guns and gunpowder similarly are brought in by the fictional character Hank Morgan coming from the United States in the 19th century where guns and gunpowder do exist, to 6th-century England where it certainly does not.

Still, the griffin, a mythical creature, ought not to fit into science fiction; one would think that would be a trope of sheer fantasy. On the contrary, the encounter with the griffin works as a proof that the griffin was in fact not a mythical creature, because there was a scientific and not a supernatural explanation to its existence. The real reason behind the myth, according to Klim, was that it actually existed in the underground of Earth. Of course, this only works within the parameters of the imaginary world, but then again, that is true of any science fiction, presenting new astonishing ideas.

There are two reasons as to why Holberg's novel is uniquely interesting in science fiction history. The first reason is that it is a journey to another planet with sentient life, which was still at the time a rare theme in literature. Christiaan Huygens (1629–1695) had only a few decades earlier written a treatise, *Cosmotheoros* (1698), about the possibility of life on other planets. The second and most important reason is that it is the first significant novel exploring the concept of a Hollow Earth as suggested by the English astronomer Edmond Halley (1656–1742) in 1692 (Fara, 2007). This kind of science fiction is what C. S. Lewis refers to as "scientific, but speculative" (Lewis, 1966, p. 63) rather than the fiction of Engineers.

So what genre is *The Journey of Niels Klim*? To Holberg it was a fictional travel narrative in the tradition of satirical utopian fiction. To Peter Fitting it is threefold, subsequently as utopia, satire, and fantasy. In addition, it is equally conceivable to interpret the novel as fantasy fiction and, in retrospect, as early science fiction. Rather than choosing one of the above as the true genre, different perspectives on Holberg's novel open up the work in different ways, although depending on the purpose, some interpretations may be more or less useful. One more way to open up this work is to take a closer look at its social criticism and satire.

Social and Religious Utopia

Ludvig Holberg was a part of the rising Enlightenment movement of the 18th century. While Holberg, as playwright, composed his didactic plays for a

Danish audience in Copenhagen, he wrote *The Journey of Niels Klim to the World Underground* in Latin for a much larger European public and published the novel outside of Denmark-Norway in Leipzig, Electorate of Saxony. The subsequent year, translations into English, German, French, Danish, and Dutch occurred, and were later followed by Russian, Swedish, and Hungarian versions (Holm, 2018). Holberg's novel was not just an innocent fairytale. It had the potential to revolutionize the foundation of European governments, structured for the most part around Kings and Nobles, and offered a radically different world-view.

It is not that Holberg was a republican or a democrat (that would have been *lèse-majesté* and treason); quite the opposite, he was a devout royalist. He was against project-makers and disapproved of commoners taking power without a traditional powerbase. Holberg demonstrates this philosophical view in his novel. In one instance, a philosopher named Rabaku ruled Potu. This did not go well because the society could not respect him since he had the most miserable upbringing and now reached the pinnacle of power. Thus, even though he was excellent at the art of governing, this alone could not ensure the dignity and admiration needed to rule the state. His equals and minions simply refused to obey his orders. First, he tried to rule with charm, and then brutality. Potu plunged into a rebellion. Rabaku abdicated so peace and prosperity could return, realizing that only a prince with birthright to the throne could in fact rule the state. Hence, ruling power is hereditary, in a straight line, with only a few necessary exceptions.

This part is not in the least revolutionary. Holberg rejects Plato's idea that the philosopher-kings ought to rule the state. Plato argued that philosopher-kings would be the finest rulers of society because they were able to recognize genuine virtuousness and righteousness since they were better educated and as a result, they could make better decisions (Takala, 1998; Plato, 2008 (original, circa 380 BC)). In Holberg's utopia, the nobility rule because they were born to do so, and this condition alone renders the king able to uphold the veneration needed to govern the state.

Nevertheless, other parts of his utopia are far more progressive. Holberg pleads for a state based on rationality and meritocracy, thinking those people who can work the hardest should get the most respect. There is no difference between nobles and commoners and as such, it is a classless society, although dissimilarity between rich and poor exists. The Potuans judge only by character and employment. As trees, the only kind of advantage children have from birth consists in the number of branches they are born with, the more the better because they will become superior craft workers. Workers earn respect for their labor. Furthermore, people with many children should be the most respected, even though they did not have to work as hard. Having many children freed Potuans from duties so they could take care of their offspring. People with many children should not work as hard, since they are working harder in order to support their family. Moreover, if a person had more than six children, then that individual did not have to pay tax at all. This means court officials should show respect to the hardworking people and people with many children. Peasants rank higher than merchants and courtiers. The more state benefits you take pleasure in, the more humble you should be. The richest bowed to the poorest. Holberg had radical humanist ideas of social justice without any Marxist influence, written a century earlier than Karl Marx made his mark in history. Holberg's ideas are still revolutionary beliefs today.

Another humanist idea clearly presents in Holberg's portrayal of gender equality. This alone makes the novel stand out. While Jonathan Swift addressed misogyny in *Gulliver's Travels* (Hawes, 1991), Holberg takes it a long step further and puts forward unreserved gender equality in his utopia. The Potuans pay no regard to gender in appointment to office and only elect those who prove most worthy after a meticulous examination. There is no glass ceiling, and women may climb the career ladder to the highest level of society based on their skills and personality. Consequently, there are equal rights for boys and girls, and men and women, to get an education as well. Again, the Potuans exclusively observe the students' capabilities, not their social position nor their gender. Holberg had exceptionally liberal views in his lifetime because strict gender equality was certainly not the rule in the 18th century.

Holberg had strong views on religion as well. Potuans view God as the creator of all things. God shall be loved and honored, and there is an afterlife in which virtues are rewarded and vices punished. However, they do not study theology. It is forbidden to comment on the Holy books. None shall debate the presence and attributes of God, or the characteristics of soul and the spirits. If they do, they are declared insane and locked up. Ironically, Holberg did not think of this as religious persecution. The Potuans do not pray pointlessly because they are convinced that piety and true worship are primarily to abide the law of God, and they certainly did not praise God for winning a war. On the contrary, they let some days go by in mournful silence as if they were ashamed to have won a bloody victory.

These religious views were not popular in Denmark. Especially among the Pietists who were not pleased with Holberg's unconventional ideas. His views were born out of the Thirty Years' War from 1618 to 1648 in which Catholics and Protestants fought against one another, Christians in battle against Christians, fighting for the right interpretation of the Holy Bible. If only they had not studied theology but loved God and followed His commands, then they might not have gone to war. This appears to be Holberg's solution to the problem. Besides, Holberg had troubles with the Pietists earlier in life. Pietism was a French idea then-recently introduced to Denmark-Norway and famous for its condemnation of theater, dance, games, etc. (Sand, 1994). In 1722, Lille Grønnegade Theatre in Copenhagen premiered with a play by Molière. Holberg followed up by writing new Danish plays for the theater such as *The Political Tinker* (1722, *Den politiske kandestøber*), *Jeppe on the Hill* (1722, *Jeppe på bjerget*), and *Erasmus Montanus* (1747). During a great fire in Copenhagen in 1728, which ravaged a third of the city, the theater was saved. However, Pietists blamed this disaster on the miserable morals of the citizens of Copenhagen, and demanded the theater be closed. When the Pietist King Christian VI (1699–1746) came to power in the 1730s, the political climate did not promote a reopening of the theater and it has never again been revived (Jensen, 1972; Holm, 2018). This explains why *The Journey of Niels Klim to the World Underground* was a subtle criticism of Pietism, and why Holberg decided to print it anonymously in Latin in the Electorate of Saxony, trying to elude government reprisal and censorship (Rossel, 1994).

Holberg tells us that in Potu it is better to employ citizens in plays and other diversions than let them stay idle, and that nobody should be considered useless. All people have qualities that may be useful to society in some way. He also warns against false humility. Knowing Holberg's views on Pietism, it becomes obvious that indeed, this social and religious criticism could potentially be explosive. Consequently, when the Danish translation of *The Journey of Niels Klim* had been published in 1742, it did not take long to figure out who wrote it. The Pietists in Denmark were furious. That is why the 1745 edition added the Apologetic Preface, which is not apologetic at all, but provokes even more by creating a fiction to declare the work an authentic testimony.

The utopia Holberg exhibits is a world of social justice, gender equality, and enlightened religious views that were not the norms and values of Denmark-Norway and the rest of Europe in the middle of the 18th century, and he created these revolutionary ideas a century earlier than the origins of Marxism.

Social Satire

There is plenty of social satire in *The Journey of Niels Klim to the World Underground*. Holberg satirizes so extensively that it would be too much to try and cover (and uncover) all of it. This, then, is a look at the social satire of Denmark and France, misogyny, and scholars.

To begin with the scholars, Niels Klim is ridiculed for being too conceited about his academic credentials. His dreams of quick career progress are questioned. First, by the Potuans who think he is overhasty, then by the Martinians who find him too slow and dimwitted, and finally, when he ends up as a malevolent tyrant. All of these are examples of how his ambitions are too huge for his own good.

In the Philosophical Region, they are supposed to value science and philosophy, but they are out of this world. A man absorbed in his own thoughts beats Niels Klim up because he took him for a pillar. He is nearly dissected out of curiosity, had he not been helped by a woman who wants to have sex with him because the philosophers are no good when it comes to the needs of a woman. These are just some of the many accounts of ridiculing scholars and academics.

There is a recurring motif of Niels Klim meeting women. At first, he climbs up in a tree that turns out to be female, only later to be judged by another female tree. In the Kingdom of Kokleku, Niels Klim encounters a tree society in which gender roles are reversed and the males cook and perform all the domestic duties, if they are not prostitutes for women. He hears about the Queen's harem with 300 attractive young fellows locked up for life. He hurries away, and later he flees the woman that saved him from being dissected by the philosophers. In Martinia, the wife of the President tries to seduce him; after he rejects her, she turns against him and tells everyone the lie that he tried to seduce her. Later, he marries a deceased emperor's daughter, denies marrying another daughter of an emperor, but ends up remarrying Magdalena back in Norway anyway. As what should now be obvious, Niels Klim has many encounters with women. Of course, the most central is his hubris when, in Nazar, he turns against women and wants them to be second-class citizens, a change from gender equality to a Patriarchal society, and for this he receives the punishment of banishment to the firmament, the inner surface of Earth.

Niels Klim tries his best but mostly fail in the end. Even his dream scenario of becoming an emperor fails. A Napoleonic figure before Napoleon, he is an anti-hero, a tragedy, a failed scholar that ends up as a custodian without the courage to tell the public about his greatest adventures.

Holberg satirizes Denmark as well. The Mardak Province is inhabited by the narrow-minded and stubborn cypresses who would rather insist on deceitful orthodoxy than learn anything new. Neophytes without qualifications, other than the trait of being obstinate, get high-ranking positions. The name "Mardak" bears a strong resemblance to (and is almost an anagram of) Denmark (Danish: Danmark), and is accordingly considered a criticism of Denmark in the 18th century (Bredsdorff and Kjældgaard, 2010).

The most unusual thing about the inhabitants of Mardak is that they all have very special eyes. Some have oblong eyes and to them everything appear oblong; some have square eyes, or very small eyes, some have two eyes turned in opposite directions, there are even some with three eyes, four eyes, and eyes that occupy the whole forehead, and finally some have only a single eye in the neck. The symbolism is clear; the Danes do not see anything clearly.

Martinia on the firmament, inhabited by the monkey-people, is an allegory of France in the 18th century (Paludan, 1878). They are the opposite of the utopian Potuans. The Martinians are superficial and are far too hasty. Klim think of them as fools because they make rash decisions. Their state is a great council selected from an old nobility. Their religion has more than 200 speculations concerning the form and being of God, and almost 400 speculations as to the nature and qualities of the soul, and many theological seminars and preachers. There are many project-makers coming up with foolish ideas, praised for their boldness even though they cannot deliver. This is Holberg's nightmarish dystopia, satirizing hurried decision-making, irrationality, nobility, project-makers, and theologians such as the French Pietists.

Adaptation

When one thinks of Jonathan Swift's *Gulliver's Travels*, there are plenty of movies going back to Georges Méliès's *Gulliver's Travels among the Lilliputians and the Giants* from 1902. The same cannot be said for Niels Klim; Hollywood has overlooked Holberg's novel. In 1984, DR (Danish television) produced a Danish three-part television adaptation *Niels Klims underjordiske rejse* (*Niels Klim's Underworld Journey*). The television series was theatrical and amateurish. No other film or television series has been produced based on *The Journey of Niels Klim to the World Underground*.

Conclusion

Ludvig Holberg's *The Journey of Niels Klim to the World Underground* from 1741 acts both as an allegorical social criticism of 18th-century kingdoms and as a subcreated world in its own right, depicting an interesting journey to a fantastic Hollow Earth world. Originally written in Latin and published in Saxony, the work was part of the European Enlightenment, and Holberg presents a harsh criticism of misogyny, social injustice, and religion in 18th-century Europe.

The Journey of Niels Klim to the World Underground is interesting because it is a travel narrative in the satirical utopian genre, like Swift's *Gulliver's Travels*. The novel is important because it is an example of either proto-science fiction or early science fiction, depending on one's science fiction perspective. It is an even more important work because it has a rare 18th-century journey to another planet, and because it is the most significant work presenting an imaginative subcreation of a Hollow Earth. It may also have included the inspiration for Tolkien's Ents.

As if this was not enough, the book represents an Enlightenment-age social reformation based on a radical notion of social justice, a century before Karl Marx, and it was a counteraction to 18th-century Pietism in Denmark. Holberg's utopia, built upon rationality and meritocracy, has far-reaching consequences, with the notion that society is fundamentally different without nobility, with a progressive respect for workers and families, and, on top of that, with a depiction of true gender equality, too.

For all of the above reasons Ludvig Holberg's *The Journey of Niels Klim to the World Underground* is a remarkable literary work, but because there are no Hollywood movies nor popular television series adapted from it, the Scandinavian novel is mostly forgotten.

Bibliography

Bredsdorff, Thomas; and Lasse Horne Kjældgaard, *Tolerance: Eller hvordan man lærer at leve med dem man hader*, Copenhagen, Denmark: Gyldendal, 2010.

Clarke, Arthur C., *Profiles of the Future*, New York: Holt, Rinehart, and Winston, 1984.

de Sousa, Elisabete M., "Niels Klim: Project Makers in a World Upside Down" in Katalin Nun and Jon Stewart, editors, *Volume 16, Tome II: Kierkegaard's Literary Figures and Motifs: Gulliver to Zerlina*, New York: Routledge, 2015, pages 65–72.

Fara, Patricia, "Hidden Depths: Halley, Hell and Other People", *Studies in History and Philosophy of Science*, Volume 38, Issue 3, September 2007, pages 570–583.

Fitting, Peter, "Buried Treasures: Reconsidering Holberg's *Niels Klim in the World Underground*", *Utopian Studies*, Volume 7, Issue 2, 1996, pages 93–112.

Fitting, Peter, "Holberg's Nazar and the Firmament" in Mark J. P. Wolf, editor, *The Routledge Companion to Imaginary Worlds*, New York: Routledge, 2017, pages 339–343.

Hawes, Clement, "Three Times Round the Globe: Gulliver and Colonial Discourse", *Cultural Critique*, No. 18, Spring 1991, pages 187–214.

Holbek, Bengt; and Jørn Piø, *Fabeldyr og Sagnfolk*, Copenhagen, Denmark: Politikens Forlag, 1967.

Holberg, Ludvig, *The Journey of Niels Klim to the World Underground*, Lincoln: University of Nebraska Press, 2004 (original: 1741/1745).

Holm, Bent; and Ludvig Holberg, *A Danish Playwright on the European Stage: Masquerade, Comedy, Satire*, Vienna, Austria: Hollitzer Wissenschaftsverlag, 2018.

Jensen, Anne E., *Teatret i Lille Grønnegade 1722–1728*, Copenhagen, Denmark: Arnold Busck, 1972.

Keen, Antony, "Mr Lucian in Suburbia, or Do the True History and The First Men in the Moon have Anything in Common?" in Brett M. Rogers and Benjamin Eldon Stevens, editors, *Classical Traditions in Science Fiction*, Oxford, England: Oxford University Press, 2015, pages 105–120.

Kincaid, Paul, "Through Time and Space: A Brief History of Science Fiction" in Andy Sawyer and Peter Wright, editors, *Teaching Science Fiction*, Hampshire, England: Palgrave Macmillan, 2011, pages 21–37.

Lewis, C. S., "On Science Fiction" in Walter Hooper, editor, *Of Other Worlds*, London, England: Harcourt Brace Jovanovich, 1966, pages 59–73.

McNelis, James Ignatius, "'The tree took me up from ground and carried me off': A Source for Tolkien's Ents in Ludvig Holberg's *Journey of Niels Klim to the World Underground*", *Tolkien Studies*, Volume 3, 2006, pages 153–156.

Paludan, J., *Om Holbergs Niels Klim, med særligt Hensyn til til tidligere Satirer i Form af opdigtede og vidunderlige Reiser. Et Bidrag til Kundskab om fremmed Indvirkning på det attende Aarhundredes Litteratur*, Copenhagen, Denmark: Wilhelm Priors Hof-Boghandel, 1878.

Plato, *The Republic*, Digireads.com Publishing, 2008 (original: c. 380 BC).

Roberts, Adam, *The History of Science, Second Edition*, London, England: Palgrave Macmillan, 2016.

Rossel, Sven Hakon, *Ludvig Holberg: A European Writer: A Study in Influence and Reception*, Amsterdam, Netherlands: Rodopi, 1994.

Sand, Erik Reenberg, "Ludvig Holbergs religionssyn som udtrykt i Niels Klim", *Religionsvidenskabeligt tidskrift*, No. 25, 1994, pages 61–81.

Takala, T., "Plato on Leadership", *Journal of Business Ethics*, Volume 17, Issue 7, May 1998, pages 785–798.

Todorov, Tzvetan, *The Fantastic: A Structural Approach to a Literary Genre*, Ithaca, New York: Cornell University Press, 1975.

Wolfe, Gary K., *Evaporating Genres: Essays on Fantastic Literature*, Middletown, Connecticut: Wesleyan University Press, 2011.

2

'A LITTLE BIT OF ENGLAND WHICH I HAVE MYSELF CREATED'

Creating Barsetshire across Forms, Genres, Time, and Authors

Helen Conrad O'Briain

Today Barsetshire and its cathedral town of Barchester are best known as the setting of a much-loved BBC costume drama, *The Barchester Chronicles* (1982) starring, among others, Susan Hampshire and a young Alan Rickman near the beginning of his career. The two novels the series dramatized, *The Warden* (1855) and *Barchester Towers* (1857) are, however, much more than the first in a series of interconnected novels by the prolific Anthony Trollope. They delineated with real depth the landscape and society of a more than what-if corner of England. Barsetshire was so well and surely drawn, so suited to narratives revolving around the tensions between preservation and change, it became, on a certain level, as material and authentic as any real-world English region, and as popular a setting for such narratives, as any of them.

Trollope was followed across genres and succeeding decades by M. R. James, Ronald Knox, and, most prolifically, Angela Thirkell, and, lest we think no train still runs to Barchester (on a Sunday or otherwise, and leaving aside the distinct possibility that that noteworthy preparatory school for young ladies, Saint Trinian's, lies within striking distance), in the 21st century by American author, Charlie Lovett, who re-imagines Barsetshire in an almost fantasy mode.

The Relative Neglect of Literary World-Building Outside the So-called Popular Genres

A consideration of Trollope's Barchester novels in terms of world-building opens up not only an important departure from novelistic narrative focus and character development, but also offers engagement with the economics of literature, the active engagement of a readership both as readers and as writers, and the development of world-building across the genres of the novels in general.

We must acknowledge, among other things, the overwhelming influence of the essentially realistic novel of the mid-to-late 19th century on all other contemporary narrative forms. No narrative genre was spared its influence on characterization, plotting, or world-building. With the exception of Balzac's *Commedie Humaine*,[1] whose influence was early recognized and accepted by Trollope himself,[2] Trollope's Barchester novels, followed by the later Palliser novels, stand very close to the beginning of a continuing and lively subgroup of literary narratives. With them, possibly influenced by multi-volume historical narratives (particularly, perhaps, Thomas Babington MacCaulay's *History of England from the Accession of James the Second* (1848–1861),[3] with its inclusion of the social setting as well as the political setting[4]), arise a progeny of similar fictional narratives stretching across the lives of generations. Such an authorial approach has become so commonplace, from Anthony Powell's *A Dance to the Music of Time* (1951–1975) to L. M. Montgomery's *Anne of Green Gables* (1908) and its sequels (including short stories in which Anne is mentioned or takes a minor role), that it is difficult now to realize the novelty multi-volume stories once had, or even the authorial concerns for their readers' ability to appreciate it. To quote Trollope himself: "the carrying on of a character from one book to another is very pleasant to the author; but I am not sure that all readers will participate in that pleasure".[5] Similarly, the current omnipresence of such continuing stories can lead reader and critic to simply and subconsciously accept, rather than appreciate, the particular possibilities offered by the interlocking of narratives of place and society into an overarching narrative carried within, and supported by, the construction of an overarching, containing world.

All narrative requires a setting, but the creative methods and purposes of narrative worlds have not received the same specific attention across all genres and forms. The study of literary world-building, in readers' and in critics' minds, has been almost exclusively associated with fantasy and science fiction. It is not so much that there is no scholarly interest in the material which forms the basis for its criticism, but rather that it is not necessarily approached as such. With the notable exception of Ellen Moody's brief but insightful "Mapping Trollope; or the Geographies of Power,"[6] in reference to Trollope and many other novelists of the mundane, it is elided into other aspects of a work. Critical analysis of what might be called the constituent elements of world-building is by no means non-existent, as, for example, in Mieke Bal's treatment of description, space, and location in *Narratology: Introduction to the Theory of Narrative*[7] particularly when Bal insists

> Description is a privileged site of focalization, and as such it has great impact on the ideological and aesthetic effect of the text. But it is also a particular textual, indispensable, indeed, omnipresent in narrative.[8]

There has been considerable critical work on the "Irish Great House" and on Virginia Woolf, who wrote both as a novelist and as a critic, dissecting the creation of meaning and atmosphere, which is at the heart of the act of world-building.[9] But such studies are not consciously situated within world-building. One might suggest the more overtly artificial nature of the setting, and the artifice generating it, in Science Fiction and Fantasy, even the selection of reality upon which that artifice works, blunt the reader's and critic's alertness to the less obvious, apparently less selective or manipulative approach of other narrative modes. This, in turn, flattens its recognition in those other narratives and their settings in an assumption of a high level of fidelity to the mundane[10] instead of seeing in them first and foremost, as worlds of artifice in a necessarily symbiotic relationship with character and action. This is despite the recognition, even in the sciences, that

> Sound observation consists of much more than an acute sensory ability, involving choices in both selection of and assignment of signification to what is seen.[11]

This is, perhaps, particularly true of the "realistic" novel, even though Gaston Bachelard laid the groundwork for such a study, across both poetry and prose, as long ago as 1958 in his *La poétique de l'espace*.[12] Nevertheless, it is obvious that the aims and methods of world-building criticism have growing relevance outside of popular literature as in J. P. Mallory's reference to it in the magisterial summation of his *In Search of the Irish Dreamtime* (2016)[13]:

> In the end the early Irish literati created a Secondary World that they passed off as the Irish Iron Age. That they did a superb job is evident in the centuries of scholars who have argued whether this imagined world was a real document from Ireland's prehistoric past.[14]

Much, then, has been recognized, but not, perhaps, its full implication as integrated into a lively conceptualization of world-building. Where the setting is clearly non-mundane or where the circumstances or needs of the narrative require elements which the audience will identify as not of the mundane, even when the setting ostensibly is our own world, the critical arena is situated within a discussion of world-building. The closer it is perceived that the narrative exists in an environment and in social categories and mores within the writer's and reader's experience, then the less likely it is to be consciously read within the distinct critical approach given to world-building, the less likely its construction and implications for the text as a whole are given their due.

Such scholarly disinterest, although culturally comprehensible, simply by its apparent lack of engagement with world-building in other modes and genres, skews and blunts our understanding of all fictional worlds. If we do not approach all narratives with a sensitivity toward setting as integral to the author's purpose, we arguably misread all of them since they exist in a continuum whether their connection is made and perceived consciously or not. The art and influence of narrative placement, consciously or unconsciously, flows, from one narrative to another across time, genre, and mode directly, indirectly, redis-covered and recapitulated. Tempe is everywhere, in every time[15] and the walls of windy Troy rise in unexpected places. We may even suggest that a greater sensitivity to setting, particularly in the realistic novel, is perhaps an ethical necessity. A reader's acceptance of the reality and meaningfulness of a book's internal world does not stay within the book's covers. We bring back to the mundane souvenirs from each journey, however brief, to secondary creations. Our time in such worlds almost invariably spills over into expectations of the mundane realities of time, place, and society. At times, insidious expectations based on the internalizing of literary world-building can have potency in the real world, as has been demonstrated of Western Orientalizing texts. The use of literary texts as primary sources for social historians and others (and we may suggest a pertinent example in Scotland's reference to *Barchester Towers*[16]) will profit from a sophisticated explication of such texts as invented within the original and present sense of the word, however closely their originators strove to make them mirrors of the mundane. The very act of verbalizing, of seizing on what to the author is most salient to his or her purpose, is no different in its aims — or even, it may be argued, in its essential techniques to high fantasy or the most outré science fiction.

By widening the remit of world-building analysis, the reader and scholar become more sensitive to the effect of a text retreating in time from its present audience as compared to that of its original one. This is a constant practice among scholars of older literatures who strive to rescue the text from anach-ronistic readings and misinterpretation. Scotland's reference to Barchester, as mentioned above, for example, considerably sharpens and underscores the rel-evance of Trollope's ecclesiastical politics in the Barchester series by insisting on the importance of radical changes in the Anglican episcopacy during the period of *The Warden* (1855) and *Barchester Towers* (1857); changes, as it hap-pened, through what we may heartlessly call "natural wastage" so sweeping, that the *New York Times* in November, 1863, republished a contemporary En-glish article on the subject.[17] Temporal distance seems to cast an afterglow of the romantic, even of the quaint, on circumstances and situations which scorched hearts and destroyed lives when those narratives were written. What was once the harsh reality of the marriage mart in Austen's England, or the bitter battles of the ecclesiastical and secular, the Evangelicals and the Oxford movement, in Trollope's time, become, for those who have experienced nei-ther, merely charming chaffing, much ado about nothing. As the 19th cen-tury retreats deeper into the past, readers, too, lose the sense of their original, sometimes extreme, modernity for their original audience. Railway timetables and the telegraph would have given the original readers a sense of the frenetic activity invading the slow episcopal calm of Barchester. The combined power of telegraph and newspaper,[18] the new speed of communication which may not be clearly communication in any real sense to the characters living with them, is woven into the setting of characters who find it difficult to communicate, who misunderstand and in their turn are misunderstood at every turn.[19] Rather than the quaint, the original reader would have recognized the playing out of exasperation and dislocation, and at times, apparently mindless energy. The world Trollope builds is one moving at different speeds, socially and regionally, in a country and society that had convinced at least a part of itself, as societies usually do, that there was an orderly past social world, where change came slowly with time to assimilate and transmute every change into a stable and traditional society. Thirkell, Trollope's most prolific and arguably most sympathetic continuator, herself, however sentimentalized her world-building might be, creates from the mundane a similar world in flux, albeit ironically one looking back to the dreaded future of the Trollope novels. She, the daughter of a classicist, must have written with *Aeneid*, Book 1, line 462: *sunt lacrimae rerum et mentem mortalia tangent* (there are tears in all that is and mortality touches thought)[20] constantly before her.

Trollope's Barsetshire in Its Time and through Time

The following, then, is a brief attempt, and no more than a brief attempt, to open up the study of world-building to include texts which lie outside of its usual purview. This is done in the belief that all narratives of whatever genre, crossing even from fiction into history itself, can only be properly understood when their created or excavated settings are understood, when a reading of the action and of the characters recognizes the powerful exegetical tool of setting.

Trollope's Barsetshire is offered as an entry into such texts because it offers: (1) an insight into an important formal development in world-building, the serial novel;[21] (2) a light on the negotiation of the boundaries between real-world settings and realistic world settings;[22] and finally (3) a new angle on the often overlooked impetus which lies behind world-building across all narratives, for readers to become writers in a desire to inhabit again another's invented world — or shire.[23] Introducing Barsetshire into the critical discussion thus offers connective pathways which may be pursued both individually and in combination with one another, elucidating Trollope's own practice, his influence on later writers, and the echo, indeed, the ripples, of practice and purpose across narrative generally. What follows, however, is again, merely an introduction to the possibilities.

Barsetshire is pivotal in the development of the serial novel and therefore of the possibility of a major shift in the dynamics of world-building. It is now difficult to remember, but at least as regards the relatively recent forms taken by the narrative,[24] that the idea of the continuing narratives across a number of short stories or novels only begins to take hold of authorial and readerly imagination in the 1850s although Balzac's *La Comedie humaine* (1830) and Poe's three short stories (1841–1844) of C. Auguste Dupin had earlier shown the way. Still as a novelty, its appearance in the English language novel must be connected first and foremost with Trollope himself in his Barsetshire novels. Oddly, the reality of the innovation apparently did not strike the author himself until *Framley Parsonage* (1860)[25] and as we have suggested above, he was not certain its full interest and possibilities were not lost upon his first readers. Nevertheless, readers of all tastes quickly accustomed themselves to it. Hence, *Tom Sawyer* (1876) was followed by *Huckleberry Finn* (1884), and *The Prisoner of Zenda* (1894) by *Rupert of Hentzau* (1898). Poovey, writing in the *Cambridge Companion to Anthony Trollope* (2010), insists it is only with *The Last Chronicle of Barset* (1866–1867) that the series, beginning in 1855 with *The Warden*, became effectively a single creation. Poovey's analysis of the creation of Barsetshire in Trollope's original series becomes focused, however, as to a great extent in their own contemporary critical reception, on Trollope's habit of sharing with his reader the realities of authorial creation of setting, character, and plot.[26]

Still, the richness of Barsetshire, as it provides a locus across genres, authors, and centuries, is a case study not merely of the multi-volume narrative of one place by one author, but of the spin-off. The Barsetshire novels are the first or nearly the first of their kind: both the multi-volume novel of one place with a recurring cast of characters and the subject of eventual re-incarnation in multi-author spin-offs (M. R. James (1910); Angela Thirkell (1933–1960); Ronald Knox (1935), Charlie Lovett (2017)). It would appear the traditional narrative curve of the novel, by the middle of the 19th century, no longer always answered the needs or interests of the writer or of his or her audience. The increasing economic concerns of publishing, with the bankable author embraced, perhaps more slowly than expected, but nevertheless surely, provided the added impetus for the bankable series. To this must be added the sense of reality, of in-ness, the fuller experience of human life, and social development. Trollope's novels provide in an unfolding series of deeply interlocked narratives, directed by a single artistic understanding, comparable to the panoramic painting popular in the 19th century,[27] as much about the time and place in which a society lives, as the individual characters that live in that society.[28] In them, as Poovey writes of *The Last Chronicles of Barset*, "the novel carries over and completes the stories from other novels without changing these characters' natures".[29] Poovey's assessment of the power of the series novel in the creation of character is worth quotation:

> By shifting the relative prominence of characters from novel to novel and by putting the character traits he has already established to various uses, Trollope was able both to create the impressions that the lives of these characters continued even when narratives stopped and to capitalize on information that readers had already gained from other novels.[30]

As we shall see, much of the same strategies apply to the creation of the place, which she calls at the end of her essay "the most vital novelistic 'organism' British readers had ever seen",[31] that these characters inhabit.

Creating a multiple-volume Barsetshire, or working within that already-created literary reality, offers not just a general form, but one as large as a shire's topography[32] and society, offering at the same time places as particular and specific as St. Ewold's parsonage in *Barchester Towers*,[33] created more by the Grantlys's reaction to it than by any specific details, except the miserable proportions of a dining room of 16 by 15 feet.[34] Trollope himself wrote in his autobiography:

> In the course of the job I visited Salisbury, and whilst wandering there one midsummer evening round the purlieus of the cathedral I conceived the story of *The Warden*, — from whence came that series of novels of which Barchester, with its bishops, deans, and archdeacon, was the central site.[35]

This approach places setting at the heart of narrative. It allows the landscape and built environment to be viewed from multiple perspectives, through different eyes each with their differently nuanced power of seeing and understanding and all in individual circumstances. It empowers the writer to look closely at one house, one room, one hill tract, one wood with attention to detail and meaning, knowing that there is a place in the literary world of Barsetshire in which it is situated and that immediately directs and contains its further definition. This gives that teller of tales a landscape with both the foundation of place similar to that immediately given to narrative in a mundane place, like London, Paris, New York, or Dublin, while adding the greater freedom of the invented. Any teller of tales of whatever sort, knowing and accepting that Barsetshire exists in some sort of symbiotic relationship with Wiltshire with its downs and chalk soil,[36] can, if they require it for their narrative or simply hanker after it for completeness, sit down with a geological survey and introduce what features they will, but selectively and not without whatever adaptations or adjustments they might need.

Deeply imbued with the power of a particular and carefully constructed setting, with some strong but intentionally vague connections to the mundane,[37] Barsetshire, ecclesiastical and below the Thames valley, would be, for its readers then (perhaps even now), more slowly paced, more deliberate, and naturally conservative. The county, the sum of all its parts, across the authors, across time, from M. R. James's short story, "The Stalls of Barchester Cathedral" (1910)[38] to Charlie Lovett's *The Lost Book of the Grail* (2017),[39] ruminates like Bede's clean beast, slowly enlarging its sympathies, as it can and will for Thirkell's Sam Adams,[40] digesting or ignoring change. And it must be admitted that, by and large, change is rarely unequivocally good in the Barchester stories — with the notable exception of Lovett's *The Lost Book of the Grail* where change is transmuted into a glorious, salvific return to the past.[41] There is little to suggest that the *Jupiter* or the Proudies, with their new and self-serving impulses toward reform, made Barchester in any appreciable way a better place. It is in individuals meeting what life brings to them and feeling their way through those things by the light of their own consciences that Barchester is left a better place, or at least a differently better place.

Trollope could burlesque an extreme antiquarian conservatism as exemplified by Miss Thorne of Ullathorne in *Barchester Towers*,[42] whose garden party with its archaic impulses leads to anarchic impulses among all the classes present, but his satire there is kindly. It has none of the distaste with which he creates Mrs. Proudie. Barsetshire as an authorial invention, however, reflects both Trollope's own political and social views, sharpened, it has been suggested, by the effect of his reengaging with his own landscape on his return from Ireland to England in 1849. Whether aware or not, he would have returned as that most puzzling and puzzled of observers, the returned expatriate. The world which he creates in Barchester is arguably the result of a bifocular vision of one who is both an insider and outsider in his own country.

At least some of the characteristics of Barsetshire must be a reaction to what must have seemed to him a deeply dystopic and largely incomprehensible Ireland.[43] A reaction to Ireland, and nostalgia for the England Trollope had left, are further influenced by his reengagement with the England to which he had returned, an England which at midcentury was undergoing phenomenal change, for better or worse. It is on this point today's readers must remember that the events that seem, at our temporal distance, slow and largely benign, did not necessarily feel either slow or benign to those who lived through them. If a writer should wish to present in a fictional narrative, a deep, albeit constructed, historical English conservatism, Barsetshire as a setting will aid and abet him/her, aid, abet, and admonish.

Trollope's followers have found just such places in the text to situate narratives. This is certainly true of James's "The Stalls of Barchester Cathedral" (1910). Its world-building is entirely integrated, as it must be, in the short story whose length dictates its other characteristics to create the desired genre-defining effect. Its intensity, however, for the reader familiar with *Barchester Towers*, is grounded within that larger act of subcreation. The Barchester setting is not a bland allusion. It draws the reader back to perhaps the true opening salvo of the Slopites against the Grantleyites. James, a parson's son, addresses, but covertly, the problems of ceremony, in a deeply schizoid church caught in the not-always-happy marriage of preservers and reformers exemplified by music. Overtly, he like Trollope, circles the problems of the temporalities of the established Church, the moral dilemmas set in motion by old men in high office dying too slowly. The stalls of Barchester Cathedral see much the same dilemmas in both works because the source of the dilemmas is not, and cannot be, addressed without radically changing the church's nature and denying its history. Trollope's Barchester, like James's, must contain these tensions or cease to command the reader's interest and sense of reality. A more perfect church, like Mr. Arabin's musings on "a church with a head" (but not the Church of Rome)[44] would not be the Anglican Church, and the writers would have departed too far from the mundane. In a similar (though freer and more expansive) manner, Lovett's *The Lost Book of the Grail*, integrating into the life and history of Barchester a century and a half of Arthurian studies and popular modern adaptations of the Matter of Britain (both of which are thriving industries), has taken the possibilities presented by Trollope at St. Ewold's and by a certain conflation and change of sex (Ewold becomes Ewolda), created a full history where before there was only a sacred lady, and a well:

> There was, he said, in days of yore, an illustrious priestess of St. Ewold, famed through the whole country for curing all manner of diseases. She had a well, as all priestesses have ever had, which well was extant to this day and shared in the minds of many of the people the sanctity which belonged to the consecrated ground of the parish.[45]

Trollope begins *The Warden* with an intellectually daring insight into his creative process:

> The Revd Septimus Harding was, a few years since, a beneficed clergyman residing in the cathedral town of ——, let us call it Barchester. Were we to name Wells or Salisbury, Exeter Hereford or Gloucester, it might be presumed that something personal was intended; and as this tale will refer mainly to the cathedral dignitaries of the town in question, we are anxious that no personality may be suspected. Let us presume that Barchester is a quiet town in the West of England, more remarkable for the beauty of its cathedral and the antiquity of its monuments, than for any commercial prosperity, that the west end is the cathedral close, and that the aristocracy of Barchester are the bishop, dean, and canons, with their respective wives and daughters.[46]

From this opening paragraph, Trollope focuses on what he sees as the heart of the invention in which he is engaging and expects his readers to recognize and engage with its artifice. That invention is not merely of human characters, but of society and environment. It is important to recognize here Trollope begins his fiction with exactly the attitude of which his contemporary critics complained. His unabashed recognition, his drawing attention to the fictive nature, even if it suggests it is only fictive for a certain meaning of fictive, is focused on Barsetshire — on his world-building, his setting as much as his character. It is in such terms that Hawthorne appreciated Trollope, writing it was, "as if some giant had hewn a great lump out of the earth and put it under a glass case, with all its inhabitants going about their daily business".[47]

Barsetshire is announced essentially as being in a symbiotic relationship, in all its elements, with the mundane. It is itself the totality of the characters which exist within it, social creatures moving through a socio-political and natural geography. They constitute a society which is above all dominated by an ecclesiastical hierarchy, not by merchants or by squires, not by industrialists or noblemen. Although couched in terms of real people who might be discommoded by a fully "real" setting, it is clear it is also insisting on the exemplary (as well as fictive) nature of his characters and narrative. Trollope is asking his readers to work with him, to integrate their experience of the mundane with his, in a shared act of creation. He expects his readers to bring a certain knowledge of places like Barchester, some of which he names, and, in fact, to bring certain attitudes and assumptions concerning such places to the story he is about to tell them. It is not an economic powerhouse, like the cities of the north of England, with their rapid growth and constant innovation in every aspect of human life. It is, frankly, quaint. Barchester could only exist in the south and west of London. It could never be several train stops from the town of Dicken's *Hard Times* (1854).[48] It is a world characterized best in the opening landscape of the hospital, the road, and the river, a passage which equally exemplifies the movement of good prose which he knew was as important as in poetry:[49]

> Hiram's Hospital, as the retreat is called, is a picturesque building enough, and shows the correct taste with which the ecclesiastical architects of those days were imbued. It stands on the banks of the little river, which flows nearly around the cathedral close, being on the furthest side of the town. The London Road crosses the river by a pretty one-arched bridge, and looking from this bridge, the stranger will see the windows of the old men's rooms, each pair of windows separated by a small buttress. A broad gravel walk runs between the building and the river, which is always trim and cared for; and at the end of the walk is a large and well-worn seat, on which, in mild weather, three or four of Hiram's beadsmen are sure to be seen seated. Beyond this row of buttresses, and further from the bridge, and also further from the water which here suddenly bends, are the pretty oriel windows of Mr. Harding's house, and his well-mown lawn. The entrance to the hospital is from the London road, and is made through a ponderous gateway under a heavy stone arch, unnecessary, one would suppose, at any time for the protection of twelve old men, greatly conducive to the good appearance of Hiram's charity.[50]

The problem in approaching this description at the onset of the reader's sojourn in Barsetshire is the richness of meaning latent in it, particularly should the reader return to it from the end of *The Last Chronicles of Barchester*. It almost asks to be dangerously over-read, but it should by no means be under-read. Here all that is stable is juxtaposed to all that is fleeting, all the mutability inherent in the human condition: the foundation, the river, and the road. Yet is it possible to be certain what is the mutable and what is not? The Hospital will, despite buttresses and gateway, change radically. The river is there as nothing else is, even the London road, yet it changes continuously. The London road is the gateway to the world which is dragging Barchester into the modernity of mid-Victorian England, but as a representative of change, it is a constant, as even hyper-conservative Miss Thorne would know from her favorite poet, Spenser; ". . . Right true it is, that these, / And all things else that under heaven dwell, / Are chaung'd of Time, who doth them all disseise"[51] until we shall pass over Jordan.[52] The built environment itself will strike up a sympathetic resonance even beyond Trollope's Barchester: Angela Thirkell will constantly employ correct architectural taste, for Trollope the 15th century, for her own novels, the long 18th century, as a shorthand for aesthetic values almost indistinguishable in her novels from ethical values.[53]

In Trollope's description (which leaves the reader to imagine specifics from their own experience), the solid cathedral, the close hospital, and the significantly one-arched bridge are not merely set against the fluidity of river and road. The details given, the buttresses, the apparently unnecessarily "ponderous gateway under a heavy stone arch", even the single arch of the bridge, all comment in retrospect on the ecclesiastical polity which must weather the storms of the narrative through six books. And when the reader reaches the last pages, all these structures will appear in a different light, less substantial, and less established; and the ever-moving, always-present river, recalling perhaps the Jordan and baptism, may seem, if it is meant so, the only true wall between the sacred and the secular, between change and eternity; as Spenser wrote:

> Then gin I thinke on that which Nature sayd,
> Of that same time when no more change shall be,
> But stedfast rest of all things, firmely stayd
> Upon the pillours of eternity,
> That is contrayr to Mutabilitie:
> For all that moveth doth in change delight:
> But thence-forth all shall rest eternally
> With Him that is the God of Sabbaoth hight:
> O that great Sabbaoth God graunt me that Sabaoths sight![54]

The physical geography of Barsetshire, as suggested above, relies on the unspoken connection with Wiltshire, but its reliance results in neither the sketchy nor the slavish in Thirkell's world as it grows across her novels. The county emerges in the narrative in many ways, all of them carefully crafted to participate in the creation of physical and built reality and the people who inhabit it, furthering the narrative at every appearance. All of these often complex, hard-working passages have their purpose, from the description of walks, to the vistas included in those walks, to the use of landscape features, as a "Chekov's gun", best exemplified by Harefield Park's lake with its spring, introduced with Mrs. Belton's worried "I was only wondering if the children would be allowed to skate on the lake this winter if they get leave."[55] to the amusing, but pointed repetition of a single landscape within the work of kind, clueless, jobbing watercolorist Mr. Scatcherd.[56] Each of these descriptions participates in, and recalls to its readers, the shadows of other books as well as the mundane, assuming as Thirkell did, a certain cultural awareness. Thirkell is not, as one would expect, above the use of pathetic fallacy,[57] but it is only one, and arguably not the most important, of her methods.

In Angela Thirkel's *Peace Breaks Out* (1946), a sister and brother, appropriately named George and Sylvia Halliday, home on leave as the war in Europe slowly comes to its end in the spring of 1945,

> prepared to go for a walk by the sunken lane which represents what is left of Gundric's Fossway in those parts, under the steep escarpment of Freshdown, once Frey's Down, and so to the bold eminence of Bolder's Knob where no tree has ever grown since St. Ewold, in an access of slum-clearance, caused the sacred oak grove to be cut down.[58]

Although the walk is never taken, the thought of such a walk says much about the characters, but even more about their world and the audience's approach to their own. This is a description whose most salient features — fosse, place names, and saint — would be almost unimaginable in Trollope, although St. Ewold, as the titular saint of Mr. Arabin's first parish, figures at least as a name in *Barchester Towers*. This is the world of the English Place-Name Society, of the renewed interest in Anglo-Saxon saints founded on emergence of medieval studies and philology, fostered by the Anglo-Catholic wing of the Anglican Church. It is Trollope's Barchester, but it is one now seen, at least here, through the lens of works like Alfred Watkins's *The Old Straight Track* (1925),[59] and Kipling's *Puck of Pook's Hill* (1906) and *Rewards and Fairies* (1910), two books which had an enormous influence on readerly expectations of presentations of the English countryside in the generations immediately following their publication.

Countryside rambles, pivoting at significant vistas, are a mainstay of Thirkell's positioning of buildings, characterization, and motivation within her invented ecumene. It is not a question of where she employs them but where she does not. She does not, however, use only the traditional walk to introduce her vistas of land and life. In *The Headmistress* (1944), Elsa Belton and Captain Hornby, sorting through family history by way of a very full attic, see from the roof of Alcot House the Saturday world of Harefield and, led by the sound of bells, walk around the roof widdershins to the west side of the house, to the sight of Elsa's not quite irredeemably lost home:

> And away up on the hill beyond was Elsa's home, almost a silhouette now with the sun behind it, its great front like a screen of stone. On a piece of level ground at one side some girls were playing netball.[60]

This is a world and its social history in miniature: the distance and elevation reduced by a setting sun to a featureless outline, its wall now only a screen, and the heedless and innocent usurpers there "at one side" because they can never truly be in that world as it was. That Elsa moves, leading her Scots lover widdershins, anticlockwise,[61] around this panorama, through her world, is telling. It is unlucky and wrongheaded, but it is also, in English and Scottish tradition, the direction into Fairie. Captain Hornby, falling in love, is another Childe Rowland.[62]

In Barsetshire, the land and the people are not only one, the land and the built environment are one in that, again and again, houses are the shape or shaping of the people who inhabit them. While never reaching the pitch of John Buchan's "little wicked house" in *Fullcircle* (1920)[63] houses do define and mold people. They can even be locked in a reciprocal, reinforcing relationship with their inhabitants. Although it is possible for houses, particularly houses that are truly homes, to be "though hideous . . . warm and comfortable",[64] that is usually not the case.

The most obvious example of unfortunate house design, deriving from and intensifying the faults of its inhabitants, must be the Tebbens's Lamb's Piece.[65] Mrs. Tebben is an academic without being a scholar. This house, "altogether Mrs. Tebben's doing",[66] "who in some ways had never developed spiritually since the days of cocoa-parties in a bed-sitting-room at college"[67] is, along with the Tebbens' home life, first introduced in *August Folly* (1936) with an extended discussion of the non-provision of a proper study for her truly scholarly medievalist/civil servant husband:

> Mr. Tebben would have preferred the lower story, from which he could escape straight into the garden and away down the valley into the woods, if pressed by enemies, but Mrs. Tebben, who liked to have her household under her eye, decided to take a piece off the dining room. The result was two rooms, both too small for human habitation.[68]

The Trollope reader coming to Thirkell, as many must have done in the 1930s, must have recalled the unfortunate dining room at St Ewold's parsonage, and been thankful Archdeacon Grantly had been gathered to his fathers before there was any possibility he would be invited to dine with the Tebbens.

The description of Gilbert Tebben's misery over the effect his wife's architectural notions have on his bookish life is perhaps the surest, albeit ironic, sign of the depth of his love for Mrs. Tebben, particularly as her idea of a good meal seems to be one which will provide left-overs. Mrs. Tebben's self-designed summer house is a projection of her own ramshackle life and character, re-enforcing the very things in her personality and behavior which makes a happy integration into the life to which she aspires difficult.

Unfortunate architecture is not, however, always the modern and incon-venient, although again it is a sad, but honest reflection on the personality for whom it was built. The Garden House, which would today probably be the only part of the Belton's Harefield Park in which the National Trust would be interested, has an escapable wrongness extending over the generations, built in folly and maintained in folly:

> A species of pleasure house or folly, built by the Nabob in his old age under the influence (we regret to say) of a French lady of great charm and beauty who was no better than she should be. . . It had also afforded scope for the undoubted gifts of the French architect and decorator . . . An exotic among dog violets and daisies, a bird of paradise among barndoor fowls, its delicate rococo graces had looked homesick and out of place from the very beginning. Now heavily overshadowed, by two drooping willows; a *cottage orne* with a pagoda roof . . . Mr Belton's grandfather had spent a good deal of money in putting it into repair in the last flare of gaiety at the end of the nineteenth century, but he would have done better to put his money back into the estate[.][69]

Just such decisions bring their descendants from Harefield Park to Arcot house. James Thurber called his home in Cornwall, Connecticut, "The Great Good Place". Thirkell would have recognized him as a kindred spirit in understand-ing the importance of the house in which one elects to live. It is a characteristic of her novels that houses are not merely signs or exemplifications of an ethical/ aesthetic sense, but can become characters in their own right. This empower-ment of the built environment is perhaps most powerful in *The Headmistress* (1944). Miss Sparling and Arcot House are arguably the two most beautifully drawn, most sympathetic characters in *The Headmistress,* perhaps in all of Thir-kell's novels. Miss Sparling, the headmistress of the Hosiers Girls Foundation School, is the antithesis of Mrs. Tebben. She is very much the true scholar, a classicist who will eventually win more than the grudging admiration of that near-caricature of an Oxford don, Mr. Caron. She also demonstrates her innate delicacy in terms of a house and the meaning of home:

> And to Mr. Belton she had shown that not only did she realize that lady's prior claim, in the eyes of abstract justice, to her own drawing room, but at the same time apologized to her for usurping it and thanked her for her friendly and generous attitude.[70]

And she is almost as quietly perfect as Arcot House on the south side of the High Street in Harefield,

> a small but handsome house in the village belonging to Mr. Belton which fortuitously fell vacant about this time, owing to the death of Old Mrs. Ellangowan–Hornby. That lady . . . had a taste for white walls, good furniture and ferocious cleanliness, . . . In the drawing-room which commanded the village street in the front and the garden with a distant view of Harefield Park at the back, a bright fire was burning, the furniture caught the gleam of the flames, Mrs. Admiral Ellangowan–Hornby's Scotch ancestors and ancestresses looked down with immense character from the walls, and tea was laid.[71]
>
> Little perhaps it was after the great rooms at Harefield Parkwith their finely decorated ceilings and furlongs of carpet, but large in its proportions and Mrs. Admiral Ellangowan Hornby's taste breathing an ordered peace which was infinitely soothing to the shipwrecked voyagers in their temporary harbour.[72]

Her "heir, a nephew who didn't in the least want to live there"[73] is the human counterpart of the house, a sensibly sized, warm, aesthetically pleasing 18th-century house at the heart of the community. Captain Hornby will have much the same effect on the Belton's daughter, Elsa, as the house has on her parents. The Beltons themselves, however much they have intermarried into the upper levels of county society, are still the descendants of a late 18th-century nabob whose Harfield Park, "a plain-faced Palladian house",[74] is a hopeless, uncomfortable money pit, even though it represents their place in society. Hornby and Arcot House seem to bring the Beltons, simply by their balance and sense, house and man's participation somehow in a Georgian apogee of England, into a proper understanding of themselves, their essential love not so much of the house as of the land, and a strengthened sense of being in the right place.

It would require a far longer and more detailed study than this to properly define and appreciate the balance between world-building, character description, and speech acts (including internal monologs) in Thirkell's novels. Their interaction is fundamental to Thirkell's creation of the narrative artifact. The impression the reader will probably bring from a Thirkell narrative is that of a rough equivalency among them. Whether there is truth in this approximation, whether it differs (and for what reasons) from novel to novel, or if we can speak of a real change in them over time, these questions require more than an intuitive response. Is there a difference in presentation of the natural and built world between the pre-World War II novels and those written during World War II, or indeed, is there yet another change between their war and postwar presentation portraits? Thirkell brought Barsetshire through the 1930s and 1940s into the postwar world, leaving it superficially in flux, but still profoundly conservative in its outlooks and methods of accommodating change and assimilating new blood into its society with men and women like Sam and Heather Adams. This conservatism is alive in the characters' behavior, conversations, and internal musings, within a built environment within a natural, largely agrarian one. But from the curving embrace of the river from the opening pages of *The Warden* to the long lost, but now rediscovered spring in the Cathedral Close of *The Lost Book of the Grail*, it is from the Earth, always threatened, always defended, that its essential continuity derives. It is only through an act of sustained world-building, not derivative in a negative sense, but reflective and deepened, that such a world and its activities are created. This is perhaps what has given the authors following Trollope into Barsetshire their desire to continue its life, this desire to demonstrate, in a sustaining environment, not the pettiness, but the small heroisms of fighting "the long defeat". Having once recognized, with them, what lies behind such an act and its importance to the narrative as a whole, it may be possible to recognize and read other novelistic lands, both on and off the map.

Notes

The quote in the essay's title is from M. Sadleir, *Trollope*, (London, 1945), p. 417.

1 The last volume of Balzac's series appeared five years before the publication of *The Warden*. The following essay will not address the possibility of the influence of the Medieval and Renaissance development of the so-called "Matters of Britain" or the fictional and historical influence of the Troy legend across European literatures, although the phenomenon has much in common with present-day sequels, prequels, and continuations both in and out of fan fiction.

2 See the opening of Ellen Moody, "Mapping Trollope; or the Geographies of Power", posted 2013/05 from the Victorian Web, http://www.victorianweb.org/authors/trollope/moody3.html

3 Thomas Babington MacCaulay, *The History of England from the Accession of James the Second*, 5 volumes, London, England: Longmans, published between 1848 and 1861. The first volume gives a condensed history of England to 1685: *MacCauley's History of England from the Accession of James II*, 4 volumes, Introduction by Douglas Jerrold Dent: London and New York: Dutton, 1953, vol. 1, pp. 1–208.

4 MacCaulay, vol. 1, pp. 209–320. The growing broadening of historical narrative has followed to some extent the broadening of focus available in the novel while the novel has absorbed some of the methods of the history in its extended observation.

5 Richard, Mullen, *Trollope: A Victorian in his World*, Savannah, Georgia: Frederic C. Bell, 1990, p. 177.

6 Ellen Moody, "Mapping Trollope; or the Geographies of Power", posted 2013/05 from the Victorian Web, http://www.victorianweb.org/authors/trollope/moody3.html

7 Mieke Bal, *Narratology: Introduction to the Theory of Narrative,* 3rd edition, Toronto, New York, and London: University of Toronto Press, 2009, pp. 35–48; 133–145; 219–224.

8 Op cit. p. 35.

9 Adele Cassigneul, "Virginia Woolf's Ruined House, A Literary Complex" in *Etudes Britanniques Contemporaines*, vol. 55 (2018), pp. 13–26, available at https://journals.openedition.org/ebc/1315

10 For the purposes of this study, *mundane* shall be taken to mean the daily perception of the Earth as it is experienced by the greater part of its human inhabitants, together with scientific descriptions of its physical appearance and processes.

11 Kenneth L. Taylor, "The Beginnings of a Geological Naturalist: Desmarest, the Printed Word, and Nature", *Earth Sciences History* 20, 2001, pp. 44–61, reprinted in *The Earth Sciences in the Enlightenment: Studies on the Early Development of Geology*, Variorum Collected Series 883, Aldershot: Ashgate, 2008, p. 2.

12 Gaston Bachelard, *La poétique de l'espace*, Paris, France: Presses Universitaires de France, 1958.

13 J. P. Mallory, *In Search of the Irish Dreamtime: Archaeology and Early Irish Literature*, Thames and Hudson: London, 2016, pp. 288–289, referencing Mark J. P. Wolf, *Building Imaginary Worlds: The Theory and History of Subcreation*, New York and London: Routledge, 2012. I would like to thank Dr. Padraig S. O'Briain for drawing this passage to my attention.

14 Mallory, *In Search of the Irish Dreamtime*, p. 289.

15 William Empson, *Some Versions of the Pastoral*, 1935.

16 Nigel Scotland, *Good and Proper Me: Lord Palmerston and the Bench of Bishops*, Cambridge: James Clarke & Co. LTD, 2000, see in particular p. 21.

17 "The Episcopal Appointments of Lord Palmerston" (from an English paper), *The New York Times*, Nov. 15, 1863, available at https://www.nytimes.com/1863/11/15/archives/the-episcopal-appointments-of-lord-palmerston.html

18 See Mr. Arabin to Mrs. Bold, Anthony Trollope, *Barchester Towers*, with an afterword by Ned Halley, Collector's Library, London, 2013, pp. 260–261

19 See, in particular, the conversations which take place at Plumstead in *Barchester Towers*.

20 *P. Vergili Maronis Opera*, ed. R. A. B. Mynors, Oxford, England: Clarendon Press, 1969, p. 117; the translation (somewhat free) is my own.

21 I use the term "serial novel" not as it is often used to denote a novel, usually 19th century, which appeared first in parts, usually in a magazine, but rather a series of novels which share a setting and a cast of characters who move in and out of prominence in the continuing narrative of that place. Pratchett's *Discworld* series is an example.

22 Discussed briefly in Bal, *Narratology*, p. 139.

23 The use of "shire" here is doubly purposeful. Obviously, Trollope and his followers invent and develop a shire, but it may also be illuminating to compare particularly Thirkell's development of Barsetshire with Tolkien's Shire, as developed through *The Hobbit* (1937) and *The Lord of the Rings* (1954–1955).

24 It could be argued that this linking of narrative and setting is an active element in the medieval Matter of Britain and to a lesser extent in the Icelandic sagas. The extent to which either may have influenced Trollope may be assumed to be negligible. It is more likely he might have been influenced by multi-volume histories, such as Thomas Babungton Macaulay's *The History of England from the Accession of James the Second* (1848), of which his biographer wrote of "the famous third chapter of the History, which may be said to have introduced the study of social history", G. R. Potter, *Macaulay* (London, England: Longmans, Green & Co., 1959), p. 29.

25 Mary Poovey, "Trollope's Barsetshire series" in Carolyn Dever and Lisa Niles, editors, *The Cambridge Companion to Anthony Trollope*, Cambridge, England: Cambridge University Press, 2011, p. 31.

26 Poovey, "Trollope's Barsetshire series", pp. 33–38.

27 See Stephen Oettermann, *The Panorama: History of a Mass Medium*, Cambridge, Massachusetts: The MIT Press, 1997, available at http://www.tate.org.uk/art/artworks/frith-the-derby-day-n00615.

28 Compare this to Terry Pratchett's *Discworld* series.

29 Poovey, "Trollope's Barsetshire series", p. 37.

30 Poovey, "Trollope's Barsetshire series", p. 39.

31 Poovey, "Trollope's Barsetshire series", p. 43.

32 The importance of this created topography is the subject of much of Moody's study, see above, footnote 7.

33 Trollope, *Barchester Towers*, pp. 256–265.

34 Trollope, *Barchester Towers*, p. 263.

35 Anthony Trollope, *An Autobiography*, Chapter 5, available at http://www.gutenberg.org/files/5978/5978-h/5978-h.htm.

36 Cynthia Snowden, *Going to Barsetshire: A Companion to the Barsetshire Novels of Angel Thirkell*, privately published, 2000, p. xi.

37 Its location is perhaps best approached through the times of railway journeys to London.

38 M. R. James, editor, *Collected Ghost Stories*, with introduction and notes by Daryl Jones, Oxford: Oxford University Press, 2011, pp. 165–178.

39 Charlie Lovett, *The Lost Book of the Grail or A Visitor's Guide to Barchester Cathedral*, New York: Viking, 2017.

40 See the thumbnail sketch of Adams in Snowden, *Going to Barsetshire*, pp. 3, 4.

41 Lovett, *The Lost Book of the Grail*, pp. 316, 317.

42 Trollope, *Barchester Towers*, pp. 273–277.

43 Robert Tracy, "Trollope Redux: the Later Novels" in Carolyn Dever and Lisa Niles, eds., *The Cambridge Companion to Anthony Trollope*, Cambridge, England: Cambridge University Press, 2011, pp. 58–70, at p. 58.

44 Trollope, *Barchester Towers*, pp. 258, 259.

45 Trollope, *Barchester Towers*, p. 255.

46 Anthony Trollope, *The Warden,* London, England: Collector's Library, CRW Publishing Ltd., 2013, p. 9.

47 (*Cowley, M. (Editor) (1978). The Portable Hawthorne. p. 688.*) Hawthorne asks his publisher, James T. Fields, in February 1860; *The Victorian Dreams of the Real: Conventions and Ideology: Conventions and Ideology,* Audrey Jaffe, Oxford, 2016, p. 27. It should be noted, however, this is still an American's assessment. On the American construction of a largely literary England, see Helen, Conrad-O'Briain, "Bookland: Building England in a Time Travel Universe in Connie Willis's *To Say Nothing of the Door*" in Mark, J. P. Wolf, ed., *Revisiting Imaginary Worlds: A Subcreation Studies Anthology*, New York and London: Routledge, 2017, pp. 310–330.

48 First published as a serial in *Household* from April 1, 1854–August 12, 1854. Published as a book by LondonEngland: Bradbury and Evans, 1854.

49 Anthony Trollope, *An Autobiography*, Chapter 12, available at http://www.gutenberg.org/files/5978/5978-h/5978-h.htm, June 2, 2018.

50 Trollope, *The Warden*, pp. 14–15.

51 Edmund Spenser, *The Faerie Queen*, Book 7, Canto 6, stanza 48. Lines 424–426.

52 Trollope, *Barchester Towers,* p. 273.

53 See Penelope Fritzer, *Aesthetics and Nostalgia in the Barsetshire Novels of Angela Thirkell*, The Angela Thirkell Society of America, SanDiego, 2009.

54 Spenser, *The Faerie Queen*, Book 7, Canto 7, stanza 2, ll 541–549.

55 Angela Thirkell, *The Headmistress*, London: Hamish Hamilton, 1944, p. 11; they will go skating, of course, with most of the village and girl's school now in Harefield Park, and someone will go through the ice and someone will save them, and everyone, almost, will be the better for it.

56 Angela Thirkell, *Peace Breaks Out*, London, England: Hamish Hamilton, 1946, pp. 17, 18, 26, 27. Mr. Scatcherd and his landscape, however, run in and out of the novel.
57 See. In particular Thirkell, *Peace Breaks Out*, p. 13.
58 Thirkell, *Peace Breaks Out*, pp. 11, 12.
59 Alfred Watkins, *The Od Straight Track: Is Mounds, Beacons, Moats, Sites and Mark Stones*, London, England: Abacus, 1974.
60 Thirkell, *The Headmistress,* pp. 119–121, quotation from p. 121.
61 Thirkell, *The Headmistress*, 119.
62 Jacqueline Simpson and Steve Roud, *A Dictionary of English Folklore*, Oxford University Press: Oxford, 2003, p. 389. See also Joseph Jacobs, "Childe Rowland", *Folklore,* vol. 2, 1892, pp. 183–197; in particular, p. 193.
63 John Buchan, *The Complete Short Stories*, edited by Andrew Lownie, 3 volumes, London, England: Thistle Publishing, 1996–1997, vol. 3, pp. 344–58.
64 Angela Thirkell, *Growing Up*, London, England: Hamish Hamilton, 1943, reprinted in 1947, p. 41.
65 Angela Thirkell, *August Folly*, North Dakota: Penguin, 1949, p. 19. Originally published by Hamish Hamilton in London, 1936
66 Thirkell, *August Folly*, p. 10.
67 Thirkell, *August Folly*, p. 14.
68 Thirkell, *August Folly*, pp. 10, 11.
69 Thirkell, *The Headmistress*, pp. 112–114.
70 Thirkell, *The Headmistress*, p. 147.
71 Thirkell, *The Headmistress*, p. 7.
72 Thirkell, *The Headmistress*, p. 20.
73 Thirkell, *The Headmistress*, p. 7.
74 Thirkell, *The Headmistress*, p. 5.

3

MYTHOPOETIC SUSPENSE, ESCHATOLOGY AND MISTERIUM

World-Building Lessons from Dostoevsky

Lily Alexander

Transparent things, through which the past shines! A thin veneer of immediate reality is spread over natural and artificial matter, and whoever wishes to remain in the now, with the now, on the now, should please not break its tension film. Otherwise the inexperienced miracle-worker will find himself no longer walking on water but descending upright among staring fish.

Vladimir Nabokov, *Transparent Things*

Nobody can understand Dostoevsky, even Dostoevsky himself.

Dmitry Bykov, *Who Killed Fyodor Pavlovich*

The Brothers Karamazov (*Братья Карамазовы*) by Fyodor Dostoevsky has grown in popularity over time, becoming a "cult classic". Written in 1880, the novel has served as an inspiration for the media industry, and its thriller and crime fiction writers. The international film and TV adaptations of *The Brothers Karamazov* count stands at 32 (on imdb.com). Dostoevsky's body of work has generated hundreds of cinematic versions around the world, creating a universe of references and resonances. (They include such screen landmarks as *The Idiot* (1951) by Akira Kurosawa; *Taxi Driver* (1976) by Martin Scorsese; and *Fight Club* (1999) by David Fincher, to name a few.) One of the top mystery books of world culture, *The Brothers Karamazov* (*TBK*), can be examined within a spectrum of contexts. This essay offers the *mythopoetic, anthropological*, and *narratological* perspectives on the novel, particularly relevant to *world-building theory* and *practice*. It is the first part of a larger work intended to continue the exploration of mythopoesis, the novel as a cultural form, and the works by Dostoevsky in the contexts of world-building and interactive storytelling.

In a nutshell, the story unfolds through the suspense of inevitable murder, with too many potential suspects to count. The psychological framing of the unpredictable cast is meant to intrigue: the character portrayals exceed the complexity levels required for a whodunit. When the unthinkable happens — but not the way one would expect — it leaves everybody puzzled, and the truth may never be revealed. Readers are left on their own to solve the story-riddle, unsure whom to trust. Implicitly but forcefully, Dostoevsky propels the themes of moral choice and conscience. Despite the tragic irony of the situation, the author shows faith in his readers, respects their dignity, and encourages them to search for the truth.

Even if a detective novel was not Dostoevsky's ultimate goal, the *deep-seated layers of hidden content* should be examined. Only by tracing the clashes among socio-cultural codes in this novel, can its meaning-making processes be revealed. *The Brothers Karamazov*, 19th-century opus of Shakespearean scale, is a recognized masterpiece of Psychological Realism and Critical Realism, accurately depicting its era, hence, a high point of the historical fiction. An influential work of Fantastic Realism, this novel is a prototype of the cultural construct we term "imaginary world". This concept belongs to the recently evolving field of knowledge, stimulated by its immense impact on media culture. Dostoevsky's masterpiece remains a subject of heated debates and conflicting interpretations. Just like any myth, the writer's last work — his testament — was designed to provoke discussions and encourage the *decoding of its concealed messages*.

This essay addresses the riddles of *TBK* and elucidates the ways of creating imaginary worlds. A part of the scholarly network for the fictional worlds-exploration, this study is meant to enrich the theory and practice of storytelling media by examining the pivotal narrative-symbolic logic which propelled *TBK* to worldwide fame. This goal is approached by interleaving several analytical methods. Dostoevsky studies, including the vast scholarship on *TBK*, envelopes the widest range of contexts possible. Yet, unlike the typically applied foci of religion, politics, and narratology, this author's goal is to examine the powerful ways mythology is integrated into the novel's imaginary world. Examined even overanalyzed in endless milieu, *TBK* is rarely explored within the realms of anthropology or folklore, and never that of fictional world-building. Yet, its locale, figures, and their actions are more than fictional: bluntly symbolic, they are a dynamic part of the (neo)mythological discourse. This essay explores the organizational principles of the imaginary world employed by Fyodor Dostoevsky, the effectiveness of mythic-symbolic codes the writer selected for his storyworld (in which historicity borders with the fantastic), and the functions of mythological references in creating the content and the far-reaching message of *TBK*.

In this volume, *TBK* serves as a case study for emerging world-building theory, a new field of knowledge this book is meant to advance. The main focus is on *mythopoesis*, understood as the engagement of the modern narrative media with myth. *Mythology* is defined here as a narrative system rooted in the worldviews, beliefs, and (proto-)religious semantics of the ancient people, expressed through a set of stories (myths). Different mythologies aligned with particular geographies and historical timelines generated distinct symbolic systems, infused with the embedded imagery and values. We don't employ here the term *mythology* in the context of ideology studies (initiated by the Frankfurt School). Yet we should not overlook that traditional mythologies and political neo-mythologies of mass societies may clash through the system of storyworld dissonances, carefully orchestrated and highlighted by the mythopoetic authors of the last centuries. In short, the old mythic beings are summoned to resolve the dead-ends of our political debates, when we don't have enough wisdom to achieve it ourselves.

This essay highlights the *building blocks*, *narrative codes*, and *algorithms of mythopoesis* employable in our era. Among them are the notions of *mytheme* (mythic theme), a recurrent transcultural theme in world myths, and *mythologeme* (the logic of plot development). Each mytheme has typically two to four transcultural patterns of story premise unfolding, or a mythologeme, which is to a mytheme what is a verb to a noun. Mythologemes activate and examine the possible ways each mytheme may unfold in culture. For example, "the brotherhood" is a mytheme, encompassing twin brothers and other brotherly ties; including such offshoots/spinoffs of Modernity and Romanticism as the Doppelgangers, or the (paradoxical/mystical) doubles portrayed by Dostoevsky's contemporaries Robert Stevenson in *Strange Case of Dr. Jekyll and Mr. Hyde* (1886) and Oscar Wilde in *The Picture of Dorian Gray* (1890). The resulting set of mythologemes sprouting from the inquiry "Am I my brother's keeper?" may range from "one sibling giving his life to save another" to "a brother killing a brother". While related to the functionality of cultural algorithms, the mythemes, nevertheless, may merge within new narrative traditions, while mythologemes may be bent or inverted by authors. No doubt, Dostoevsky employed the mythopoetic elements thoughtfully, yet creatively and often astonishingly.

Mythopoesis is a vital subject for the success of contemporary world-building practices. Hence, this article examines the mythopoetic depths and engines of the novel, paying special attention to Dostoevsky's mythopoetic resources, tactics, and strategies. *Mythopoetic tactics* help to skillfully organize a storyworld, while *mythopoetic strategies* are meant to influence the larger cultural (and political!) discourse. The writer was exceptionally well-read in world literature. Mythological resources available to Dostoevsky in the late 19th century include the world myths and fairytales, the Hellenic and European narrative traditions, Slavic mythologies and Russian folklore, as well as the neo-mythologies emerging in the European Modernity and the literature of his time. The mythic motifs he selected may have been employed either subliminally or intentionally. We need to examine the plausible sources to understand his strategic choices.

From what cultural depths did the mythopoetic tropes emerge; which ones, when, and why? What unsolved historical problems prompted specific elements to surface, in response to the call of our cultural needs?

This essay is meant to stimulate world-building theory and practice by drawing attention to three mythopoetic cultural mechanisms as essential and instrumental. The highlighted notions include the proposed concept of *mythopoetic suspense*, and the nearly forgotten but valuable concepts of *mythological eschatology* and *misterium* (or *mysterium*). Mythopoetic suspense, while bestowing the aesthetic pleasure of "story magic", creates sudden perception shifts, instrumental in building dramatic, semantic, and axiological tensions. It aligns with Aristotle's emphasis on *astonishment* and the Formalists' *making strange*. Mythological eschatology is instrumental is clarifying and resolving those tensions, while tracing each story figure's moral steps through the revelations of consequential logic. Misterium provides the unique conditions for these processes to take place and climax to (cathartic) resolutions. These concepts-blueprints arise as the instrumental symbolic frameworks or operating systems, which are vital for the compelling world-building.

The above-highlighted useful notions will serve to solve the riddles of *TBK* and outline the potential of mythopoesis as the meaning-making mechanism of culture. The proposed interdisciplinary approach is hoped to illuminate the "hidden corners" of the novel and its symbolic discourse, perceptible only within the realms of mythology. The world narrative heritage represents a colossal and powerful resource for emerging storytelling media. Hence, learning from the classical writer how to employ this treasured cultural reserve is important. It is from this perspective that we will attempt to "understand" Dostoevsky, the brothers Karamazov, and the role of myth in Fantastic Realism and fictional world-building.

A magnum opus of 800-plus pages, *The Brothers Karamazov* includes 12 books, an Epilogue, and a promise of a sequence, embodying a consequential imaginary world with a provocative fusion of the real and the fantastic. The novel, often viewed as a narrative maze and animated riddle, was indeed designed as a multi-layered mystery, enigmatic on many (symbolic) levels. The puzzling and dynamic world of *TBK* keeps "spinning", forcing manifold characters to toss and turn, revealing their conflicting sides. Some storyworld edges are polygonal and see-through, opening (into) new startling depths and emerging into "other realms". To this day, the commenters argue why the God and the Devil "visit" this crime scene, and disagree on whether the supernatural encounters "really" occur in the storyworld or if they are fruits of characters' imaginations.

Rooted in the ritual riddle, all mystery genres operate by means of "secret codes". Narration in *TBK* is channeled via a *nameless* figure with a mysterious identity, a mediator between the Author and the readers. The action takes place in the *imaginary* provincial town; but its name is so ill-omened that the enigmatic Narrator admits to fear to even utter it. The location of *TBK* is a metaphor of a town in 19th-century Russia, as well as a typical "transnational" settlement of any repressive unfair society, the ill-fated "any town" of the humankind. The name of this locale is Skotopogonievsk, which represents a sort of (intentionally) awkward-by-design verbal construction, bleeding with the author's spiteful sarcasm. Such name cannot exist in its language, exposing the impossible, insulting, humiliating place the semantic abyss. The town name literally means "the place where the cattle is chased toward. . . (slaughter)". Clearly, by "the cattle" the writer means men, "all of us", the people. This locale is his dystopian metaphor for the "place of hell".[1] Each story character even when confessing hidden feelings, troubling thoughts, or shameful deeds reveals alternative identities, never being "equal to Self" (resonating with Dostoevsky's most notorious protagonist Raskolnikov, the Split Man of *Crime & Punishment* (1866)). When introduced to a crowded social storyworld, we observe the imaginary psychological projections of living-breathing humans, throwing goliath mythic shadows. To deepen the poetic mystery of *TBK*, some storyworld inhabitants unveil (a presence of) fantastic silhouettes behind them.

The threads of mythology are naturally woven into the mythopoesis of the modern novel. Mythic characters in Fantastic/Magic Realism preside over the dramatic action from Great Time, the timeless Olympus of sorts.[2] This powerful team does not promise to debate Keynesian economics or solve our socio-political problems. Alert and supportive, the mythic beings watch from the cloud-balcony to calmly remind the humans that our challenges, dictators, and seeming "dead-ends" are temporal; but we should continue looking for answers ourselves.

The mythic contours of this novel channel a whole world of influences. The mythological circuit to be utilized in the studies of Dostoevsky encompasses the three symbolic orbits: Slavic mythology (native to Dostoevsky), pagan beliefs, and Russian fairy tales; the mythic pantheon of Hellenism promoted to a transcultural code that buoyed Renaissance and Classicism; and the cultural-political neo-mythology of European post-Enlightenment. Through multiple sources, mythopoesis affects reality by re-creating the symbolic community in unimaginable fusions and odd political alliances. Magic Realism plays with our expectations by invoking resonances and dissonances of mythic images, which unexpectedly sync or clash, yet inciting our compassion toward the afflicted fictional populace. Mythopoesis astonishes by re-aligning the storyworld groupings, untangling friends from foes, and revealing which characters cannot be forgiven and which ones should be saved.

TBK is famous for its symbolic and paradigmatic value: it has the transcultural, proverbial significance, addressing issues topical for all generations and eras. The pivotal theme of fathers and sons is manifest in the title, referencing the influential novel *Fathers and Sons* (1862) by Ivan Turgenev.[3] *TBK* may be viewed as a modern take on King Oedipus's *familial* problem, aligned with the themes of murder and guilty conscience. All brothers, in some way, find the figure of their patriarch intolerable. What would they do?

The mythic tale of Oedipus is rooted in the conflict between cultural codes. This is the central idea in the first structural study on the subject, Vladimir Propp's "Oedipus in Light of Folklore" (1944).[4] As Propp notes, the Oedipus tale's dramatic trigger was the crisis in the ancient world, which represents the clash of two social orders: the matrilineal and patrilineal. As will be shown in this essay, *TBK* reveals a clash of *several cultural codes*, although different from those of Oedipus's mythic era. Let us extend Propp's idea by suggesting that any culture clash, that is, between influential cultural codes, which deeply affect societies, is first tested and symbolically "resolved" (in hypothetical ways) within a narrative. Only later the conflicts are approached by logic and law, while their resolutions in reality may follow the proposals from the fiction.

The crisis of *Oedipus* was triggered by the social condition in which the *father was not recognized*; in a sense, the male parent's identity was largely unknown to his offspring, and if known, it meant little in all matters of legacy, heritage, and succession. For emerging civil society, this "mystery" had many consequences, both predictable and tragically unforeseen. The Riddle of the Sphinx, therefore, "challenged" the evolving civilization to define the (life-asserting) essence of manhood. One assumes that social harmony needs fathers to take full moral responsibility for their children. The mythological, historical, ethical, political, and philosophical meaning of *fatherhood* (the fathers' impact on the world) was at the heart of the classic tale (*The Odyssey* and its referential framework addressed the same theme, but from a different narrative perspective). What kind of world do fathers leave for the new generation? Predictably, this story signified the birth of tragedy. The myth of Oedipus foresees and "projects" the imaginary, long-term, catastrophic "butterfly effects" of existential memory gaps between generations and within the family, a keystone of society.

The two epigraphs for this essay, chosen for setting up a discussion, highlight the clash of opinions represented by contemporary literary critic Dmitry Bykov (b. 1967) and renowned novelist Vladimir Nabokov (1899–1977). Their aesthetic views diverge on whether we should simplify the approach to such a puzzling, multifaceted narrative as *TBK*. Nabokov is a writer whose imagery and sentence structure are more than metaphorical; they overflow and burst with the sprouting seeds of mythopoesis. The apt image-concept "transparent things", envisioned by Nabokov, implies that the modern novel serves as a veil, concealing yet vaguely revealing the rich symbolic imagery of myth, while its deep-seated codes and values *transpire* through the literary text. Employing the metaphor of *transparent things*, this essay highlights the mythological undercurrents of the novel and show that *TBK* transcends the crime fiction genre, opening for us the *transpiring contours of myth*, with its immense depth of field and "forgotten" value systems, which have "something to say" about Modernity. Regardless of how subliminal the flow of images was in the author's mind, the mythic themes are instrumental, playing a dynamic role in the meaning-making of *TBK*.

A narrative puzzle, the novel is designed to be complicated. Should the tactics of a simplified analysis of *TBK*'s multifaceted nature prevail? Nabokov favors embracing the poetic complexity. Conversely, Bykov reduces Dostoevsky to a postmodernist, while concluding that *TBK* is essentially just an early "whodunit" and imitation of Dickens.[5] However, the crime investigation with multiple suspects emerged as a cultural form rooted in the 19th-century socio-economic reality.[6] The genre's dissemination was not due to one writer's influence on another. Bykov insists that there is no answer: we *will never know* who the killer is because none of the characters, even while confessing, is a "reliable narrator". This is a neo-postmodernist interpretation of *TBK*. (The postmodernist era lasted from the 1960s to 1990s, and was replaced by new aesthetic paradigms.) To some extent, it may be true: Dostoevsky's humans are not equal to themselves; they all are the "underground" and "split" types (as per *The Double* (1846), *Notes from the Underground* (1864), and *Crime and Punishment* (1866), where the antihero's surname means "split").

Yet, essentially to Dostoevsky, each personality is shaped by one's precious deeper truth, which channels his whole worldview, held up by the gravity of a person's sacred faith based on individual values. Dostoevsky's characters take their beliefs seriously and argue about them fiercely. A mischievous provocateur and performance artist, Bykov half-jokingly exclaims that Dostoevsky may have been unaware of the content he himself created: "Even Dostoevsky does not understand Dostoevsky", Bykov says. The idea that much of the imagery may emerge from the artist's subconscious is neither new nor lessening his creative achievement. Mythological consciousness has a capacity of facilitating understanding of complexities, according to Lev Vygotsky (a founding father of modern psychology who commented on *Primitive Mentality* (1922) by Lucien Levy-Bruhl). Hence, we will undertake a journey away from postmodernism and toward mythopoesis, into the realms where mythology nurtures the artist's imagination and his search for the higher truth.

When 19th-century mythopoesis met the novel, two influential cultural forms merged to create the complex storyworlds of Fantastic Realism. (This encounter had already happened before, with the similar poetic tour-de-force in the post-Hellenic era of Apuleius's *Metamorphoses* and the post-Medieval era of Rabelais's *Gargantua & Pantagruel*, as explored by Bakhtin.) What is revelatory in Dostoevsky's experimentations with the novel and today's world-building is the idea of poetic persuasion through structure. In Modernity, matters of social significance increasingly come to light via the novel, a cultural form suitable for investigating behavioral puzzles and multiple points of view. While skillfully designed as a murder investigation, *TBK* is also a mockery of crime fiction genres. In other words, Dostoevsky builds his Temple, yet not without self-irony, decompressing his authorial self-importance, as suitable to the witty modern man. Layered upon his pathos and aspiration toward tragedy, self-parody and hidden laughter are essential to his fictional world-building.[7] Bakhtin also insisted that world mythology is revealed in his interpretation, via carnivalesque humor, and intrinsically present in the structure of Dostoevsky's novels. Bakhtin's theory of polyphony (his theoretical metaphor means the integral sum of politically diverse points of view embedded within a storyworld) remains the most influential in Dostoevsky studies and among the theories of the novel. Thus, the real and the fantastic, pathos and irony, all converged in a dynamic fusion in *TBK*.

Astonishingly (as per Aristotle, who emphasized perception shift as a poetic necessity), in Dostoevsky, irony does not take away from pathos, but also from mystery. Much of the implicit "clever" irony comes from the novel's world-model, in which what *transpires* for readers is that each (clueless) fictional character cannot see what his storyworld neighbor is doing, behind a story corner, even if only a few pages away. For such an "all-round" vision, narrative culture would employ the prying-everywhere Private Investigators and... supernatural beings. The present essay is meant to supplement Bakhtin's model of the novel as a political chorus. The active voices from multifaceted world mythology transpiring though the text and illuminating with their "truths" should be added to the Bakhtinian polyphony of social voices, while assembling a panorama of multiple perspectives on reality within a fictional world.

This essay also initiates an inquiry into the diversity of cultural codes which are both set to clash and synchronized in *TBK*. How do disparate modeling systems, such as ritual, myth, storyworld, genre, polyphony, and spiritual quest, become coordinated and "work in concert" while generating this influential novel with a strong spiritual center? The imaginative modalities, to be references, include several types and levels of mythology: the *transnational*, explored by structural studies of myth; the *classical European*, with the roots in the Greek tradition; the *post-Enlightenment European*; and the poorly studied *Russian folklore* informed by early man's *ritual-mythological practices* and *pagan religions*. This layering allows one to discover the stratification and hierarchical organization of diverse symbolic elements, employed for ontological timeless inquiries and for a candid appeal to the contemporaries via fictional world-building.

Secret Codes, Ritual Riddles, and Symbolic Resonances

The massive text is roughly structured by the arc of three mythologemes (types of action, recurrent in myth and narrative): (1) The abusive Father-Tyrant is asking for trouble: he is almost "a dead man walking"; (2) Tensions rise, and the family is entangled in the knots of greed, hubris, and lust; emotions reach a boiling point and the Father is killed; and (3) One of the brothers, presumably innocent but framed, is arrested and put on trial. All participants of the murder investigation and court proceedings, including authorities, remain clueless, never coming close to solving the *mystery*. Formally, plot development encompasses the author's designated 12 volumes, defined as separate "books", with the 13th titled "Epilogue". The novel's 800-plus page length, many books in one, and a promise of a sequel, makes this work a precursor to a serial drama, linked by one original storyworld. Recent adaptations of *TBK* explicitly took the shape of a film series.

The Brothers Karamazov remains a mystery on many symbolic and diegetic levels: those of mythological consciousness, the ritual riddles, the embedded openness to variable interpretations and hermeneutics, the mastery of suspense, a craftsmanship of genre-writing of the murder mystery, and crime investigation (although they are "secretly" parodied). *TBK* represents, employs, and mocks, for all intents and purposes, the formula of the "whodunit". The myth of the City-Jungle, emerging in the 19th century, laid the foundation for the helpless anticipation that neighbors won't be their *brother's keepers*. This abysmal fear that "anyone might have a motive" in the crowded yet anonymous urban space became a cultural premise for the rise of crime fiction with its embedded social riddles. Yet, Dostoevsky implies the nascent "whodunit" recipe and also challenges it. *The Brothers Karamazov* is also a skillful thriller: its storyworld is clouded by feverish anticipation. The narrative suspense occurs when the audience knows about the looming dangers, yet the characters don't (as Hitchcock famously said). To rephrase, Dostoevsky amasses information on tacit malicious thoughts and sinful plans which is so *excessive* that the heads began to spin, not only those of the wary characters, but also those of the readers. The audience is gradually burdened by knowing "too much". Suspense in this novel is manifold, transpiring on levels from zoological fear to philosophical angst.

The world-building of Modernity (including our own era of globalization) operates on the level of cultural codes, which are braided together, demonstrating multiple perspectives on, and conflicting interpretation of, the same story events, often creating both: defamiliarizing effects and stunning revelations. The codes' fusions, conflicts, and counter-influences implicitly work on grand levels, redefining cultures. Yet these codes also work on the explicit levels of the plot, prompting characters to "disagree with themselves" and "suddenly" commit acts, confusing even to Self. This *tragicomedy of errors* helps in the uncovering of macro-cultural and social changes. Via story structure, the author comments on how the world is organized, yet also reveals how it is falling to pieces. In *TBK*, the symbolic codes are aligned with the margins and centers: the image-symbols are set to move in two defining trajectories: decentralizing and pivoting or focalizing. The centrifugal force launches into narrative orbit a startling and lavish variety of mythic imagery. The centripetal force tirelessly rearranges symbols, while building what we will call here *the axiological axis mundi*. (While tautological, this phrase highlights how both meanings, the system of values and the pillar of the world, are essentially the same thing.) Applying symbolic anthropology, this essay discloses several "hidden" codes and story forces, facilitating access to obscured layers of content.

Hitchcock defined *suspense* as the effect when the reader/audience's knowledge exceeds that of those characters on-screen or "on-stage" (and in danger). Conversely, the (proposed here) mythopoetic suspense accompanies guests from the realms of mythology, who see infinitely more than the (mortal) story characters, and similarly naïve readers. We know that the visitors know what we don't and cannot know, and it is frightening. We are in awe about the inevitable shift in perception and meaning, our incompatible scales of space-time, and how a mythic character would choose to act in our questionable social reality. Besides, the fictional "sightseers" are on the otherworldly side of life and death, hence, possess supernatural might we can't imagine. When the Devil arrives in the world brutally oppressed by the tyrant-Stalin, what would he do? The Devil "would be shocked"! (As per Mikhail Bulgakov's novel, *The Master & Margarita* (1967), banned for thirty years (1937–1967), a direct reference to *The Brothers Karamazov*). Incomparable realms, values, and powers create mythopoetic suspense, in which the audience's thrill, excitement, thirst for magic, hope for liberation and catharsis, but also the infernal fear, are all fused together.

How do writers find and employ deep-seated mythological codes? To what extent are artists and audiences aware of the archaic symbolism employed in the media of modernity? Mythologies penetrate and empower modern texts through the artistic efforts, both conscious and subconscious. Some of us extensively research mythologies, yet many motifs penetrate our minds subliminally, via the local or transcultural layers we absorb. Readers/audiences may recognize mythological codes in artistic structure. When they don't, the gaps in understanding trigger the adventurous experience and stimulate imagination, via mythopoetic suspense. Such codes may manifest in portions by explicit or implicit mythic imagery, effects of estrangement or defamiliarization, or a story's mysteries, riddles, and twists. Overall, the cultural codes of mythological or religious symbolic frameworks effectively function through artistic structure, influencing readers with strategically imbedded puzzles or revelations, all of which subliminally enhance the total impact. Unlike in Hitchcockian suspense, where the readers notice dangers but characters remain perilously clueless, in mythopoetic suspense of Dostoevsky, Joyce, Bulgakov,

Borges, Marques, or Tolkien, the readers are astonished and enchanted, but don't grasp with cognitive lucidity all the symbolic meanings, which may appear illogical to the modern mind. Conversely, the many-faced Janus characters (part-mythic) are privileged to the secret/sacred knowledge of archaic mythological systems and values, to be gradually revealed through storyworld structure, or *transpire*.

For example, a sum of money continually surfaces and disappears in the character communications in *The Brothers Karamazov*. The figures in the storyworld, related or distant, crave, steal, bribe, tease, plan murder, frighten, or attempt to buy love by means of notorious money. So many memorable situations and passions are attached to these fiercely emotional interactions that a reader may miss the point (or notice it!) that the amount remains the same in various scenes: about 3,000 rubles. It is with tragic irony that Dostoevsky makes a reference to the *30 pieces of silver*, an ominous fetish employed among humans, while they betray or enslave each other.

This money, which everyone needs and thinks would save him, echoes the Golden Calf's symbolism of the "wrong god". This "talisman" is also reminiscent of magic coins from folktales, which cannot be lost or exchanged, always returning to its owner (presumably moved around by a dark spirit of sorts or a "laughing demon"). Yet, nothing (good) can be bought using it. While seldom this *recovering* coin may help "deserving characters", more often this (cursed?) money plays tricks with naïve but obsessively greedy humans. Flowing through many lives, but avoiding all eager hands, this money brings luck to none of the undeserving. The wishing coin in folklore is *acting differentially*, rewarding or punishing based on the hidden truth of each person's moral essence. This symbol is instrumental in *TBK*'s story development, performing diverse yet dramatically important roles, and always drastically shifting a social situation. This is only one example of how Dostoevsky plays with the visibility/obscurity of his symbolic images, hiding them in plain view. This sum of money with the ill-omened number becomes an *agent of change*, although nobody seems to notice this infernal entity's persistent presence and a menacing role in the storyworld.

Researchers infer that the books by Dostoevsky have layers of hidden symbolism. For example, in Yuri Marmeladov's *Dostoevsky's Secret Code: The Allegory of Elijah the Prophet* (1987), Marmeladov is correct in tracing the connections between Ilya the Prophet and characters in Dostoevsky's fiction.[8] It has been a well-known conclusion (as per the Chicago School of Religious Studies of the 1960s–1980s) that in various cultures, mythic figures of the pagan gods of Thunder, such as the Slavic Perun, were gradually converted into the Elijah the Prophet within the evolving Christian contexts. Yet, there are many more mythological connotations or "secret codes" to be discovered in *The Brothers Karamazov*.

Vital Interpretations: Decoding Nature's Tests

Why so many secrets? And why are we enthralled with storytelling full of riddles and puzzles? Early man's interactions with his habitat were defined by the need for deciphering or "cracking the codes" of his natural environment. Secret signs and symbols "emitted" by his surroundings were believed to transpire and come to light, to be decoded (deciphered); and relied on for survival. Since the dawn of the "mythological mind", it was assumed that the very interpretation of reality must include decrypting Mother Nature's subtle signifiers and passing her implicit tests. The ancients depended on the faith that reality *continuously speaks to them* in many "natural languages". Early man viewed these communications as "organically" obscured, because they were channeled through the inborn manifestations of nature, its sounds, movements, touches, colors, and shapes.[9] Even before *reading between the lines* (of books), people had hopes of *getting a whiff* of change from Nature's many communication channels. These subtle "micro-messages" which the Nature-gods and Spirits leave for the humans to grasp, encompass the sudden thunder, the flood, birds' love songs, the raining toads, or the advent of the apple-clasping snake. Only through these signs, the "marks of gods", could predictions be deemed reliable, while hidden truths about reality were revealed (or so our ancestors believed). Thus, the need for learning biosemantic communication with Nature later extended to mythology and narrative culture.

Various deities (initially, the animal-sprits) spoke different "natural" languages, and their dissonant chorus "had to" be synchronized. It is with the idea of the world governed by these diverse and "mysterious" semantics hence, in need of translation that a special deity was appointed (in the Hellenic tradition) to perform the clarification function, for both his fellow deities and the subordinate humans. The Olympus assigned the god Hermes a mission to launch hermeneutics, the activity of interpretation, endowed with "divine" revelatory power. Just as mythological image-concepts had formed a symbolic framework for the people at the dawn of culture, mythic subtexts function as a connecting tissue in much of modern storytelling.

To complicate things further (on purpose!), some spirits-deities, the entities of supernatural power, *intentionally clouded* their communication. They *had* to establish boundaries of understanding for humans, because the gods belong to the highest realm of powers set in Nature; while the mortals were expected to have a limited access to the (sacred) knowledge, unless they were "initiated".[10] Hence, the natural "hard to decode" languages and the "intentionally obscured" communications (symbolic, metaphorical, and proverbial) had set the foundations for the *ritual riddles,* a framework which shaped the ensuing mystery genres and the (metaphorical) language of art per se. Looking at the roots of mythological consciousness, which define its semantics, we can better grasp its functionality within narrative contexts. Everything appears to be (and is expected to be) a dynamic "sign" a signifier in the operational system of mythology; the more important and vital whenever it enables "survival". The Renaissance, Baroque Art, and Romanticism facilitated interest in myth, which then soared during Modernism. Among the programmatic goals of emerging Modernism in the late 19th century was that of learning and employing various organic (expressive) and intentional (metaphorical) languages of the natural world, also mediated by ancient art. Dostoevsky lived and worked in the age spanning from Romanticism to Modernism. Unsurprisingly, cultural codes were on his mind.

What's in a Name?

The inquisitive reader, who suspects that the word *karma* resonates with the title, is right. A careful examiner of Dostoevsky's fictional worlds notices his numerous tale-telling signs in *naming*. The ritual origin of naming is in the "mystical" linking of a person to powerful natural forces or spirits, with the purpose of establishing rewarding and safeguarding identification (as in *naming* European cities Berlin and Bern to ensure their citizens' protection and ritual empowerment expected in the Bear-totem era). Authors often use a name to (subliminally) reveal a hidden truth about its *bearer*.

Karamazov, Karamzin, and Karamazin are real Russian surnames (of the Turkic linguistic roots). Yet, the writer chose a family name with a revelatory message about his protagonists. The surname Karamazov unsurprisingly shares etymological roots with the concept of *karma* (via Indo-European linguistic connections). The Russian noun *kara* means the (deserved) punishment from the higher powers (pagan gods, God, or fate) for committed sins and crimes. The verb *mazat* means to paint, draw, chart, and also to stain or pollute. The family name Karamazov, therefore, may be interpreted as "the fate is drawn or tarnished" or possibly "to draw/taint one's fate with this person's choices or actions". The name explicitly points to the "karmic" meaning and the spiritual purpose of the novel. The protagonists are the brothers whose futures are being determined and drawn (on the scrolls of their timeless legacy, on some invisible tablets of Providence). Hence, the novel's title is linked to such notions as Fortune, also highlighting that it is our life choices that shape our futures. "Fate is predetermined" is echoed in the family name Karamazov. Yet the novel implies that by means of decisions and actions people draw their own destiny; *while the gods are watching.*

Just by *naming* the family and *casting* his characters, Dostoevsky lets the air and shadows from mythological realms into his storyworld. His cast of characters, entangled in tragedy and mystery, includes the antihero father; his sons; the four women who fatefully influenced the lives of the Karamazov men; the town's spiritual mentor; the locals and officials; several "weird" enigmatic types; as well as God and the Devil. Fyodor Dostoevsky's arch-villain is Fyo-dor Karamazov. The story's villain and the author teasingly "exchange masks": they wear the same name, which in this context sounds tragic-ironic: the "gift from God" Theodoros (Fyodor in Russian). It is hard to overlook the fact that of all possible names, the author gave his antagonist *his own name*, with a whiff of self-irony ("How far is Everyman from society's antiheroes?" is a lingering question).[11]

A few more tale-telling names have a Greek origin (Zosima, Dmitry, Kat-erina, Grusha, Alexei, and Ilya). In other novels, many names and surnames are symbolic. In *Crime and Punishment*, Rodion Raskolnikov's given name means "he is born" while his surname means "split man"; Sonya, Sophia the Wise, Razymikhin means "sensible"); in *Poor Folk* (1846), there is Devyshkin ("girl-ish, gentle like a girl"); in *The Idiot* (1869), there is Myshkin ("little mouse"), Nastasia ("eternally growing"), and Rogozhin ("cheap rug"). Let's look at other connotations with the potential symbolism bursting forth into the *TBK* plot functionality. Zosima, spiritual mentor, means *life* and *the living* (Forever?). Dmitry, the brother to be framed and sentenced, is *the Earthly Man*, the off-spring of the Nature-goddess Demetra, and his love Agrafena "feet first", the walking, *wanderer on the earth*. Ivan is symbolic of the Russian Everyman and the folktales' Ivan the Fool. Alexei is *the defender of man* (a short version of Alex-ander). Katerina the Pure (vs. the Impure) connotes purification and catharsis (as in Mary Douglas's *Purity and Danger: An Analysis of Concepts of Pollution and Taboo* (1966)). Ilya is from the Hebrew Eliah, *the son of God*.

It is worthwhile to further analyze what significance, if any, naming may have in this novel; and how names abet the storyworld's complex system of meanings. Through nearly all the names in his novels, Dostoevsky adds some symbolically *elevated* perspective on a character's nature or path in the world. Importantly, the novel generates its own narrative hermeneutics, which is grounded, implicitly, in the deep layers of existing symbolic systems, ascending from mythologies and religions. The game of decoding and meaning-making in *TBK* goes much deeper than the "whodunit?".

Who is Who? The "Threshold" Characters: Between Myth and Literature

The cast of characters consists of a very elaborate system of contrasting and resonating figures; almost like a chess set, ready for battle; and with carefully set traps. The inner circle is the Karamazov family, with the Father-tyrant, the main cause of the plot disequilibrium and a man impossible not to hate. This emotion is craftily provoked for readers to feel, which the younger generation of the Karamazov family predictably shares. The (folktale's) three sons are of course at life's crossroads, as mythic, journeying heroes should be. The old-est, Dmitri, is the Passionate one. The middle brother, Ivan, is the Smart and

Educated one. The youngest, Alexei, is the Truth-seeker and a Kind Soul. The heart, the mind, and the soul. So far, good-old reliable clichés and unashamedly blunt symbolism. The devilish math of "How many brothers are in the novel?" is designated to be a separate puzzle to solve. There will *transpire*, through the storyworld folds, an yet unknown brother, Pavel, unrecognized on many symbolic levels. Part of the transcultural mytheme of *the lost relative*, returned to the family in a *fateful manner* (or by Fate with a karmic intension), this "secret" brother will play a pivotal role in the novel. His storyline was developed a century later into a separate work, and likewise "more-than-whodunit", revolving around the tragic "bastard" figure (or the despised son-servant, who may explode one day), in *Gosford Park* (2001), directed by Robert Altman and written by Julian Fellowes.

The Karamazov men are involved with four women, who cannot be more different from each other. Two of them oddly have the same name, Liza. Of these Karamazovs's "significant others" (for the men and for the plot), two are rich, two are poor, two are healthy, two are sick, two are loved, while two barely tolerated; traits come in unexpected sets. The math is getting more ominously playful. Three of the four *femmes fatale* would be "fatefully" involved with more than one of the Karamazov men, in various unforeseen combinations, but ensuring the chaos and fury of passions. *Cherchez la femme*, that is, ironically invoked by Dostoevsky.

The mythic and (near) supernatural figures include the God, the Devil, the Holy Sage, the chilling Grand Inquisitor, and the few Holy Fools, believed in Russia being "the children of God". The strange, threshold silhouette the ghostly Narrator is neither here nor there, and is neither the author, nor a story character, despite his claim of living in the same town and being a neighbor, an "eyewitness" of sorts. While he conveys his cheeky comments on the story events, he is strapped in the limbo of the proscenium, between the real writer-Dostoevsky and generations of his infinite readers. Any *liminal personae*, residing in the mysterious place of betwixt and between, according to the founder of symbolic anthropology Victor Turner, transpires as a figure of ritual influence, sparking magic-infernal expectations.

Most ancillary figures fittingly for the novel step on the stage precisely to ricochet. The Brownian Motion they cause is one of accidental influences, in which one chance encounter or an explosive secret may have a long, fateful impact on this fictional world. The storyworld's external circle consists of local residents of all ranks, and the officials, who enter the stage for the murder investigation and the court hearings. The townsfolk and administrators are mostly clueless and apathetic regarding God and the Divine perspective. The background social circles are painfully unaware, being deaf and blind, of the signs of Fate, meanings of the events, and higher truth. Some are confused about even basic facts of life and its social foundations. (Examples include the monks' expectations that their devout peers' bodies after death would not decay, or the spoiled rich girl's belief that the Jews steal babies to drink their blood.)

Among the townspeople, a special place is allocated to one family, who are marginal in every way; the poor, suffering yet honorable father and his little son. Their surname, "Snegirev", means *of the bullfinch kind*, a tiny snowbird, a vulnerable cold-weather survivor. The deep bond between the Snegirevs is a striking contrast to the toxic relations of the father and sons in the wealthy Karamazov family. Snegirev is a retired army officer: his social identity belongs to the transcultural narrative type of the "war veteran", ascending to a heroic scale. This symbolism transpires through the pantheon of powerful, near-shamanistic *old warriors* of world mythology, which include the humble *old soldier*, invincible and wise, who can solve any problem in the Russian folklore. (Warriors who survived many battles are believed to *have had many lives*, or to be sort of "immortal".) The veteran's mythic-symbolic status would be even more elevated in the subsequent literature, from Leo Tolstoy's *War and Peace* (1865) (with Platon Karataev), to the novels by Erich Maria Remark. All the diverse characters of *TBK* are brought, or thrown, together to take part in the story's intrigue and action, to express unique voices (the Bakhtinian polyphony or multiple point of view of reality), and via *mythological eschatology*: to be compared, to stand the tests, to measure up, to be assessed, and to be *judged before gods.*

Of Conscience and Shame: Mythological Eschatology Becomes "NarratoLogical"

The story characters act, hence, claim a position on life, and must be evaluated. One of the core paradigms of mythology is its innate eschatology, Mother Nature's habit of keeping records and scoreboards of human deeds. The social connection with the members of the tribe in the presence of the worshipped anthropomorphic natural environment was the starting point of the "moral record keeping". The concept of eschatology is rooted in the ritual paradigm of death-rebirth, a key concept in symbolic anthropology. Eschatology, initially, a human response to the crises of survival, which unleashed fears, began to grow into a moral framework, as vivid in the late Hellenic orphic tradition. Yet, the micro-elements of moral self-assessment could be traced back to the dawn of mythological consciousness. Humans were trying, desperately, to guess what Mother Nature considers "right and wrong". The scholarly concept of mythological eschatology was developed by classicist and structuralist Olga Freidenberg in the 1930s to highlight that within all mythological frameworks, the idea of "keeping score" has always been implicitly embedded, and regulated by native moral systems. (It is tragic-ironic that in the darkest hours of

Stalin's purges, the scholar who would soon be ostracized, banned from visiting the university library, and fired for being Jewish (or "cosmopolitan" in Stalinist terms) developed the idea that even in the worlds of tyrants *someone is watching*).[12]

Mythological consciousness embraces the belief that *someone is always watching* be it a tree, a cloud, a sacred animal, the divine light, or anthropomorphic deity. This *Observing Mind* (Nature's integral multi-source POV) keeps track of everyone's deeds on the moral grid; with the counts to be announced when the mortal pleads for the afterlife. Christian eschatology would make this threshold even more rigid: one way or the other; heaven or hell. Yet, in the world of early religions, this accumulation of decrees and penalties/rewards prevails as the subtle yet omnipresent buildup (i.e., *karma*). The outcomes may vary for one's afterlife; and the "informers" may similarly diverge Nature's eyewitnesses, the multiple evidence sources for the verdict.

These *silent witnesses* may contribute from the manifold mythological layers of culture. In sum, the whole world of mythologies in the moral symbolic ecosystem of humanity may "judge" any character in the plot. (This is exactly the point in J.R.R. Tolkien's *The Lord of the Rings* (1954–1955) and *Spirited Away* (2002).) Mythological eschatology is the bridge to understanding how ethics gradually evolved, connecting the logic of living Nature, the emerging mythological consciousness and the perceived "narrative justice". An intriguing detail about the evermore symbolic expression of mythological eschatology in the narratives of Modernity, particularly in the novel, is its manifestation by means of Fate. This "goddess" no longer reveals her face or persona, transpiring only through the turns of the story. Story twists, in the disguise of *chance* no more the explicit agent of the divine Nature or Fate, come to represent a narrative function.[13] Story twists expose the limited *partial truths* the storyworld mortals are doomed to possess. Narrative peripeteias and accidents also symbolize the continual *tests by reality,* which Fate forces characters to take, entailing the "score keeping" for the records.

Mythological eschatology (derived by Freidenberg from her studies of the Classics) is not too distant from the notion of karma, devised by the religious consciousness of India. This multifaceted stream of cultural meaning-making in the global mythology grew over time, and multiple semantic streams established that the worlds of supernatural beings (even before monotheism) have implicit, invisible to the human eye, mechanisms of judging all living beings in respect to the morality of their actions and *organic responsibility* for the world. Mythology makes it clear that these Irrational Forces (as Bakhtin called them, to fit in with the anti-religion phase in Stalinist discourse) would carry out justice, without hesitation or delay, through various "accidental" and natural-looking occurrences. In sum, mythological eschatology means that "Nature is watching" and the verdict will be quickly executed. The "Nature-Judge" has infinite means to implement her sentence.

The early representation of this eschatological effect is the "accidental" *death by the falling wall* in the proverbial tale of Cain and Abel (according to the *Book of Jubilees* 4:31). God specifically banned anyone's interference with the destiny of the brother-killer (the theologians debate "why" to this day); perhaps to check if there is indeed karma in the natural course of the universe. Dealing with the archetypal moral dilemma of being one's *brother's keeper*, the tale implies the spectrum of possible relations between the symbolic brothers, expanding from the familial to the social scale. Cain kills his brother. Yet, the divine punishment was intentionally "postponed". It was the narratological consequential punishment that eventually transpired: Cain oops was accidentally killed by the wall, which he, himself, erected. Already in the (mind behind) the Bible, we see how the *mythological eschatology* morphs into the *religious eschatology* and into the cultural logic of *narrative justice*.

Dostoevsky was a devoted Christian; however, he was curious about many diverse belief systems. Admittedly, he was also *pochvennik* (deeply rooted in the native soil), a member of the intellectual movement which treasured the "organic" growth of cultures and civilizations as well as all transhistorical values of the native land, including ancient beliefs, myths, and folklore. In 19th-century Russia, there was no sharp contradiction, as typical for the Slavic world, between the pagan and Christian faiths, particularly, among the peasants and the intelligentsia. Conversely, the major rift emerged between the believers-Slavophiles, and their opposition, the Westerners, those who aligned only with the European values, rationality and science. Hence, the traditional mythologies and mythological consciousness were part of Dostoevsky's interests as a writer and thinker.

The intrinsic logic of myth, with its keen attention to the Nature's balance and the tendency of harmony-restoration mythological justice was gradually replaced by the composite reasoning embedded in the complexity of fictional worlds, termed here "narratological". This dynamic type of model, called "novel", traced the restoration of justice through the social knots of long-winded trajectories, which were impossible for a single pair of eyes to see. Dostoevsky, along with the novel-writing giants of the 19th and 20th centuries, was one of the creators of this vital moral framework at the dawn of mass society.

The Brothers Karamazov adheres to the *mytheme of the lost brother*: the accepted/alienated and the brother known/unknown. Brought up separately and finally meeting, each young Karamazov tries to explain himself to his siblings, yet remaining unsure what really is on the other brother's mind. The dilemma of one's brother being *recognized/unrecognized* (in every sense, also syncing with the unrecognized father of *Oedipus*) has the eschatological implications. In *TBK*, readers are positioned to wait-and-guess which of the brothers would kill their father, and on what page (already!). But their predictions may fail because it might be an (unknown) brother (they don't know) who kills his father and frames his (known) brother for this crime. The plot distraction, or the red herring (the author-planted false assumption) is the Father-Son's ruthless and known rivalry for the same woman. And while they are a step away from killing each other, there is the foreshadowing of the even deeper hatred that would erupt into a crime. Just as Nature used to *observe everything*, a new agency, the mind of the novel, now keeps the scoreboards of all brothers' actions, intentions, and hidden thoughts.

Moving from Mother Nature's woodland into the City-Jungle, the characters in the novel are now tested by, and seek "vital signs" for survival in the grimaces of urban environment. The revelatory semantics are emitted here by the crossroads, chances, accidents, the Many-Faced Janus's nature of humans, hypocritical "masks", role-playing, eavesdropping, ominous anonymity, and all other hidden corners and folds of the city, from where anyone could "suddenly" attack.[14] Therefore, it is in the nature of the novel to oversaturate the mythologized city narrative with the tale-telling and warning signs. Such is the imaginary world of *TBK*. In the emerging cultural form of the novel and its essential variety, the crime novel, eschatology and score-keeping are manifest in the investigation (where the clues, red herrings, accidents, chases, and confessions encompass the zigzag streams of revelatory information, essentially, all the helpful "vital" signs).

The enigmatic contours of the City-myth already transpire from the geometrical uncertainty of the Baroque and Piranesi's ominous fantastic prisons; this distinct aesthetics later extends through the daunting urban tales of French Naturalism and Film Noir. The fogged city-image not only warns of looming dangers but also of the difficulties in moral judgment and finding the truth. How to correctly assign the "guilt" to the wrongdoers? They may include the accidental criminals or those fighting back to survive; the uncaring or empathetic witnesses; and even the victims, those vicious whom "anyone could kill". The Whodunit story pattern, when many have a motive, serves as a backward mirror, showing the victim's own crimes, in reverse. The readers are given tiny bits of the puzzle through hints and clues, so they may begin to explore the hidden realms of the storyworld. Intuition is engaged as an important mode of perception in this ritual riddle-cracking, so the keen reader/audience would exclaim with excitement "I knew it!" — before the characters do. Therefore, a super-novel like *TBK* would have to stockpile an enormous quantity of the subtle tale-telling signs, from all realms of mythology and contemporaneity, and gradually release them, making the storyworld-decoding a tough yet thrilling experience.

Eschatology, as mentioned earlier, is a moral grid by which one's life is assessed at the threshold, as per mythologies and religions. In crime fiction, eschatology is both simplified and complicated. It becomes more straightforward since the goal is to catch the criminal and put him in jail, using the reliable legal apparatus of our civilization. Conversely, the good fiction tends to problematize the clichés, and add the "it's not that simple" perspective, continuing the inquiry beyond the letter of the law. What if it is unclear who is to blame? Where the limits are in (life-long) self-defense? And how do misdeeds accumulate, unchecked in life, in the family, and in social reality?

Misterium as a Genre and Beyond

The Brothers Karamazov, clearly "more than crime fiction", may be viewed as a multi-genre enterprise. It has elements of crime drama, detective novel, coming of age, Bildungsroman, or the novel of education, romance, thriller, tragedy, confessional prose, and even farce or the "tragicomedy of errors". Recognized as a psychological, philosophical, political, and historical novel, *TBK* is also a diatribe against social injustice, intact with its era's Critical Realism. Yet, while pondering on the nature of *The Brothers Karamazov*'s genre, and acknowledging its experimental aspirations, we must invoke a notion of *misterium*, a near-forgotten yet enduring cultural form that has always remained timely.

The umbrella concept, central paradigm, and pivotal force which ties diverse elements together is *misterium*. *The Brothers Karamazov* cannot be understood without clarifying this notion, in both the historical and theoretical contexts, including an anthropological angle. This essay proposes restoring the Latin spelling *misterium* for the theoretical term referring to the phenomenon, which signifies the related cultural paradigm, while transcending chronologies. The word's original Latin spelling helps to distinguish this important notion from the word *mystery*, recently overused, and a subject of heteroglossia: it conveys too many different meanings to remain a useful and clear term. Misterium (plural *misteria*, adjective *misterial*; from the Greek *mist* to squint, "shut", or "eyes shut") connotes the phenomenon both historical and timeless / transcultural, also meaningful for creating imaginary worlds.

What is misterium? Why did Dostoevsky need it, and how can world-building benefit from this forgotten cultural form? From the perspective of misterium, it does not matter whether the mythic beings visit the storyworld "for real" or as the ghosts of characters' imagination. In misterium, which affords a sort of (religious) trance, the *eyes are shut* (this is what the word means, as its original Greek language etymology alludes). By its nature, one experiences the world that transpires through the eyes "wide shut". In this "betwixt and between" liminal world,[15] the characters bare their souls and conscience for judgment, before the diverse (newly assorted) gallery of mythic deities. Hence, their presence in the (modern) novel is justified. They oversee the court of divine justice, which unlike trial by humans, mocked in *TBK* by Dostoevsky, can determine what the truth "really is".

Historically, misterium refers to the ancient Greek and Roman public celebrations, performances and festivals, devoted to the local gods; the most well-known are the Eleusinian and Dionysian mysteries. (Classicists continue using the term "mystery" in respect to the public rituals of Antiquity/ancient Greece and Rome.) The established postulate of the anthropology of performance traces the origin of theater to ritual. But there was something else, in between, astonishingly poorly studied, yet of foundational significance. The transitional historic phase between ritual and theater, which lasted centuries, was misterium (ranging about a millennium BC and two centuries AD). Yet even with the emergence of stage arts, as we know them, misteria did not disappear from the realms of culture and religion, still influencing art, media, and narrative culture in many predictable and unexpected ways. Misterium has emerged as a media construct and a profound (timeless, rather than displaced from the historical arena) cultural paradigm, particularly revelatory for world-building theory and practice.

Ritual as a predecessor of theater art (and its heirs, film, television, and video games) is a well-established postulate of symbolic anthropology and performance studies.[16] The influence of the initiation rituals on culture has been thoroughly studied. Named by Joseph Campbell, the "hero's journey" has had a far-reaching impact on media culture. Less-known is the significance of the later phenomenon, misterium, which still overlaps with ritual, and therefore, was predictable, while already adding a specifically urban dimension to its essence. Emerged as a form of collective rituals in the settings of the first towns, misteria were devoted to synchronizing individual ritual actions of diverse participants in the growing settlements they all called home. A single-hero's lonely journey of the earlier ritual culture was followed by socializing procedures, which took forms of coming together as a group in celebration of the native gods, the patrons of the settlement, and the surrounding nurturing fields.

The key features of misterium include: the simultaneous and parallel "journeys" of many participants who seek the acceptance through initiation; and the expression of loyalty to specific, locally valued gods, chosen with expectations of domestic benefits from the richly populated and diverse pantheon of Hellenic polytheism. There was also the invocation with invitation: the chorus of neighbors calling for the deity to arrive (in earlier rituals, the higher powers arrive when they see fit). The revelers also opened themselves to judgment in the effort to purify their souls and match the moral requirements from the beyond to ensure the "good life" in the afterlife. The moment of increasingly active participation of the community in relations with the patron deity was a subtle yet vital new aspect in the emerging town-culture misteria.

Gradually, transforming from the calendar-linked or the harvest-focused celebrations intended to ensure plentiful food supplies, misteria began to develop dramaturgy, at first re-playing key moments in the worshipped deity's biography, and later presenting various human social situations to be examined and judged before gods. This branch evolved into man-authored drama and comedy (resolvable by human efforts, including laughing at oneself) and tragedy (typically unresolvable without the involvement of the gods from the machines, and their cathartic enlightening of human minds). We may say that the "eschatological" impulse (to be judged and corrected before too late) was now coming from the humans themselves.

The eyes were supposed to be shut as a mark/device of entering the other dimension, stepping from the profane/ordinary world through the portal of misterium into the sacred/divine realm, where the two kinds the gods and mortals can meet and resolve looming problems. With (symbolically) closed eyes in a mysterious mood the magic action of stepping across the threshold was expected to occur. We now employ for this purpose the "magic moments" of rising theater curtains, screens lighting up, and books opening. The key defining features of misteria include group participation; concern for the local home environment; the addressing of the pressing issues of social life; the human initiative in appealing to, and bringing in, the higher powers; readiness for moral judgment; and choosing the ever-increasing pantheon of gods (when civilization expanded) to be addressed from all realm/resources of the world mythologies and religions, to whom these newly re-elected individual deities the people would plead allegiance. This is what we observe in *The Brothers Karamasov* and perhaps what contemporary world-building aspires to achieve. In *TBK*, the author and his multiple characters (including his alter egos) cross the textual threshold (enhanced by multiple stories-within-stories) and invoke various higher powers, while seeking help in addressing the pressing social questions (in this case, Russia's unresolvable political problems of undying Feudalism before the dawn of the 20th century).

Certainly, not all historically performed misteria were of the spiritual quality, as designated. There were different traditions and the bad apples, such as the violent or criminal Roman bacchanalias, "which were periodically banned, whether for their excessive violence or politically subversive messages." (It is important to mention that the "corrupt" or the exploitative use of the powerful misterial form, governed by flawed moral or political aims, may happen in any century). Yet the fruitful traditions flourished around ancient Greece and the Mediterranean of late Antiquity, as described in Apuleius's *Metamorphoses* and his biographies, depicting the writer's real-life journeys and explorations of diverse deities' cults, popular around the Mediterranean in the 2nd century AD. In essence, misteria have never left the realm of art entirely. Consider, for example, the key dramatic functions of the Ghost, the fertility god's offspring Queen Hecuba, the Goddess Hecate, the Thunderstorm, and the array of mythic beings in Shakespeare's *Hamlet* (1609), *Macbeth* (1606), *King Lear* (1606), and *Midsummer Night's Dream* (1605), respectively. Add to this the movement to restore ritual in the theater, pioneered in the 20th century by Artaud, Meyerhold, Grotowsky, and Brook; and the new tradition of screen *passions* (misteria!), directed by Dreyer, Pasolini, and Tarkovsky. The rise of Fantastic Realism, following European Romanticism and the vestiges of Modernism (the looming aesthetic revolution), encouraged experimentations with reality, myth, and fantasy.

It is important to add the notion of the misterial, as an adjective (as per the French and Italian roots). It applies to the quality proven to remain transhistorical and transcultural that has transpired in multiple cultural phenomena since the rise of the town-cultures of the Mediterranean before Hellenism, to modern-day media. The elements of the misterial beyond the Antiquity were later manifest in a variety of cultural expressions. They include the adventuristic novel, Medieval Cathedrals (some with their sentinels–gargoyles), church passion plays, Renaissance paintings, Cervantes's self-ironic quest for the ideal Self in *Don Quixote* (1605), and Vermeer's challenge to bend geometry for peeking into the other dimensions.

The mysteriousness of the Baroque and Gothic art was also part of this avenue, making a shift from the pathos of sacred mystery to the pragmatism of crime fiction in the narrative discourse. Initially, the dangerous, mythic shadows appeared invincible; later, the story efforts focused on finding and destroying the foes of society, however natural or supernatural they turn out to be. As emphasized by Bakhtin and Deleuze, it was the Baroque era which gave birth to crime fiction.[17]

The City-culture, with its overwhelming mosaic and multiple vistas, simply was in need of the spiritual centers. Therefore, misterium returns in Modernity not merely an aesthetic (theatrical, narrative), but a cultural phenomenon. And it is not authored or pioneered by individuals but represents the spiritual modality that aspires to find an embodiment in response to our cultural needs. Urban growth is overwhelmed with its rag-bag of the newly arriving townsfolk; hence, the sundry set of multifarious mythic deities is a proper match to the diversity of the city-culture. Just as in the turbulent Hellenic world of late Antiquity, strange types from the neighboring religions/cults may end up in the revised collections of active gods, mythopoesis of Magic and Fantastic Realism may parade the peculiar, quirky, offbeat, weird, and eccentric mythic powers/beings, encompassing the walking Nose, the giant talking black cat, the jailed god, and the omnipresent inquisitor.

The influence of the (macro) cultural form of misterium on Dostoevsky, an avid reader of world literature, reveals a long-term trajectory, via European heritage implicitly, but also via a short arc, explicitly, in the 1880s. When he was working on the novel, emerging French Symbolism was raising a question of the intrinsic religiosity of theater, or *stage art as ritual*.[18] The echo of Symbolism profoundly influenced the Russian and Scandinavian dramatic art; as demonstrated by the Modernist theater experiments, and writings on the philosophy of art by Henrik Ibsen, August Strindberg, Vladimir Soloviev, Nikolai Berdyaev, Nikolai Evreinov, Pavel Florensky, Marc Chagall, Pavel Filonov, and later Antonin Artaud and Sergei Eisenstein.

The Baroque, Romanticism, and French Symbolism implicitly placed the stories in realms observable by the supernatural figures. These were metaphorical constructs, yet ones preserving the religious impulse, as is typical for any ritual process overlapping with art. In the decades preceding the 20th-century threshold, the cultural agenda of the misterium restoration was already explicitly discussed by artists and philosophers of the late 19th century, particularly in France and Russia. The restoration of misteria was one of the explicit core projects of Symbolism and Modernism, widely discussed in the theater and aesthetic circles. Symbolism, while not being explicitly religious, sought the understanding of the profound and meaningful symbolic (spiritual) processes of reality, through art.

The Modernists sought to weave trance-inducing experiences by invoking cosmic image-signs from the entirety of nature and culture to convey, via artistic mosaics, subliminal messages of revival and rebirth. These discussions were part of the public discourse among the artists, writers, cultural philosophers, and, of course, religious thinkers seeking to find innovative ways to restore religion in view of the dangerous trends of mass society. Russian thinkers and artists eagerly supported this movement (leading to the prominent Russian Symbolism of the Silver Age and also its forerunner, Fyodor Dostoevsky).[19] The desired syncretism of the Arts proposed to fuse poetry, theater, literature, music, visual arts, and other multi-sensory experiences of synesthetic stimulation and total immersion. The motives behind this movement encompassed the concerns of the aesthetic, spiritual, and political nature, at the dawn of the 20th century.

Originating as a religious-performative experience, misterium evolved as the paradigmatic and transhistorical cultural form. It branched away from ritual, with its syncretic unity of "art-religion-knowledge" into the realms of narrative and theater, developing as a symbolic algorithm of culture. This split could be dated to the Renaissance, when misteria's secular aspirations began to sprout in many artistic directions. Yet, while the religious impulse may take metaphorical expressions in the Arts, by its ritual nature, the axiological perspective of the gods, watching. . . can never be eliminated from the story framed by misterium (even if these higher beings take the identities of mythic entities or aliens). Misterium was repeatedly activated as a cultural tour-de-force by geo-political changes, associated with rapid expansions. When distant populations had to become one people under the umbrella of new ideas or governments, their beliefs and values were set to fuse or clash. "The wisdom of synchronization – the solution effective in both nature and culture – in its optimal forms leads to the advancements of individuals and groups." The necessary mutual sharing and absorption of foundational myths led to the new empowerment of misteria, caused by the cultural need. Such eras include the late Antiquity, the Renaissance, the 19th-century threshold between the French Revolution and the Napoleonic Wars, and the dawn of the 20th century, with the looming shadows of world wars. Our era of globalization is certainly part of this historical chain of expansions. Unsurprisingly, the modern-day world-building movement (already) has invoked the misterial elements in its media language and practice.

The joy of the locals for coming together in a communal event of spiritual unity (something Dostoevsky cared for deeply) morphed into the forms of virtual collectivity and collaboration on-line. Yet, there are also the real-world fan movements, carnivals, and conventions. Global media encourages sharing favorite stories and adopting the foreign-born magic friends from other cultures (or planets, or species). In place of the gods, any authority figures from the world mythologies may come into play; and we see many spectacular, influential characters from the fantasylands who teach us good lessons about humanity. Dramas, thrillers, and mysteries do not let us forget about our human flaws and unpredictability of the natural world. And here transpires the mechanism of mythopoetic suspense: elucidating the dark corners of respective cultures with hidden biases, envy, hubris, delusions, and dangerous ambitions. Mythological eschatology that insists on karmic revelations transforms into savvy narratological scoreboards, while the entire foundation of interactive storytelling is based on (moral) choices, social pathfinding, and consequential logic. Aspiring media artists and game designers may fantasize freely, engaging the treasures of world myths. The axiological framework and operating system of symbolic misterium will keep them grounded in moral values, which we continually reassess as an evolving global community.

Notes

1 This imaginary dystopian locale resonates with the Glupov-town of Mikhail Saltykov-Shchedrin's *The History of a Town* (1870), a grotesque satire, politically risky novel relating the tragic-farcical chronicles of the fictitious Foolsville or Stupid Town, a caricature of the Russian Empire, with its sequence of monstrous rulers tormenting their hapless populations. This neo-mytheme also connotes Kurt Vonnegut's *Slaughterhouse Five* (1969).

2 In his body of work, Bakhtin proposed and employed a notion of Great Time (*Bolshoe vremya*). This (metaphorical) concept implies symbolic–axiological eternity. The enormous, infinite realm of time is conceived by Bakhtin as populated by archetypal mythic figures and serving as a precious reserve of the most important values and perspectives on the world. What is interesting for the study of mythopoesis is that Bakhtin alludes that this enigmatic realm of Great Time is implicitly but actively present in all (best) narratives of humankind as a latent, deeply embedded POV. A philosophical anthropologist and predecessor of the semiotics of culture Bakhtin developed his own conceptual apparatus which integrates a poetic and a philosophical language. His conceptual system was enthusiastically reemployed by "the Bakhtin industry" in the humanities of the 1990s, particularly, in France, the United Kingdom, and the United States. See: M. M. Bakhtin, *Rabelais and His World*, translated by Hélène Iswolsky, Cambridge, Massachusetts: The MIT Press, 1968; M. M. Bakhtin, *The Dialogic Imagination: Four Essays*, edited by Michael Holquist, translated by Caryl Emerson and Michael Holquist, Austin, Texas, and London, England: University of Texas Press, 1981.

3 Ivan Turgenev's classical novel *Fathers and Sons* (1862) had initially shaped the public discussion on intergenerational ideological tensions in Russia; shortly thereafter Dostoevsky began to write *TBK*.

4 For the seminal international collection, *Oedipus: A Folklore Casebook* (1995), on the archetypal myth, its co-editor, Alan Dundes, the leading American theorist of folklore, commissioned the translation of the influential work by Propp, the founding father of narratology and the structural studies of plot. See Allan Dundes and Lowell Edmunds, editors, *Oedipus: A Folklore Casebook*. Madison, Wisconsin: University of Wisconsin Press, 1995.

5 See Dmitry Bykov, *Who Killed Fyodor Pavlovich*, Audiobook lecture, Moscow, Russia: Litres, 2019. Bykov suggests that *TBK* was largely inspired by Charles Dickens's similarly unfinished experiment, *The Mystery of Edwin Drood* (1870).

6 See Lily Alexander, *Fictional Worlds: Traditions in Narrative and the Age of Visual Culture*, Charleston, South Carolina: CreateSpace, 2013, and Lily Alexander, "The Hero's Journey" and "Mythology" in *The Routledge Companion to Imaginary Worlds*, edited by Mark J. P. Wolf, New York, New York: Routledge, 2017, pages 11–20 and 115–126.

7 Mikhail Bakhtin, *Problems of Dostoevsky's Poetics*, edited and translated by Caryl Emerson, Minneapolis, Minnesota: University of Minnesota Press, 1984. This now-classical work on polyphony in Dostoevsky and its anti-totalitarian ideas, first published in 1928, landed Bakhtin in the exile under Stalin, after he miraculously escaped a concentration camp sentence in 1928, with secret help from the Minister of Culture, Anatoly Lunacharsky. While Bakhtin spent 30 years behind the Ural Mountains (in Kazakhstan and Mordovia), banned from entering the European part of the Soviet Union, Dostoevsky, his subject and mentor, was largely banned from educational institutions during the Soviet era, with the exception of *Crime and Punishment*, taught as a moralizing parable.

8 Yuri Marmeladov, *Dostoevsky's Secret Code: The Allegory of Elijah the Prophet*, Coronado, California: Coronar Press, 1987.

9 Lucien Levy-Bruhl was the first explorer of mythological consciousness. While at the brink of World War II, the anthropologist admitted having regret for employed "politically incorrect" terminology; his rich and original theoretical heritage is currently being effectively reevaluated in view of recent studies on the diverse forms of cognition and consciousness. See his book *Primitive Mentality* (1922).

10 The pioneer of initiation studies, and the first to discover "the hero's journey" ritual paradigm, was Arnold Van Gennep, with his book *Rites of Passage* (1909), Chicago, Illinois: University of Chicago Press, 2nd edition, 2019.

11 It is another example of Dostoevsky's "carnivalesque" humor, as outlined by Bakhtin (1928) 1984. The book "Problems of Dostoevsky's Poetics" by Mikhail Bakhtin was first published in 1928; translated into English in 1984.

12 Olga Fridenberg, *Image & Concept: Mythopoetic Roots of Literature*, London and New York: Routledge, (1955) 1997.

13 Mikhail Bakhtin, *The Dialogic Imagination: Four Essays*, edited by Michael Holquist, translated by Caryl Emerson and Michael Holquist, Austin, Texas, and London, England: University of Texas Press, 1981.

14 See Vladimir Toporov, *Myth, Ritual, Symbol, Image*, (in Russian), Moscow, Russia: Progress, 1995. While Toporov was not the first to discover that Dostoevsky used the word "vdrug" (suddenly) hundreds of times throughout his fictional worlds, he does a comprehensive overview of this discovery and its significance.

15 Victor W. Turner, *The Ritual Process: Structure and Anti-Structure* (1969), Piscataway, New Jersey: Aldine Transaction, 1995 paperback; and Victor W. Turner, *The Forest of Symbols: Aspects of Ndembu Ritual*, Ithaca, New York: Cornell University Press, (1967) 1970.

16 See: Vladimir Propp, *The Morphology of Folk Tale*, Minneapolis, Minnesota: University of Minnesota Press, (1928) 1984; Victor W. Turner, *The Anthropology of Performance*, New York, New York: PAJ Publications, 1987; Victor W. Turner, *From Ritual to Theatre: The Human Seriousness of Play*, New York, New York: PAJ Books, 1982. Also see Lily Alexander, "The Hero's Journey" in *The Routledge Companion to Imaginary Worlds*. Specifically, on Greco-Roman mysteries, see the works from Classical Studies, for example: Walter Burkert, *Ancient Mystery Cults*, Cambridge, Massachusetts: Harvard University Press, 1987; Jaime Alvar Ezquerra, *Romanising*

Oriental Gods: Myth, Salvation, and Ethics in the Cults of Cybele, Isis, and Mithras, Leiden, The Netherlands: Brill Publishers, 2008; and Hugh Bowden, *Mystery Cults of the Ancient World*, Princeton: Princeton University Press, 2010.

17 The Baroque generated crime fiction, as per Bakhtin (1981) and Gilles Deleuze, *The Fold: Leibniz and the Baroque*, Minneapolis, Minnesota: University of Minnesota Press, 1992.

18 The 19th-century literary group known as Symbolists include Belgian/Flemish writer Maurice Maeterlinck, and the French authors Charles Baudelaire, Arthur Rimbaud, and Stéphane Mallarmé.

19 One such misterium-experiment, *Vespers* or *The All-Night Virgil* (1915) by Sergei Rakhmaninov (Mass for Unaccompanied Chorus) was recently performed in New York in St. Paul the Apostle Church, in February 2018.

4

BUILDING THE VORKOSIGAN UNIVERSE

Edward James

Lois McMaster Bujold is one of the most popular writers in the world of science fiction and fantasy. The Hugo Award for Best Novel, based on a popular vote among science fiction fans, has been won by her four times, more than anyone else apart from Robert A. Heinlein; three of the wins were for novels in the Vorkosigan sequence. The Hugo Award for Best Series was created recently, and she won it in the first two years it ran: in 2017 for the Vorkosigan Saga and in 2018 for The World of Five Gods.

Apart from her early novel *The Spirit Ring* (1992), which was set in a fantasy version of Renaissance Italy, all her published books have been set in one of three created universes. The World of Five Gods books, sometimes called the Chalion series, so far consists of three novels and six novellas, set in a secondary fantasy world, which features not only magic but also the active participation of gods. The Sharing Knife sequence, which Bujold calls the "Wide Green World", currently consists of four novels (or one long novel in four parts), and one long novella (or short novel). This is mostly interpreted as a fantasy set in a version of the American Midwest; I have argued elsewhere that it fits just as well in the long American tradition of post-apocalyptic science fiction, in which people live in a rural post-industrial world where "wild talents" such as telekinesis develop.[1] And, finally, the series with which she made her name, the Vorkosigan Saga, whose first novels were published in 1986 and the most recent addition (the novella *The Flowers of Vashnoi*) in 2018: currently it runs to 16 novels and five short stories or novellas. It is set in a future in which humans from Old Earth have colonized numerous planets, and in which control of the wormholes which allow interstellar travel is crucial for ambitious planetary governments. The Vorkosigans are a leading family on one of those ambitious planets: Barrayar.

After the first few novels in the series it was generally categorized as "space opera", because of its affinity with the science-fictional subgenre known for its "colourful action-adventure stories of interplanetary or interstellar conflict".[2] However, with *Mirror Dance* (1994) and *Memory* (1996), the books had started transforming into something much more interesting. Miles Vorkosigan, whose adventures as a self-styled Admiral had occupied much of the attention in the earlier books, reconciled himself to abandoning his career commanding a space fleet, and in the rest of the books a spaceship became just a convenient way to travel rather than a locale for action. The later books vary between political thrillers, comedies of manners (*A Civil Campaign* (1999) was even subtitled *A Comedy of Biology and Manners*) and detective novels. Miles Vorkosigan's new career as Imperial Auditor — essentially a plenipotentiary investigator — allowed the series to escape the label "space opera", but also to add a new dimension of plotting and character development. The appeal of the Vorkosigan novels to its fans is largely the result of Bujold's attention to character, and of her ability to place them in interesting ethical dilemmas.

Before considering world-building in the Vorkosigan series, it is worth taking a brief look at how she did it in the Chalion books, as it is both a contrast and an interesting comparison. In both cases, the building blocks were to be found in our world. In the case of Chalion, the inspiration was a university course on medieval Spanish history which Bujold attended several years before she began writing the series. Chalion is a deliberately distorted and distorting image of the kingdom of Castile, in the generation before the marriage of Isabella of Castile and Ferdinand of Aragon paved the way for the creation of modern Spain. There is systematic distortion. The points of the compass have been reversed, to begin with: the Roknari princedoms to the north correspond to the Muslim kingdoms in the south of Spain or North Africa, with a dash of Viking. Darthaca in the south corresponds to France. Bujold's own map, at www.dendarii.com, shows clearly that Chalion itself lies within an upside-down Spain, to its south, with a mountain frontier separating it from Darthaca. Other forms of disorientation were applied, such as using the word *roya* instead of "king" or *royesse* instead of "princess". Some of the characters in the first two novels, *The Curse of Chalion* (2001) and *Paladin of Souls* (2003) clearly have their parallels in 15th-century Spain: Ferdinand and Isabella become Bergon of Ibra (Aragon) and Iselle of Chalion (Castile). The counterpart to Juan's favorite Alvaro de Luna is Arvol dy Lutez, and Juana la Loca, Joanna the Mad, has two incarnations in Chalion, either Ista or Catillara. The world seems well-planned compared to the Vorkosigan universe, which seems to have gradually accreted, but Bujold remarked that stealing it from history wholesale "saves a lot of steps".[3] The really original part, which makes Chalion special, is the creation of the polytheistic theology; and there Bujold owes nothing to medieval Spain. With the Vorkosigan sequence, of course, Bujold is mostly dealing with alien planets (though in *Brothers in Arms* (1989) we do visit an Old Earth which has been seriously affected by climate change and a rise in sea level). There are some nods in the direction of the scientific details with which science fiction writers traditionally dealt with imaginary planets. Thus, the Barrayaran day is 26.7 Old Earth hours long; Sergyar has slightly less gravity than Beta Colony; Beta Colony has an atmosphere too poisonous and solar output too extreme for people to live on the largely desert surface for long; you need breathing apparatus to leave the domed cities of Komarr. Bujold is not particularly interested in alien zoology; her first novel introduced us to vicious six-legged crab-like predators and vampire balloons, but such exotica are not found again, although their presence in great numbers is mentioned in *Gentleman Jole and the Red Queen* (2015). There we briefly visit the Department of Biology at the University of Kareenberg (on Sergyar), which has a team that classifies and catalogs about 2,000 new species a year. Jole ventures to remark that it sounds impressive. "Does it?" is the response. "At this rate, we should have Sergyar's entire biome mapped in about, oh, roughly five thousand years" (p. 206).

Bujold does recognize that environments can have a direct impact on the way those human societies develop, however. Beta Colony, for instance, had a high level of social cohesion in part because it was settled by slower-than-light generation ships, meaning that the colonists had a long time to develop cooperative systems in a closed environment. And once the planet was settled, that tendency was strengthened. Because the surface is so hostile, Betans live underground, and continue to restrict reproduction just as they had done in the even more cramped conditions of the generation ships. A desire to be protected from the environment was in part responsible for the near-universal use of the uterine replicator — an ideal environment for the development of a fetus during its first nine months of growth. But on the whole, environments do not play a large role in Bujold's narratives, particularly for Barrayar, where the majority of plots unfold: to all intents and purposes, the landscape of Barrayar is indistinguishable from that of North America. On the whole, Bujold is much more interested in constructing imaginary societies than in imagining exotic planetary environments.

I am going to split my discussion of Bujold's creation of the Vorkosigan Universe into two. First, I am going to look at the historical inspirations for her planetary cultures; and second, I will examine the way in which she slowly creates these cultures over multiple novels, or, at least, slowly reveals them to her readers. John Lennard, who has written on Bujold, suggests that there are two types of imaginative writers: the icebergs and the searchlights. Tolkien was an iceberg, in that much of what he wrote about Middle Earth — the languages, the history — did not appear in *The Lord of the Rings* (1954–1955) at all, but remained beneath the surface, in his notes and his memory. Much of this work was completed even before the publication of *The Hobbit* (1937). Bujold is a searchlight: "imagining only what necessarily fell within protagonists' experience."[4] The Vorkosigan Universe (or Vorkosiverse, as some fans with no feeling for the English language call it) was created over several decades, with new parts being created when needed.

There are multiple forms of world-building involved. Our first protagonist is from Beta Colony, and in the first novel, *Shards of Honor* (1986), she meets her future husband, who is from Barrayar; they meet on the newly discovered planet that is later named Sergyar. In the very first novel, therefore, we are introduced, however superficially, to three different planets. In the sequence as a whole we get to know — again, sometimes superficially — some nine planets (including Old Earth) and three space stations. Three of the novels — *Barrayar* (1991), *Cetaganda* (1995), and *Komarr* (1998) — are named after the planet on which the action takes place. Beta Colony and Barrayar are exceptions in Bujold's world-building, in that the Vorkosigan family members who are the protagonists of most of the early novels are so intimately connected with them: all our focalizing characters are either Barrayaran or Betan. (The exceptions are *Ethan of Athos* (1986) and *Falling Free* (1988), which is set at least 200 years before all the others.) The first novel, *Shards of Honor* (1986), which establishes the narrative background for what follows, is focalized through Cordelia Naismith, a Betan, and the next few novels are focalized through her son Miles, whose parentage is mixed and who is portrayed as a Barrayaran who often sees things through Betan eyes. He has spent some time on Beta Colony as a teenager, and even manages to maintain the Betan side of his personality by masquerading as a Betan, Admiral Miles Naismith. This masquerade lasts for six books, and it is only in *Memory* (1996) that he finally gives up his Betan persona and resigns himself to taking up his father's role as a Barrayaran aristocrat. Even so, he has imbibed enough of his mother's attitudes, and traveled enough, to be very different in his views from the average Barrayaran.

I have suggested that the differences between Beta Colony and Barrayar might be seen as representing different facets of American society, "which may very loosely be regarded as its progressive, egalitarian, and democratic aspects faced with the conservative and hierarchical".[5] But it is more helpful to think of all the varying cultures of the Vorkosigan Universe as having elements of applicability to contemporary Earth cultures; there is no direct relationship to any one of them. Bujold's cultural creations are intended to force us to think about our own world, which is why I called the chapter in my book on Bujold which discussed her various cultures "Cultural Critique".

Beta Colony is, in fact, the only extraterrestrial planet to be colonized directly from the United States. It is technologically predominant within the Vorkosigan Universe, both in military and medical technology, which is why the Betan dollar — and that is the word Bujold uses — is the strongest currency in the Vorkosigan universe. Like America too, or like America's vision of itself, Beta Colony is very egalitarian. One of its earliest appearances in the narrative is when the Barrayaran Aral Vorkosigan makes fun of the Betan military's tendency to argue rather than to obey: "You are no better trained than children at a picnic. If your ranks denote anything but pay scale, it's not apparent to me" (*Shards of Honor*, p. 11).[6] There is no hereditary aristocracy, and an elected president, though "I didn't vote for him" becomes almost a catch phrase in Cordelia's mind. The egalitarianism brings with it a political transparency unknown on Barrayar: Betan public ceremonies are all seen on "holovid" (3D television), and commented on at length. And with egalitarianism also comes a lack of deference. Miles, in his Betan guise, is instructed by a Barrayaran officer on the respect owed to a Barrayaran count: with the Betan half of his mind, Miles translates this into "*Call him sir, don't wipe your nose on your sleeve, and none of your damned Betan egalitarian backchat, either*" (*The Vor Game*, p. 320; Bujold's italics).

Along with egalitarianism came universal civil rights. An important element in the Vorkosigan family is the equal rights given to clones, thanks to which Mark, Miles's clone, becomes recognized as his legal brother. Hermaphrodites, created by Betan science, have civil rights too; to Bel Thorne, who becomes a significant character in the Vorkosigan Saga, Miles reveals that he is not pure Betan by showing unconscious inability to accept hermaphrodites as naturally as Betans do. Criminals have civil rights too: crime is a disease, to be treated as such, by therapy. Aral gives the Barrayaran response: "at least we kill a man cleanly, all at once, instead of in bits, over years. . . Beheading. It's supposed to be almost painless." "How do they know?" asks the Betan Cordelia (*Barrayar*, p. 122). Betan medical technology gave the Vorkosigan Universe the uterine replicator, but also gave its citizens much longer lives: "all Betans expect to live to be 120. . . they think it's one of their civil rights" (*Warrior's Apprentice*, p. 47). Betans have a right to live without poverty, and with proper medical care. For Cordelia, the definition of poverty is "not owning a comconsole" (a personal computer with Internet access); and is horrified that for Barrayarans poverty may mean having no access to shelter, food, clothing or medical care.

Betan sexual customs are more relaxed than those elsewhere in the Universe. Sexual availability is advertised by clothing, or lack of it, or, for girls and women, the wearing of earrings. Cordelia is fitted with a contraceptive device at the age of 14, at the same time that her hymen was cut and her ears pierced; the event was celebrated by a coming-out party (Barrayar, p. 154). Because of the general permissiveness (and an aversion toward exploitation of any kind), the sexual role of prostitutes in fulfilled by Licenses Practical Sexuality Therapists (LPSTs)— men, women, and hermaphrodites who have gained licenses after a period of training.

To some Barrayarans, particularly women, Beta Colony appears almost utopian. Women seem to be treated as real equals, unlike the subordinated women of Barrayar. Cordelia becomes a role model for Elena Bothari — a Barrayaran daughter of a soldier forbidden by Barrayaran custom from going into the military — not just because Cordelia had chosen to go into the military, but because she had *choice*. However, Bujold has exercised her own choice to show Beta Colony as falling short of any utopian ideals. As early as *Shards of Honor*, we see that Betan security forces can be as amoral and ruthless as their Barrayaran or Cetagandan equivalents. Elena Bothari, on the point of visiting Beta Colony, is enchanted by the notion of "Betan freedom". Miles has to correct her. Betans do not have "freedom" in the abstract. They cannot have children without applying for a license first. And because they live on a planet with a hostile planetary environment, Betans "'put up with rules we'd never tolerate at home. You should see everyone fall into place during a power outage drill, or a sandstorm alarm. They have no margin for — I don't know how to put it. Social failures?'" (*Warrior's Apprentice*, p. 53). Despite the caveats, Betans stand for a level of freedom which has been aspired to, but never attained, by American radicals or utopians. In the two early books, with Cordelia as focalizer, we are inclined toward her evaluation of the levels of Betan civility and Barrayaran barbarism. And then, with some shock, the non-vegetarian reader realizes that Cordelia finds Barrayaran primitive cooking procedures, which involve taking protein "from the bodies of real dead animals", really disgusting (*Barrayar*, p. 79); and all of a sudden we realize we are barbarians too.

Beta Colony seems to reflect many of the ideals of the United States, in however distorted a fashion. One might then presume that Barrayar reflects European ideals, or at least the attitudes common in Europe in the 19th century, since most of its colonists were of Russian, Greek, French, or British origin. One of the main themes underlying the whole Vorkosigan Saga, however, is that these attitudes are changing quite fast, under the influence of Beta Colony and other galactic powers. There is an historical event that was largely responsible for Barrayaran backwardness: the Time of Isolation. It is a reference to the historical event that was largely responsible for this backwardness. After the first 50,000 colonists had arrived on Barrayar — the Firsters — the wormhole through which they had come closed down. Their easy route to the rest of the human-settled Galaxy had disappeared, and the Firsters had to fend for themselves. The emergent terraforming program collapsed; imported Earth species broke loose, and largely wiped out native flora and fauna; and the Barrayarans did not share in Galactic scientific advances for 700 years. The Time of Isolation only ended just over a hundred years before the birth of Miles Vorkosigan, and revival and recovery was then set back by the Cetagandans, who invaded and attempted to colonize Barrayar, taking advantage of the newly opened wormhole. There is tangible evidence remaining on Barrayar of the wars fought with the Cetagandans, in the shape of areas devastated by nuclear attacks, whose radiation levels still exclude human habitation. In the past, mutations were a direct result of this pollution, and mutants were ruthlessly eliminated; now, in Vorkosigan time, the problem is rather how to stop people killing mutants, as we see in the novella *The Mountains of Mourning* (1989). The latest novella in the sequence, *The Flowers of Vashnoi* (2018), shows the attempt to cleanse affected areas of their radiation.

The Firsters had been drawn from various ethnic groups on Earth. Russians seem the predominant group, and many of the aristocrats have surnames derived from Russian. The name Vorkosigan was inspired by the name of Alexei Kosygin, a leading Soviet politician in the post-Khrushchev era. All aristocratic families have names preceded by the Vor suffix: when devising the Vor system for Barrayar, Bujold had not known that *Vor* was Russian for thief, although now she finds it strangely appropriate. Although most of the Vor names recall Russian origins, there are Vorsmythes, Vormuirs, Vorgustafsons, and Vorvilles. Most of these appear in the background, but two aristocrats presumably from a French tradition appear in the narrative: Etienne Vorsoisson and René Vorbretten. Other than the Russians, the group that maintains its sense of identity the most are Greeks, mostly associated with rural areas. Lady Alys Vorpatril diplomatically remarks that a particular custom has died out "except in some of the backcountry districts in certain language groups", and frowns when her son Ivan adds "she means the Greekie hicks" (*A Civil Campaign*, p. 41).

Crucial to the story arc of the Vorkosigan Saga as a whole is the role of Cordelia in importing Betan ideas to Barrayar and thus bringing about a change in Barrayaran society. One of the sub-plots of later Vorkosigan novels concerns the impact of uterine replicators on Barrayaran society, as a direct result of Cordelia's decision to import them: indeed, her son Miles would never have survived as a fetus without the uterine replicator. But the uterine replicator is just a symbol of the scientific and other advances which could be made on Barrayar with the judicious introduction of scientific techniques and social change. Aral is not averse to such changes, and change is greatly facilitated by Emperor Gregor, who as a child saw a lot of Aral and Cordelia, the Regent and Regent-consort. There are several rebellions led by conservatives when Aral as Regent tried to push through reforms; but the rebellions fail, and slow progressive reform does take place. One example: he makes it easier for ordinary Barrayarans to switch their oaths to a different district count, thus giving incentives to counts to actually attract new residents, by offering lower taxes, for instance. And the reforms continue after Aral resigns as Regent. In *CryoBurn* (2010), the novel which in terms of internal chronology is the penultimate one, Miles Vorkosigan is in charge of a committee designed to make the laws on reproductive technology as up-to-date as those in the rest of the Galaxy.

Barrayar appears so European in its make-up that it is a slight shock to realize that the inspiration for Barrayaran society comes actually from Japan. The clue was in the phrase Time of Isolation. "Isolation" is a word frequently used for the period in Japanese history between the 1630s and 1853: in that year four American warships arrived off Edo/Tokyo in order to force an ending to the maritime restrictions that had largely isolated Japan from the rest of the world. Bujold has explained that although the Barrayarans have the European culture inherited from the first settlers, in terms of history and "the shape of their culture", it was Meiji Japan which provided the inspiration. She wrote: "It had its own time of isolation; it had its development of a military caste; and it had its very traumatic re-opening to the outside world."[7] She added that Japan did not almost immediately suffer an invasion (as Barrayar did from Cetaganda); but Russia has been invaded many times. "It is a blending of these two histories, of Japan and of Russia, with various and sometimes logical results — not always salutary results, but always logical results."[8] The young Emperor Gregor, then, stands in for the young Emperor Meiji, who in his long reign between 1868 and 1912 introduced reforms, many of which involved implanting in Western ideas in Japan, and built up the Western-style military forces that inflicted stunning defeats on China in 1894–1895 and above all on Russia in 1904–1905.

The second major culture in the Vorkosigan universe that owes something to Japanese culture and history is that of Cetaganda. We learn about this mostly in *Cetaganda* (1996), which recounts the visit of the young Miles Vorkosigan and his cousin Ivan Vorpatril to the Imperial Palace on Eta Ceta IV, from which the Empire's eight major worlds, and various other dependent planets, are governed. We learn nothing about ordinary Cetagandans: only about the two different levels of the aristocracy, and about the ba, who are the neuter servants of the upper aristocracy. The lower-level aristocrats are the only ones whom most outsiders encounter: the ghem, whose men form the core of the armies that established the Empire, but who have, in recent years, met with a number of political reverses. Ghem warriors are distinguished from each other by bizarre and colorful patterns painted on their faces, which relate to their status and/or their grouping within the armed forces. The ghem are to be found in security positions on Eta Ceta IV itself: Miles finds Ghem-Colonel Benin, who interviews Miles in connection with a murder, to be not unlike a senior security man on Barrayar — in other words, a type that Miles had met many times before, and whom he therefore found both congenial and predictable. Benin wears face paint that indicates his Imperial allegiance rather than his clan: "a white base with intricate black curves and red accents that Miles thought of as the bleeding-zebra look" (*Cetaganda*, p. 116). Miles predicts, correctly, a promotion in Benin's future; and thinks that perhaps Benin would be rewarded by having his genes taken up for inclusion in the genome of the upper aristocracy.

Genetic manipulation is at the heart of the Cetagandan system. Ghem ladies vie against each other in producing exotic creations, though using genetic material from animals and plants rather than humans. Miles and Ivan attend an exhibition of these creations (*Cetaganda* pp. 164–166), and Ivan is attacked by a hyperactive climbing rose. When he encounters a tree from which small kittens hang in pods, he assumes that they are glued in, and rashly attempts to rescue one: it dies in his hand as soon as he picks it. More fundamental, but equally questionable, genetic engineering is carried on by the haut, the upper level of the aristocracy, who seem to be invisible most of the time as far as ordinary Cetagandans are concerned. The haut are themselves the result of a program of genetic improvement — of eugenics — over several centuries. There is a question as to whether they are actually human any longer, but their long-term goal is certainly to create a post-human species. It was already flagged in *Ethan of Athos*, and alluded to in *Cetaganda*, that the Cetagandans might experiment with the importation of genes for telepathy into the genome. The genetic work is carried on by the Star Crèche, an all-female and all-haut group of scientists, ultimately under the control of the Emperor, but in practice under the direct control of the mother of the Emperor, or the mother of his heir. The Star Crèche controls the genome of the haut very strictly, allowing it to develop in part by the insertion of promising ghem genes. Each year, the Star Crèche on Eta Ceta IV send out haut fetuses to the eight planetary governors and their consorts (who are all themselves haut women closely associated with the Star Crèche). The story behind *Cetaganda* is the plan to decentralize this system, and to allow the consorts to take charge of genetic developments on their planet; however, one of the planetary governors wants to subvert this plan, and centralize matters on himself, with the help of senior ghem; *Diplomatic Immunity* (2002) revolves around a different attempt to subvert the genetic plans of the Star Crèche.

Cetaganda is immediately reminiscent of traditional Japanese culture: there is an Emperor; there is an apparently rigid aristocratic or caste system, and a military class; ceremony is an important part of aristocratic life; and there is high respect given (by aristocrats at least) to every aspect of art and aesthetics. Bujold has said that it was partly the Japan of Lady Murasaki Shikibu, who wrote the *Tale of Genji* in the early 11th century which lay behind Cetaganda (which might explain the importance of haut women in Cetagandan culture), but some elements were taken from Imperial China of the late Manchu period. There are no apparent clues from Cetagandan names, however. If the name of Ruyst Millisor, the first Cetagandan we meet in the Vorkosigan saga, has any ethnic origins it would appear to be European rather than Asian. Other names we encounter (in *Cetaganda*) are Fletchir Giaja, the Emperor; Lisbet Degtiar, his mother; Ilsum Kety; Dag Benin; and so on. They look very much like the made-up names of people in a Jack Vance space opera. If there is a specific Earth culture from which Cetagandans are intended to derive, it is concealed in points of detail. Indeed, that may be the purpose: after all, it is the policy of the Cetagandan Empire to develop and indeed evolve away from its primitive Earth roots, in the direction of the post-human.

There are other cultures that Bujold creates, for Komarr such as the Kiboudaini (another culture heavily influenced by Japanese culture), but perhaps one more is worth mentioning in detail here: Jackson's Whole. Bujold's cultural worlds frequently force us to think about our own world by taking facets of it and exaggerating or extrapolating them to extremes. Jackson's Whole is a nightmare world in which free-market capitalism has been allowed to develop without any legal restraints. Bujold has commented: "Everybody says they want a world with no government. Here's a world with no government. How do you like it?"[9] It is run, if at all, by a relatively small number of desperately competing Great Houses, most of whose fortune is based on what other worlds would probably regard as criminal activities. A century or two before Miles's time it was little better than a base for space pirates. Since then it has "senesced", as Miles puts it, into a collection of syndicates which are "almost as structured and staid as little governments", and Miles wonders whether one day they will all succumb to "the creeping tide of integrity". Miles lists the main houses, when he first comes across them, in the story "Labyrinth":

> House Dyne, detergent banking — launder your money on Jackson's Whole. House Fell, weapons deals with no questions asked. House Bharaputra, illegal genetics. Worse, House Ryoval, whose motto was "Dreams Made Flesh," surely the damndest — Miles used the adjective precisely — procurer in history. House Hargraves, the galactic fence, prim-faced middlemen for ransom deals — you had to give them credit, hostages exchanged through their good offices came back alive, mostly.
> (Borders of Infinity, pp. 103–104)

While Miles's clone brother Mark was himself being grown on Jackson's Whole, he learns about House Bharaputra's life extension business, whereby wealthy people have their brains, with their personalities and memories, transplanted into the bodies of young clones in order to extend their lives. The operation is not always successful, as a certain percentage of the patients die: "*Yeah,* thought Miles, *starting with 100% of the clones, whose brains are flushed to make room. . .*" (*Borders of Infinity,* pp. 116–117). Jackson's Whole is, of course, very useful to the rest of the galaxy, because it does offer services and products that are unavailable elsewhere. Jackson's Whole has many skills; it is merely that those do not include any sense of corporate or medical ethics. Bio-engineering is particularly advanced on the planet, and in the course of the Vorkosigan books we meet a number of its products. Miles's clone-double Mark heads the list, but there is also Sergeant Taura, who is constructed to be the ultimate warrior: when she dies, she says that she wants her ashes to be buried anywhere in the universe — anywhere except Jackson's Whole. Gupta, whom we meet in *Diplomatic Immunity,* is an amphibian human, with gills and webbed extremities, created by House Dyan on Jackson's Whole. Jackson's Whole also creates slaves, either by conditioning or by genetic manipulation: they are called jeeveses (possibly Bujold's only direct Wodehouse reference). "They're said to pine if they are separated from their master or mistress, and sometimes even die if he or she dies" (*Captain Vorpatril's Alliance,* p. 41). The jeeves is a symbol of the creative, yet totally exploitative and immoral, spirit of uncontrolled capitalism on Jackson's Whole.

For the second part of this paper I want to look at the way in which Bujold introduces her planetary cultures. She does not use some of the familiar methods: brief extracts from a text-book or scientific manual or long expositions within the text (the "as-you-know-Bob" technique which used to be common in early science fiction). She drops slow hints, and misdirections, and then (usually by visiting the planet in question) fills in the details. It allows her to invent the details as she goes along, of course, but also enables readers to find out about other cultures in a slow and natural way. I shall take examples from the way in which she builds up the readers' knowledge of Beta Colony, Barrayar, and Cetaganda.

The first three Vorkosigan books all appeared in 1986: *Shards of Honor* (June), *The Warrior's Apprentice* (August), and *Ethan of Athos* (December). None are direct sequels. The first deals with the meeting of Cordelia Naismith, from Beta Colony, and Lord Aral Vorkosigan, from Barrayar, and ends shortly after their marriage. *The Warrior's Apprentice* describes the early years of their son Miles (the main protagonist for eight of the novels), and the origins of his career in space. *Ethan of Athos* has Elli Quinn, one of Miles's officers sent on a mission to Kline Station; as the book's title suggests, she is not the main protagonist, and Miles does not appear at all. *Ethan of Athos* is an interesting book, and deals in passing with Athos, possibly the only planet in popular science fiction inhabited solely by gay males, but in terms of the building of the Vorkosigan Universe, the other two are much more significant, and introduce us to the two most important characters in the whole saga — Cordelia Naismith and her son Miles Vorkosigan — and to the worlds they inhabit.

Shards of Honor begins with Cordelia Naismith on the surface of an unnamed planet, with just one comparative detail: "the gravity of this planet was slightly lower than their home world of Beta Colony" (p. 3). They are in the mountains. There is forest, and dense vegetation; beyond rocky mountains with a central peak "crowned by glittering ice" (p. 4). The sun shone in a turquoise sky, onto banks of white clouds below the mountains and onto the grasses and flowers. So far there is little that could not be a description of Earth (Bujold is in fact not good at visual descriptions of otherness). They discover that their camp has been destroyed while they were away. "Aliens?" (p. 5), queries Cordelia. And then "Multiple choice, take your pick — Nuovo Brasilians, Barrayarans, Cetagandans, could be any of that crowd" (p. 6). There are actually no intelligent aliens in the Vorkosigan Universe, and no further reference to them throughout the Vorkosigan Saga; indeed, as far as I can see Nuovo Brasilians are not mentioned again either. But we have learned for the first time that there are rival political groups in space (two of these are going to be important later in the series). Before the end of Chapter One, Cordelia realizes that the aggressors are Barrayarans, has met Captain Aral Vorkosigan, and discovered that he commands a Barrayaran war cruiser, and we learn that she is in command of a scientific team under the auspices of the Betan Astronomical Survey. From the beginning, Betans are categorized as peaceful, and Barrayarans as aggressive; and Cordelia and Aral have a conversation that shows the contempt of the Barrayaran military officer for the lack of discipline and military training of the Betans. Before the end of the chapter, we have discovered that Betans are sympathetic to the injured or disabled; the Barrayaran suggests putting the wounded Betan out of his misery. Another crucial piece of information comes in Chapter Two. Aral has been talking about his family. His maternal grandmother turns out to be Betan; the grandfather met her while serving as Barrayaran ambassador on Beta Colony. "'Outsiders — you Betans particularly — have this odd vision of Barrayar as some monolith, but we are a fundamentally divided society. My government is always fighting these centrifugal tendencies'" (p. 33). Aral is addressing Cordelia, of course; but Bujold might well be addressing her readers. It had long been one of the failings of space opera to imagine that each planet, if inhabited by an intelligent species, had one language and one culture. *Star Trek* was a major offender, and Bujold had been an enthusiastic fan as a teenager (she was co-founder of a fanzine, *StarDate,* which was possibly only the second fanzine in the United States to be devoted to a single TV show).[10]

The world-building of the two main planets of Beta Colony and Barrayar is conducted mainly in terms of comparisons and contrasts between the two, and above all in *Shards of Honor.* Much of it is stems from conversations between Cordelia and Aral, although we do also see the inner thoughts of Cordelia, on whom the narrative focalizes in both *Shards of Honor* and its immediate sequel *Barrayar.* Sometimes we learn about Barrayar from odd facts that Cordelia dredges up from her memory. Interestingly, the dialog between Beta Colony and Barrayar does not end when, with *The Warrior's Apprentice,* Miles Vorkosigan takes on the focalizing role, because, as we have seen, he belongs in both cultural worlds.

In terms of world-building, however, it is a slow build-up of information, which continues throughout the series. One crucial fact about Beta Colony, for instance, is as far as I can see, not mentioned until the most recently published Vorkosigan novel, *Gentleman Jole and the Red Queen* (2015): it is revealed that on Beta Colony, unlike Barrayar, there are no clearly distinguished ethnic groups: "the Betans had been using gene cleaning and rearranging for generations, which meant anyone's ancestors could be anything" (p. 25).

Our knowledge of Barrayar increases once Cordelia actually arrives there, which does not happen until two chapters before the end of *Shards of Honor.* There are some verbal descriptions of the countryside and of the capital city, but, as before, much of what we learn about Barrayarans comes through Cordelia's reaction to them when she meets them: first Sergeant Bothari and Aral's father, Count Piotr, and then Prime Minister Vortala and Emperor Ezar. This increased density of reality continues in the novel which is the direct sequel,

Barrayar. But that sequel (really the second half of one long novel) did not arrive until 1991, by which time the conscientious reader has already learned a lot more about Barrayar through Miles's eyes, in the four Miles-centered novels which intervened.

Part of the learning process is through the device of a travelog: that is, as the protagonist travels about the planet, we learn more. Although Cordelia ventures into the countryside in *Barrayar* (thanks to a revolt which causes her to go into hiding), we had already seen something of the countryside beyond the boundaries of aristocratic villas through the eyes of Miles. The true state of Barrayaran backwardness, for instance, is not really apparent until Miles is sent, for his own education as much as anything else, on a mission deep into the countryside, in "The Mountains of Mourning", a novella in the Vorkosigan sequence.[11] He is sent as "the Voice" of his father, Count Aral Vorkosigan, to Silvy Vale, to investigate the murder of an infant with a hare-lip. That he himself is a cripple, whose growth was stunted by being poisoned in the womb, is very relevant. Country people regarded him with horror as a "mutie", a mutant. (Disability and people's reaction to disability are major themes throughout Bujold's work.) He, in his turn, is horrified at the poverty, and at the absence of an electrical supply, but above all at the backward attitudes of these people from the "backbeyond". The dead baby was "only a mutie" (p. 55). Miles sees the ignorance of the hill-folk not as their fault, but as shaming the Vorkosigans. It is an event crucial to his own education, and for his preparation as the future Count.

Cetaganda has been introduced slowly too. As we have seen, in *Shards of Honor*, Cordelia at first wonders whether her encampment had been destroyed by Cetagandans. Later in that novel, we learn two further things about the Cetagandans: that Aral's grandfather was an ambassador to Beta Colony before the First Cetagandan War (p. 32), and that the old Emperor Ezar had fought in the war as the military apprentice to Aral's father (p. 234). *The Warrior's Apprentice* adds more details, with Miles's grandfather reminiscing about fighting the Cetagandans in the Dendarii mountains, in Vorkosigan territory (p. 14), and Aral himself remembering the Third Cetagandan War. The city of Vorkosigan Vashnoi was destroyed by a Cetagandan nuclear bomb (p. 67); Miles pledges the worthless real estate to a Betan in return for a spaceship. And, much later in the same novel, "Admiral" Miles Naismith discovers that he has recruited into his mercenary force "two dozen Cetagandan ghem-fighters, variously dressed, but all with full formal face paint freshly applied, looking like an array of Chinese temple demons" (p. 212). A certain amount of tension follows, but no more information, and no explanation of that word *ghem*.

This slow drip of information reaches a different level in the third novel published in the Vorkosigan Universe, *Ethan of Athos*. The action takes place almost entirely on Kline Station, a space station, and the protagonist Ethan is being chased by a Cetagandan counter-intelligence team led by ghem-colonel

Millisor. And it is here, at the very end, that Commander Elli Quinn, acting for Miles Vorkosigan, shows us that Miles has an interest in Cetaganda. (It is not for another ten years that Bujold would publish *Cetaganda*, revealing that Miles had visited Cetaganda on a diplomatic mission *before* the events of *Ethan of Athos*.) Quinn refers to Cetaganda as "a typical male-dominated totalitarian state, only slightly mitigated by their rather peculiar artistic cultural peculiarities" (p. 65), which is because Miles has not told the details of his mission, or (more likely) because Bujold had not yet worked out the complexities of Cetagandan society. But we do learn a crucial fact about Cetaganda here, that *Cetaganda* only reinforces: that they have a serious interest in genetic engineering. Millisor was in charge of security for a military-sponsored genetics project, and "Millisor and his merry men have been chasing something around the galaxy ever since, blowing people away with the careless abandon of either homicidal lunatics, or men scared out of their wits" (p. 65).

We learn little about Cetagandans in subsequent books, except that they are clearly the villains who can be blamed for anything, such as the kidnapping of Miles, and his subsequent cloning (in *Mirror Dance* [1994]). In 1987 Bujold published "The Borders of Infinity", in which Miles organizes an escape from a brutal Cetagandan prison; in *Brothers in Arms* (1989) Miles has to dodge Cetagandans in London (of all places); and in *The Vor Game* (1990) he foils a Cetagandan invasion of Vervain. Cetaganda only comes to the forefront in *Cetaganda* (1996). This contains a scene which retrofits the action very carefully in relation to the previous novels. Miles overhears a mysterious communication from ghem-colonel Millisor, who is in pursuit of some very important missing genetic material (p. 153). Clearly this is before the events of *Ethan of Athos*, but only just before: Miles has time to send Commander Quinn to follow Millisor as far as Kline Station to discover what has been lost, and thus to meet Ethan of Athos. Miles is 22 when he and his cousin Ivan Vorpatril are sent to a state funeral on Cetaganda to represent Emperor Gregor. He already shows the talents for which he was a few years later appointed as Imperial Auditor, solving a murder and getting mixed up in Cetaganda's internal politics, and coming out of it, to his embarrassment, with a Cetagandan Imperial Order of Merit. When, ten years later in Vorkosigan time, Miles, his wife Ekaterin, and the Betan hermaphrodite Bel Thorne, all help save Cetaganda's bacon for them a second time, in *Diplomatic Immunity* (2002), only Ekaterin and Bel get the Imperial Order of Merit; Miles is asked to donate a genetic sample to the banks of the Star Crèche, the highest honor that Cetagandan can conceive. That Miles is aiding the traditional enemies of Barrayar is certain; that he does it for reasons of Barrayaran policy is also clear. Miles's main worry is that the haut would lose control over the ghem in this struggle for genetic power. The ghem have an aggressive expansionist past, while the haut were much more concerned with their genetic project than with extending the Cetagandan Empire.

We began by seeing Cetaganda as yet a rather brutal militaristic society intent upon expanding across the Galaxy, and ended by realizing it is a complex, tiered society, devoted to artistic and scientific endeavors, which is ultimately under the control of a secretive group of aristocratic women. Bujold has worked this sort of switch before: Barrayar initially appeared as similarly brutal and militaristic, and it was only gradually that it was revealed to be a complex and many-layered society with much to admire. Do not judge people or societies until you have grown to know them might be one of the lessons of the Vorkosigan Universe.

First Publications of the Vorkosigan Saga, in Order of Internal Chronology

"Dreamweaver's Dilemma", in Bujold, *Dreamweaver's Dilemma: Short Stories and Essays,* edited by Suford Lewis (Framingham, MA: NESFA Press, 1996), pp. 69–103.

Falling Free (Riverdale, NY: Baen, 1988). Previously serialized in *Analog,* December 1987–February 1988.

Shards of Honor (Riverdale, NY: Baen, 1986).

Barrayar (Riverdale, NY: Baen, 1991). Previously serialized in *Analog* July–October 1991.

The Warrior's Apprentice (Riverdale, NY: Baen, 1986).

"The Mountains of Mourning" (novella), *Analog* May 1989, pp. 14–74.

"Weatherman" (novella), *Analog* February 1990, 12–75.

The Vor Game (Riverdale, NY: Baen, 1990), incorporating "The Weatherman".

Cetaganda (Riverdale, NY: Baen, 1996). Previously serialized in *Analog* October–mid-December 1995.

Ethan of Athos (Riverdale, NY: Baen, 1986).

"Labyrinth" (novella), *Analog* August 1989, pp. 2–84

"The Borders of Infinity" (novella), in *Free Lancers,* edited by Elizabeth Mitchell (Riverdale NY: Baen, 1987).

Brothers in Arms (Riverdale, NY: Baen, 1989).

Borders of Infinity (Riverdale, NY: Baen, 1989), incorporating "The Mountains of Mourning", "Labyrinth" and "The Borders of Infinity".

Mirror Dance (Riverdale, NY: Baen, 1994).

Memory (Riverdale, NY: Baen, 1996).

Komarr (Riverdale, NY: Baen, 1998).

A Civil Campaign (Riverdale, NY: Baen, 1999).

"Winterfair Gifts" (novella), in *Irresistible Forces,* edited by Catherine Asaro (New York, New York: New American Library, 2004), pp. 1–71.

Diplomatic Immunity (Riverdale, NY: Baen, 2002).

Captain Vorpatril's Alliance (Riverdale, NY: Baen, 2012).

The Flowers of Vashnoi (novella) (Riverdale, NY: Baen, 2018).

CryoBurn (Riverdale, NY: Baen, 2010).

Gentleman Jole and the Red Queen (Riverdale, NY: Baen, 2015).

Notes

1 Edward James, *Lois McMaster Bujold* (Modern Masters of Science Fiction), Chicago and Springfield: University of Illinois Press, 2015, pp. 62–72. Parts of this chapter are drawn and repurposed from this book, with permission of the publisher.
2 Brian M. Stableford and David Langford, "Space Opera" in *The Encyclopedia of Science Fiction*. edited by John Clute, David Langford, Peter Nicholls, and Graham Sleight. Gollancz, 21 May 2019, available at http://www.sf-encyclopedia.com/entry/space_opera.
3 James, *Bujold*, p. 53.
4 J. Lennard, "(Absent) Gods and Sharing Knives: The Purposes of Lois McMaster Bujold's Fantastic Ir/Religions" in *Lois McMaster Bujold: Essays on a Modern Master on Science Fiction and Fantasy* (Critical Explorations in Science Fiction and Fantasy, p. 37), edited by Janet Brennan Croft (Jefferson, NC: McFarland, 2013), pp. 172–194, at 176.
5 James, *Bujold*, p. 75.
6 All quotations come from the first editions listed above.
7 Bujold, *Dreamweaver's Dilemma: Short Stories and Essays*, edited by Suford Lewis (Framingham, MA: NESFA Press, 1995), p. 210.
8 Bujold, *Dreamweaver's Dilemma*, p. 211.
9 *Dreamweaver's Dilemma*, p. 212.
10 James, *Bujold*, p. 6.
11 Published in *Analog* May 1989, and later forming part of *Borders of Infinity* (also 1989). It won both the main science fiction awards, for Best Novella, in 1990: it was the first of her seven Hugo Awards, and the second of her three Nebula Awards.

Audiovisual Worlds

5

OUR WORLD

World-Building in Thornton Wilder's *Our Town*

Mark J. P. Wolf

Imaginary worlds have been around as long as storytelling itself, and have appeared in every medium that stories have, though the possibilities and peculiarities of each medium directly affect what kind of world-building can be done in it. While literature, film, television, and video games have evolved greatly over time and have increased their capabilities as venues for imaginary worlds, the theater stage has remained a more difficult place to world-build, especially when compared to other audiovisual media. Popular worlds from other media have been adapted to the stage, but far fewer worlds have originated onstage, without pre-existing incarnations of them in other media to carry the burden of exposition and introduce worlds that will already be well known to the audience by the time they appear in the theater. Thus, plays which are the origin of new, detailed worlds are few and far between.

Thornton Wilder's Pulitzer-Prize-winning *Our Town* (1938), arguably one of the greatest plays of the 20th century, presents a fictional town, and perhaps no stage play attempts as much world-building as *Our Town* does. Nor does any play depend on world-building so much for the exploration of its theme and its philosophical outlook; the fictional town of Grover's Corners itself is the play's main character, as the title indicates. Though loosely based on Peterborough, New Hampshire, where Wilder wrote part of the play as a fellow of the MacDowell Colony, an artists' retreat center, Grover's Corners is a place all its own, with its own geography, history, and families of residents, all described and built up in the imagination of the audience during the course of the play's performance which is usually between two and three hours on average. Before examining the world-building present in the play itself, however, we should consider the relationship between world-building and theater in general.

World-Building and Theater

A dramatist is one who believes that the pure event, an action involving human beings, is more arresting than any comment that can be made upon it.
—*Thornton Wilder,* Writers at Work *Interview, 1958*[1]

Imaginary worlds have appeared on stage since ancient times, such as Nephelokokkygia (Νεφελοκοκκυγία) or Cloudcuckooland from Aristophanes's *The Birds* (414 BC), and throughout history, including Prospero's Island from Shakespeare's *The Tempest* (1611), Barrie's Neverland from *Peter Pan* (1904), the island in Karel Čapek's *R. U. R.* (1920), and others, as well as stage versions of imaginary worlds originating in other media, like the adapted stage plays of *The Wizard of Oz* (1902), *The Hobbit* (1953, 1967, 1968, and more), and even *The Lord of the Rings* (1981, 1988, 2001, 2002, 2003, 2006, and more). But world-building faces several challenges on the stage; the size of the stage and the sets built on it, the life-size nature of the performers, the real-time nature of the live performance, and the fixed point of view of the audience. While the liveness and actual presence of the actors are the advantages of the stage (the "pure event" that Wilder speaks of in the above quotation), the disadvantages limiting storytelling and world-building are usually compensated for by the theatrical conventions understood by the audience that allow certain things to be implied and inferred.

World-building in literature is accomplished through description, while an audiovisual medium like theater can present sets, costumes, and props which can be seen directly by the audience, but these are limited in scope due to the limitations of the size of the stage. While some stages and sets can be very large, like the venues used for the Passion Plays at Oberammergau, Germany; Greenville, North Carolina; Eureka Springs, Arkansas; and formerly at Spearfish, South Dakota, the distance between the audience and performers still limits the scope of the presentation, and thus the size of the visible portion of the diegetic world of the story being presented. This can be expanded, however, through the use of a narrator (a stage convention going back at least to the Greek chorus in early theater), who can, as in literature, verbally describe as large a world as is needed. The possibility of description means even a small stage can be used, or a nearly empty one, leaving the world to be almost completely described by a narrator. This occurs frequently in shows with only one performer, who acts out the parts and narrates the rest to the audience, as found in stage plays like Don Berrigan's *St. John in Exile* (1986), William Luce's *The Belle of Amherst* (1976), and Rob Inglis's one-man stage adaptations of *The Lord of the Rings* (1981). Such performances are more reliant on verbal description than stage sets, making them arguably more like radio plays or audio books; but they are able to evoke larger worlds as a result.

Likewise, the timeframe of the play's action is not necessarily limited to the real-time length of the performance itself, since scenes can be set at different times, and span; however many years are needed, though such information must also be conveyed to the audience in some way. Thus, world-building to any degree in theater will likely depend on metatheatrical devices such as direct address, the acknowledgment of conventions, and other self-reflexive gestures that risk diminishing the very immersion that world-building strives to achieve. The incorporation and effacement of these devices, then, becomes another obstacle for the playwright who wishes to engage in world-building.

World-Building in *Our Town*

Thornton Wilder's *Our Town* (1938) takes place in Grover's Corners, New Hampshire, a fictional though typical American small town, so it is not an imaginary world with an enormous size or scope or great depth of invention; it is meant to be ordinary and relatable, and relies heavily on real-world defaults, audience imagination (due to its minimalistic set and lack of scenery), and a narrator, the character of the Stage Manager. Wilder had used a Stage Manager character in his earlier, one-act plays *The Happy Journey to Trenton and Camden* (1931) and *Pullman Car Hiawatha* (1932). These plays also had minimal sets, the latter used direct address as well, and at the beginning of both *Pullman Car Hiawatha* and *Our Town*, the Stage Manager gives the audience a verbal tour of the location, indicating where everything is in relation to everything else. According to Takuji Nosé,

> The Stage Manager in *Pullman* is given both pseudo-narrator-like and pseudo-director-like status on the stage, which indicates that he carries out not only a functional role in the mediating communication system but also has one in creating a dual time scheme in the play. Whereas in one time scheme, the characters within/around "Hiawatha" convey the events on stage through their actions, in the other time scheme the Stage Manager directs the entire story through his explanations about the plot to the audience and also through his instructions to the other characters about such matters as entering/exiting and starting/stopping their performances.[2]

The Stage Manager of *Our Town* guides us through the play, tying the infrastructures together into a world, and acting as the author's onstage world-building alter ego, even to the extent of setting out the furniture as the play opens, before he says anything. In his opening lines, he sets up the two of the three main infrastructures of the play's imaginary world, geography (space), and history (time): "The name of the town is Grover's Corners, New Hampshire, just across the Massachusetts line: latitude 42 degrees 40 minutes; longitude 70 degrees 37 minutes. The First Act shows a day in our town. The day is May 7, 1901. The time is just before dawn". Both of these facts, locating us precisely in space and time, turn out to have something curious and contradictory about them, as we shall see. The sections that follow will examine these two infrastructures, along with the third one, genealogy (characters), separately, so as to be able to show how each of them is used to build the world of the play.[3]

Geography (Space)

While most authors are vague as to the precise locations of their imaginary worlds, in order to keep them inaccessible, Wilder begins with what appears to be great precision: Grover's Corners is in New Hampshire, "just across the Massachusetts line" at the coordinates "latitude 42 degrees 40 minutes; longitude 70 degrees 37 minutes". These coordinates, however, are not even in the United States, but in rural Kazakhstan, in the Zhualy district in the southern part of the country. For a location in North America, the longitude coordinate should be −70′ (not positive 70); but even then, 42° 40′, −70° 37′ is not on land but in the Atlantic Ocean, in Sandy Bay just north of the coast off of Rockport, Massachusetts. The precision of these coordinates gives the location the concreteness of a real place, and at the same time the coordinates could not have been checked by the audience as they sat in the theater, at least in 1938, when the play debuted. The Stage Manager then goes on to lay out the whole town for the audience, with stage directions indicating where he points:

> The sky is beginning to show some streaks of light over in the East there, behind our mount'in. The morning star always gets wonderful bright the minute before it has to go, — doesn't it? [*He stares at it for a moment, then goes upstage.*] Well, I'd better show you how our town lies. Up here — [*That is: parallel with the back wall.*] is Main Street. Way back there is the railway station; tracks go that way. Polish Town's across the tracks, and some Canuck families. [*Toward the left.*] Over there is the Congregational Church; across the street's the Presbyterian. Methodist and Unitarian are over there. Baptist is down in the holla' by the river. Catholic Church is over beyond the tracks. Here's the Town Hall and Post Office combined; jail's in the basement. Bryan once made a speech from these very steps here. Along here's a row of stores. Hitching posts and horse blocks in front of them. First automobile's going to come along in about five years — belonged to Banker Cartwright, our richest citizen. . . lives in the big white house up on the hill. Here's the grocery store and here's Mr. Morgan's drugstore. Most everybody in town manages to look into those two stores once a day. Public School's over yonder. High School's

still farther over. Quarter of nine mornings, noontimes, and three o'clock afternoons, the hull town can hear the yelling and screaming from those schoolyards. [*He approaches the table and chairs downstage right.*] This is our doctor's house, Doc Gibbs'. This is the back door.

At this point, before the action begins, the town's geography is laid out in a series of tightening concentric circles, beginning with the coordinates situating it in the world overall, with each location or set of locations providing the context surrounding the next one presented, with the level of detail also increasing, The quote above begins with the distant mountain as a backdrop beyond everything, then moves closer to the outskirts of town "across the tracks", gradually drawing into the more central part of town (the Town Hall and Post Office). After this description, he indicates the Gibbs's house and yard, and the Webbs's house and yard. After this quote, we are told what is growing in Mrs. Gibbs's garden, "This is Mrs. Gibbs' garden. Corn . . . peas . . . beans . . . hollyhocks . . . heliotrope . . . and a lot of burdock", and Mrs. Webb's garden, which is "Just like Mrs. Gibbs', only it's got a lot of sunflowers, too". The concentric circles of description, growing in detail as we approach the center, focuses the audience on the area of the town being represented onstage, after we are able to imagine what lies beyond it.

After the scene at the Gibbs's house, the Stage Manager brings out Professor Willard, who gives more geographic detail, beyond what we might expect to get about the town. Professor Willard: "Grover's Corners lies on the old Pleistocene granite of the Appalachian range. I may say it's some of the oldest land in the world. We're very proud of that. A shelf of Devonian basalt crosses it with vestiges of Mesozoic shale, and some sandstone outcroppings; but that's all more recent: two hundred, three hundred million years old. Some highly interesting fossils have been found . . . I may say: unique fossils . . . two miles out of town, in Silas Peckham's cow pasture". We learn about the literal bedrock upon which the town was built, giving it a figurative and literal foundation within the play.

At the beginning of Act Three, we are in the graveyard at the top of a hill, and once again the Stage Manager gives us a situating description, which builds the world around us:

You come up here, on a fine afternoon and you can see range on range of hills awful blue they are up there by Lake Sunapee and Lake Winnipesaukee . . . and way up, if you've got a glass, you can see the White Mountains and Mt. Washington — where North Conway and Conway is. And, of course, our favorite mountain, Mt. Monadnock, 's right here — and all these towns that lie around it: Jaffrey, 'n East Jaffrey, 'n Peterborough, 'n Dublin; and [*Then pointing down in the audience*] there, quite a ways down, is Grover's Corners.

While no stage directions are given for all the other locations (several of which are real), the only one given is for Grover's Corners, which is literally where the audience is sitting. At this point, then, the audience can be said to be *in* Grover's Corners, viewing the graveyard from the point of view of the town (although the Stage Manager also says the graveyard is "an important part of Grover's Corners", which would seem to include it in the town as well). Later during Act Three, the left half of the stage will become Main Street and the Webbs's home in the scene in which Emily goes back to her 12th birthday, but the initial positioning which brings the audience's own location into the town adds to the immersion already established in other ways.

All these details — and *Our Town* is constantly giving us concrete details and instances that represent universal, general things, and concepts for which we substitute our own lives' specific details — together present a rich, full world onstage and in our imagination, which overlaps our own Primary World situation. The way these details are presented, using the concentric circles described above, along with positioning just described, has the overall effect of locating us in the center of the world, even as we are viewing it, just as Jane Crofut's letter is addressed to The Crofut Farm; Grover's Corners; Sutton County; New Hampshire; the United States; Continent of North America; Western Hemisphere; the Earth; the Solar System; the Universe; the Mind of God.[4] The play also uses similar world-building strategies when it comes to history and time.

History (Time)

> *On the stage it is always now; the personages are standing on that razor-edge, between the past and the future, which is the essential character of conscious being; the words are rising to their lips in immediate spontaneity.*
>
> —*Thornton Wilder,* Writers at Work *Interview, 1958*[5]

Just as the beginning of Act One situates us precisely with geographical coordinates (albeit specious ones), the same opening statement does so with time, telling us "The First Act shows a day in our town. The day is May 7, 1901. The time is just before dawn". This day, however, turns out to be problematic later; on the evening of that day, characters are commenting on how "terrible" and "wonderful" the moonlight is, at 8:30 pm; but moonrise on May 7, 1901, at latitude 42.6666, longitude −70.6166, was actually at 10:23 pm; which means the moon would not rise for almost two hours *after* the characters' statements about the moonlight were made.[6]

Despite this error, almost all of the events of the play do fit into a coherent time structure, to the point that one can generate a timeline from all the lines which attribute specific years or even dates to events which occur or are discussed in the play. Compared to other plays, *Our Town* has an unusually high number of statements regarding events and their times, which is necessary here for the temporal world-building that gives Grover's Corners its detailed history within the confines of the play's dialog. Some of this is done very directly, as when the Stage Manager gives us a capsule history, for example, in Act One, that of Joe Crowell, Jr.: "Joe was awful bright—graduated from high school here, head of his class. So he got a scholarship to Massachusetts Tech. Graduated head of his class there, too. It was all wrote up in the Boston paper at the time. Goin' to be a great engineer, Joe was. But the war broke out and he died in France". Most of the time, however, years and dates are casually given in character dialog, or inferred from references to ages and past years. Putting all these references together, we can generate the following timeline of events:

200–300 million years BC = Pleistocene granite forms with shelf of Devonian basalt and Mesozoic shale and some sandstone outcroppings.

10th century AD = Earliest evidence of the Cotahotchee tribes in the area.

17th century AD = Migration occurred near the end of this century.

1670–1680 = Earliest tombstones in cemetery on the mountain are Grovers, Cartwrights, Gibbses, and Herseys.

1864 = Myrtle Webb begins cooking three meals a day for 40 years.

1871 = Howie Newsome is born around this time (he is said to be "about thirty" in 1901).

1884 = Julia Gibbs begins cooking three meals a day for 20 years. Hank Todd is on the baseball team.

1884 = George Gibbs is born.

1884 = Bessie, Howie Newsome's horse, is born.

1887, February 11 = Emily is born.

1890 = Rebecca Gibbs and Wally Webb are born.

1899, February 11 = Emily's 12th birthday.

    7:00 am = The Webbs have breakfast.

1900, June = Emily likes George a lot, but then George starts spending all his time at baseball.

1900 = Sam Craig goes out East, ends up in Buffalo.

1901, May 7, (Day seen in Act One)

    1:30 am = Frank Gibbs gets a call to come deliver the Goruslawski twins.

    "just before dawn" (sunrise was 4:29 am that day[7]) = Frank Gibbs returns home after delivering the twins.

    5:45 am = Shorty Hawkins takes the train to Boston

    7:00 am = Emily and Wally Webb are called to breakfast.

    10:00 am = Wally has a test on Canada.

    11:00 am = Mrs. Wentworth comes over.

    "late afternoon" = Children return home from school.

"evening" = Children are doing their homework. Choir practice is going on.

8:30 pm = Frank and George Gibbs have a talk, and choir practice ends. George says he is "almost 17".

1901, June = George and Emily are juniors in high school and elected to school government positions.

1904, July 7, (Day of the wedding in Act Two)

"early morning" = It is raining.

5:45 am = Whistle heard from train to Boston. Mrs. Gibbs and Mrs. Webb make breakfast.

7:00 am = George goes to call on Emily.

12:00 pm = The wedding of George Gibbs and Emily Webb.

1906 = First automobile, belonging to banker Cartwright, comes to town.

1909 = George and Emily Gibbs's son is born.

1910 or 1911, summer = Julia Gibbs dies.

1913, summer = (Day of the funeral in Act Three)

"afternoon" = The burial of Emily Gibbs is held in the cemetery.

1930 = Frank Gibbs dies. (At an unspecified time later, the hospital is named after him.)

2901 = The time capsule in the cornerstone of the Cartwright Bank is expected to be dug up.

Before we examine the timeline as a whole, there are a few interesting things to note about these entries. To begin with, there is an inconsistency regarding Emily's age. In Act Three, we are given the actual date of Emily's birthday; she was born on February 11, 1887. This agrees with the statement made on July 7, 1904, Emily's wedding day, when Mrs. Webb says: "It came over me at breakfast this morning; there was Emily eating her breakfast as she's done for seventeen years and now she's going off to eat it in someone else's house". Both figures would imply that Emily is 17 at the time of the wedding, on July 7, 1904. George, who is in the same class in high school with Emily, says during Act One, in a scene occurring on May 7, 1901, that he is "almost 17"; thus his 17th birthday is most likely during 1901, which would mean that the year of his birth would around mid-1884, making him between two or three years older than Emily. Contradicting this, a stage direction in Act One (on the same day of May 7, 1901) says "*Right,* GEORGE, *about sixteen,* and REBECCA, *eleven. Left,* EMILY *and* WALLY, *same ages*". This means Emily would have been born in 1884, like George; yet in Act Three we are specifically given February 11, 1887 as Emily's birthday. Since the date in Act Three is so precise (and matches the comment made in 1904), it seems like it would take precedence over more vague ("*about sixteen*") information given only in a stage direction. If we go with the latter year of 1887 for Emily's birthday, then this would mean, since George and Emily are juniors in high school and elected to school government positions in June of 1901, that Emily is a high school junior at the age of 14, which would put her three grades ahead of her contemporaries. In Act One, Emily does say "I'm the brightest girl in school for my age. I have a wonderful memory", but it also seems unlikely that she is actually three grades ahead of others her age. Due to the stage direction that says "*same ages*" and the fact they are in the same class together, one does get the impression that Wilder intended George and Emily to be the same age, but the information he gives us implies otherwise, or is simply inconsistent.

The years of two other events are implied in the dialog; Sam Craig must have went out east in 1900 before ending up in Buffalo, because in Act Three, which is summer of 1913, he says he has been gone "over 12 years"; if he had been gone longer, one would expect him to say "over 13 years" or something like that; so it is likely that 1900 is the year he left. Likewise, Joe Stoddard says "Yes, Doc Gibbs lost his wife two-three years ago . . . about this time", so her death must have been summer of either 1910 or 1911. Finally, there is an error in what the Stage Manager says; he claims that Emily's 12th birthday, February 11, 1899, was a Tuesday, when in fact it was actually a Saturday.

As a whole, this collection of events, stretching across millions of years, with events ranging from the geological to the mundane, may remind one of the book-length expansion of Richard McGuire's *Here* (original six-page comic strip, 1989; book, 2014), which imagines all the events to take place on a small section of land throughout the history of the world.[8] Just like the concentric circles of geography are increasingly detailed as we move toward their center, the events on *Our Town*'s timeline extend from the prehistoric to the futuristic, with the majority of the events falling between 1899 and 1913, and especially on the days of the wedding, the funeral, and May 7, 1901, the last of which can even be laid out in a timeline on an hourly basis. Professor Willard's description of the land is followed by other details of the Native American tribes, the first humans in the area, the migrations of later immigrants, and the tombstones of the oldest families (all of which still have descendants in town, as we discover), and so on, leading up to the turn of the 20th century, the present time of the play. We also move forward in time, with the changes the Stage Manager mentions at the start of Act Three:

> This time nine years have gone by, friends — summer, 1913. Gradual changes in Grover's Corners. Horses are getting rarer. Farmers coming into town in Fords. Everybody locks their house doors now at night. Ain't been any burglars in town yet, but everybody's heard about 'em. You'd be surprised, though — on the whole, things don't change much around here.

Of course, the play appeared in 1938, when much turn-of-the-century life was already gone, and the worsening situation in Europe threatened to change things even further. And three out of four of the last items on the timeline also involve change; the deaths of Julia Gibbs, Emily Gibbs, and Frank Gibbs. All of the details and events referred to beyond the events of the main storyline are necessary for world-building and context, especially since the town itself is the play's main character.

Finally, the last event on the timeline, set far ahead in the year 2901, is the expected digging up of the time capsule, which will be buried in the cornerstone of the Cartwrights's new bank in Grover's Corners. The Stage Manager tells us about the preparations for the future discovery:

> And they've asked a friend of mine what they should put in the cornerstone for people to dig up. . . a thousand years from now. . . . Of course, they've put in a copy of the *New York Times* and a copy of Mr. Webb's *Sentinel*. . . . We're kind of interested in this because some scientific fellas have found a way of painting all that reading matter with a glue — a silicate glue — that'll make it keep a thousand — two thousand years.

The discussion of the silicate glue that will preserve the paper, keeping it intact for perhaps as long as 2,000 years, could be seen as implying that the capsule's contents could remain on display in a museum for another 1,000 years, bringing the timeline to an end as late as the year 3901. Finally, there is the last item mentioned that will be put into the time capsule; according to the Stage Manager, in Act One:

> And even in Greece and Rome, all we know about the *real* life of the people is what we can piece together out of the joking poems and the comedies they wrote for the theatre back then.
>
> So I'm going to have a copy of this play put in the cornerstone and the people a thousand years from now'll know a few simple facts about us — more than the Treaty of Versailles and the Lindbergh flight.
>
> See what I mean?
>
> So — people a thousand years from now — this is the way we were in the provinces north of New York at the beginning of the twentieth century. — This is the way we were: in our growing up and in our marrying and in our living and in our dying.

A copy of the very play being "performed for (or read by) the audience." is one of the written works being placed in the time capsule; interestingly, written works are the only things mentioned as the capsule's contents. That *Our Town* itself will be included means that the last remaining vestiges of Grover's Corners, apart from the time capsule itself, as an object, will be the very play the audience has now; we are, in a way, like that future audience, since that is all we presently have to represent the town. Finally, the people mentioned by the

Stage Manager brings us to the third main infrastructure of imaginary worlds, which is that of characters, and the webs of relationships which give them their context.

Genealogy (Characters)

Just as the play gives us a broad but limited background geographically and historically, we likewise get similar information on the background of the people of Grover's Corners. Again, it is Professor Willard who establishes the deep background in Act One:

> Yes . . . anthropological data: Early Amerindian stock. Cotahatchee tribes. . . no evidence before the tenth century of this era. . . hm . . . now entirely disappeared . . . possible traces in three families. Migration toward the end of the seventeenth century of English brachioce-phalic blue-eyed stock. . . for the most part. Since then some Slav and Mediterranean —

We are also told that the earliest tombstones in cemetery on the mountain, from 1670 to 1680, contain the names of Grovers, Cartwrights, Gibbses, and Herseys. The first surname, Grover, provides a possible origin of the town's own name, tying it closer to its inhabitants. The last three names are names which reappear in the present-day portions of the play, showing that the families have remained in the area; the Cartwrights are said to have had the first automobile in town, and it is also their new bank building which will contain the time capsule, so they are expected to be around for some time.

The Gibbs and Hersey families, of course, have intermarried; we find out that Hersey is the maiden name of Frank Gibbs's wife Julia. Julia's grandmother is mentioned as Grandma Wentworth, and another Wentworth, no doubt a descendent or relative, is said to be coming to visit the Gibbs's house at 11:00 am on May 7, 1901. We also discover more genealogical connections throughout the play; Julia's cousin is Hester Wilcox, Julia's sister is Carey, and Carey's son is Samuel Craig. Frank and Julia Gibbs, of course, have a son, George, and a daughter, Rebecca. George has an Uncle Luke, who is mentioned four times, along with the fact that George wants to work on his farm and that his uncle may one day give it over to him.

The other major family of the play is the Webb family; Charles and Myrtle Webb, who have a daughter, Emily, and a son, Wally. We are told Emily and Wally have an Aunt Carrie and an Aunt Norah, though through which of their parents they are related is not indicated. George and Emily marry, uniting the play's main two families, and have two children of their own, neither of which is named; Emily dies after giving birth to the second one, and the first is a boy who is born four years earlier. Thus we have traced three generations of family, and a number of collateral relations as well. Apart from that, there are other indications of relationships, even to characters we may not meet; for example, Mrs. Soames mentions Mr. Soames, Mrs. Goruslawski is the mother of twins, and Joe Crowell, Jr. and his brother Si Crowell must be the sons of Joe Crowell, Sr. Likewise, the play is rich in background detail as well; over the course of the three acts, we are given no less than three dozen surnames of the town's inhabitants: Carter, Cartwright, Corcoran, Craig, Crofut, Crowell, Ellis, Fairchild, Ferguson, Forrest, Foster, Gibbs, Goruslawski, Greenough, Grover, Gruber, Hawkins, Hersey, Huckins, Lockhart, McCarty, Morgan, Newsome, Peckham, Slocum, Soames, Stimson, Stoddard, Todd, Trowbridge, Warren, Webb, Wentworth, Wilcox, Wilkins, and Willard.[9]

The genealogical background places the characters in the context of families from which they have descended; George and Emily's children can trace their roots to the Gibbs, Webb, and Hersey families, perhaps even back to those whose graves are marked by the early tombstones. The background details, and events we have witnessed, give us a familiarity that the play encourages; not only does the Stage Manager speak to us directly, but occasionally characters address the audience, including Professor Willard, Charles Webb when he answers questions posed by the faux audience members during the question-and-answer session in Act One, and Mrs. Soames at George and Emily's wedding in Act Two, as her chatter (addressing us and her neighbors) drowns out the clergyman. By Act Three, we are seeing the graveyard from the point of view of Grover's Corners (as mentioned earlier), and the Stage Manager shows us various graves and says "Here's your friend, Mrs. Gibbs" and "And Mrs. Soames who enjoyed the wedding so — you remember?", the first comment casually supposing familiarity and a relationship, while the second comment suggests a nostalgic recollection of an event from the past, both comments encouraging our emotional involvement with the play's characters and history.

And through the intimate knowledge of the characters, along with the town's geography and history, by the end of the play the audience will likely have established a close connection and familiarity with the town itself; indeed, it is not just "their town", but "Our Town". After that, it is merely another step to consider our own hometown, its history, layout, and inhabitants, the comparisons causing us to reflect on the universal and eternal qualities that the play is discussing.

Transmedial Adaptations of *Our Town*

Our Town was first performed January 22, 1938, it later found success on Broadway, and won the Pulitzer Prize for Drama. Thornton Wilder also had a hand in the transmedial expansion of the play and its world into film, and recognized the peculiarities of that particular medium. Audiences may be surprised to find that the 1940 film adaptation differs from the play; apart from a number of other changes, perhaps the greatest one is that Emily lives at the end. At first this may seem like typical Hollywood meddling to bring about a happy ending, but Wilder himself approved the idea. Producer Sol Lesser and Wilder discussed the film adaptation of *Our Town* in a series of letters. As Edward Burns and Ulla E. Dydo write in an edited collection of those letters,

> Wilder was consulted by Lesser about the film script. Their letters concern problems faced in transforming a play into a film. On the major change of the added happy ending, Wilder commented to Lesser on Easter Night 1940, "In the first place, I think Emily should live. I've always thought so. In a movie you see the people so *close* that a different relation is established. In the theatre they are halfway abstractions in an allegory; in the movie they are very concrete. So insofar as the play is a generalized allegory, she dies — we die — they die; insofar as it's concrete happening it's not important that she die; it's even disproportionately cruel that she die.
>
> Let her live — the idea will be imparted anyway."[10] The changed ending still has Emily undergoing a near-death experience, allowing the graveyard scene in the play to occur, before Emily returns to the living. As Donna Kornhaber writes,

> Wilder's argument, is, in essence, based on the different properties of film and theater, on a belief that the intimacy and proximity of film forces it into the status of a "Concrete Happening" that does not offer the same allegorical possibilities as the stage. The changes to which he consented were an attempt to render *Our Town* anew in a manner appropriate to cinema. Wilder's concessions did not mean he was entirely satisfied with Wood's adaptation, although it was well received at the time and was nominated for six Academy Awards. But the playwright took from the experience a deeper appreciation of the specific strengths and capacities of filmic storytelling and a willingness to adjust his working methods to the demands of the screen, even if that meant reversing some of his most closely held principals. Wilder learned that film is a medium that must tell its stories differently and that, contra the theater, must find its power in the particular.[11]

The adaptation of *Our Town* raises other questions and issues pertaining to the adaptation of an imaginary world originating on the theatrical stage to various media; for example, the interaction with the faux audience members, which helps bring the audience into closer connection with the town, will likely be lost. So far, *Our Town* has been adapted to radio in 1939 and 1940;

film in 1940; television in 1955, 1977, and 2003; ballet in 1994; and opera in 2009. The operatic version of the play, the 1955 television adaptation, and the stage adaptation called *Grover's Corners* (1987) were all musical adaptations of the play, demonstrating its flexibility and continuing durability. The play itself continues to appear onstage, and in 1989 it won the Drama Desk Award for Outstanding Revival and Tony Award for Best Revival. In 2017, *Our Town* was even performed in American Sign Language and English, by the Deaf West Theater and Pasadena Playhouse in California.

While theater places its own limitations on world-building, it also provides an immediacy and presence which other media do not. Perhaps playwrights have still not fully made use of the unique world-building possibilities that the live theater stage can provide, although *Our Town* has arguably made the best use of them so far.[12] By cleverly managing to include a large amount of world data which, while perhaps not immediately pertinent to the advancement of the storyline, is still necessary to the world-building needed to give Grover's Corners its detail and verisimilitude, *Our Town* demonstrates that the stage can deliver unique imaginary worlds that become our world as we attend the performances occurring there.

Notes

1 Malcolm Cowley, *Writers at Work: The Paris Review Interviews*, New York, New York: Penguin Books, 1958, page 108.
2 Takuji Nosé, "Speech System of the Stage Manager in Thornton Wilder's Pullman Car Hiawatha", *On-line Proceedings of the Annual Conference of the Poetics and Linguistics Association* (PALA), 2008, available at https://www.pala.ac.uk/uploads/2/5/1/0/25105678/nose2008.pdf.
3 Elsewhere I have written extensively about the infrastructures of imaginary worlds; see Mark J. P. Wolf, *Building Imaginary Worlds: The Theory and History of Subcreation*, New York: Routledge, 2012.
4 There is no "Sutton County" in New Hampshire; Sutton is a town in Merrimack County, New Hampshire, which is made up of the villages of Sutton Mills, North Sutton, South Sutton, and East Sutton; see https://en.wikipedia.org/wiki/Sutton,_New_Hampshire.
5 Malcolm Cowley, *Writers at Work: The Paris Review Interviews*, New York: Penguin Books, 1958, page 108.
6 Moonrise on May 7, 1901, according to the Keisan Online Calculator, available at https://keisan.casio.com/exec/system/1224689365.
7 Sunrise on May 7, 1901, according to the Keisan Online Calculator, available at https://keisan.casio.com/exec/system/1224686065.
8 Richard McGuire's "Here" began as a six-page comic strip in *Raw*, Volume 2, #1, in 1989, and was expanded to the book-length work *Here* from Pantheon Books in 2014.
9 Assuming that Professor Willard and Professor Gruber, who have researched Grover's Corners, are also residents; but the play does not specify exactly one way or the other.
10 From *The Letters of Gertrude Stein and Thornton Wilder*, edited by Edward Burns and Ulla E. Dydo, with William Rice, New Haven and London: Yale University Press,

1996, page 256. Available at https://books.google.com/books?id=SHOPenESaHQC& pg=PA256&lpg=PA256&dq=%22different+relation+is+established.+In+the+ theatre,+they+are+halfway+abstractions+in+an+allegory,%22&source=bl&ots= ctEokyiIXa&sig=b8Cd7b0Bm1cMTMItawIFeeuCwnc&hl=en&sa=X&ved=2ah UKEwi7-_iStpzeAhXM7VMKHctGBdsQ6AEwAXoECAgQAQ#v=onepage& q=%22different%20relation%20is%20established.%20In%20the%20theatre%2C% 20they%20are%20halfway%20abstractions%20in%20an%20allegory% 2C%22&f=false.

11 From Donna Kornhaber, *Hitchcock's Diegetic Imagination: Thornton Wilder, Shadow of a Doubt, and Hitchcock's Mise-en-Scène*, November 2, 2015, e-book, available at https://books.google.com/books?id=z-vZCgAAQBAJ&pg=PT12&dq=the+idea+ will+be+imparted+anyway&hl=en&sa=X&ved=0ahUKEwiGy5-RubjeAh Wuc98KHYxDBwEQ6AEIMzAC#v=onepage&q=turns%20pivotally&f=false.

12 Due to the errors regarding the chronology, it would appear Wilder did not lay out all of his events on a consistent timeline, the way world-builders would do to-day. Still, the timeline is fairly detailed compared to the existing imaginary world chronologies of its time, especially in theater, and holds together well enough for the purpose of the story.

6

"SUCKLED ON SHADOWS"

States of Decay in Mervyn Peake's *Gormenghast* Novels

Edward O'Hare

> What was I after anyway? I suppose, to create a world of my own in which
> those who belong to it and move in it come to life and never step outside into
> either this world of bus queues, ration-books, or even the Upper Ganges — or
> into another imaginative world.
>
> —Mervyn Peake, in a letter to Gordon Smith[1]

In the autumn of 1943 Mervyn Peake sent a manuscript to Graham Greene
for his appraisal. When Greene, by then not only a famous novelist but also an
influential figure in British publishing, wrote back, his "mercilessly frank"[2]
comments must have been the very opposite of what Peake had hoped to hear.
Even though he had been intrigued by the opening sections of the work, which
the young author had entitled *Titus Groan*, Greene found it marred by extreme laziness and awash with "really bad writing, redundant adjectives, [and] a
kind of facetiousness, a terrible prolixity in the dialogue".[3] For everything that
he considered to be "immensely good"[4] about the book, Greene complained
that there was an equal amount that was "trite, unrealized [and] novelettish".[5]
Weighed down by "about 10,000 words of adjectives"[6] which he felt were entirely superfluous, he regarded *Titus Groan*'s prospect of publication as doubtful,
to say the very least.

Having labored enthusiastically on the novel for almost four years, Peake
must have been particularly stung by the initially well-disposed Greene's dev-
astating verdict and by the series of rejections the book subsequently received
from leading publishing houses. For Peake, the novel was not merely another of the many projects that became the focus of his multifaceted creative
talent; it was his first sustained attempt to represent the world of his richly

strange and gloriously macabre imagination in words. Thankfully for modern literature Peake persevered, and *Titus Groan* was published three years later in March 1946 and was later followed by two sequels. Although the book received some glowing accolades, Peake must have been dismayed that even after his substantial revisions many reviewers voiced opinions strongly reminiscent of Greene's, often in similarly trenchant terms. The Irish writer Kate O'Brien called it "a large, haphazard, Gothic mess",[7] while the British playwright Charles Morgan argued that although Peake's novel was undoubtedly an astonishing display of the "forces of dream, vision and language"[8] its overall effect was weakened by his indulgence in "shocking affectations and sudden pedestrian vulgarisms".[9]

Of all the critics who reviewed *Titus Groan* upon its original publication, the renowned novelist Elizabeth Bowen came closest to identifying the true nature of Peake's accomplishment. Bowen observed that *Titus Groan* was "one of those works of pure, self-sufficient imagination that are from time to time thrown out",[10] and she correctly predicted that in the decades to come this highly unusual new author would enjoy "a smallish but fervent public, composed of those whose imaginations are complementary to Mr Peake's".[11] Over the years the ranks of this deeply devoted and continually expanding group has included an eclectic assortment of cultural luminaries such as C. S. Lewis, Orson Welles, John Betjeman, Peter Sellers, Anthony Burgess, Michael Moorcock, Sting, Terry Pratchett, Joanne Harris, and Neil Gaiman,[12] all of whom have praised the marvelous idiosyncrasy and deliciously dark wit of Peake's creation.

Following Bowen's example, many of Peake's admirers have tried to define exactly *what* kind of text *Titus Groan* and the other novels which form the *Gormenghast* sequence are. To do this, they have consistently tried to bundle them into the genres of Gothic fiction and Fantasy literature, often implicitly assuming that there exists some critical consensus as to what those terms signify. This has proven especially misleading in the case of Peake, since his books contain none of the uncanny or preternatural elements traditionally thought of as intrinsic to the Gothic genre, nor do they feature any of the wizards, dragons, or invented languages which readers commonly associate with Fantasy novels. Another frequent approach to the *Gormenghast* sequence has seen critics interpret it simply as Peake's nightmarish depiction of the events of his own age, a period of history characterized by unparalleled destruction, violence, and social upheaval. An otherworldly creative figure who discovered the extent of mankind's barbarity while traveling through Europe in the immediate aftermath of World War II, there has been a tendency to conclude that the *Gormenghast* sequence is really Peake's cathartic bid to transmute the incomprehensible monstrousness of this conflict into a work of art.

If neither of these conventional forms of analysis has succeeded in capturing the artistry of these most wildly overdetermined and uproariously eccentric of texts, an alternative critical strategy is needed for examining the *Gormenghast* books. The objective of this essay is to formulate such a strategy in order to explore the many sides of Peake's imaginative vision. It aims to trace the origins of the Groan family saga in Peake's varied artistic and literary influences, as well as in the details of his extraordinary upbringing; to examine the grotesque style and ornate sensibility which are unique to his fiction; to assess Peake's ability to defy the constraints of genre and create characters who are both utterly alien and yet curiously familiar; ultimately, I intend to demonstrate how the land of Gormenghast occupies a singular place in 20th-century fiction.

The *Gormenghast* sequence comprises the three original novels published in Peake's lifetime, *Titus Groan* (1946), *Gormenghast* (1950), *Titus Alone* (1959), the short narrative *Boy in Darkness* (1956),[13] and (in the view of a select group of critics and aficionados) *Titus Awakes* (2011), a novel written in the years after Peake's untimely death by his widow Maeve Gilmore and based upon his notes. The first two novels are set in an imaginary realm dominated by Gormenghast Castle, an impossibly vast edifice which has been in a state of decay as far back as anyone can remember. The castle is home to Sepulchrave, the morose 76th Earl of Gormenghast, his formidable wife Lady Gertrude, their petulant daughter Fuschia, the Earl's cretinous, doll-like twin sisters Clarice and Cora, and a rigidly stratified society made up of different classes of servant. Daily existence for the Groans and their legion of loyal retainers consists of an endless series of interminable and esoteric ceremonies, since tradition must be fastidiously adhered to at all costs. Everything that happens in this dreary, cloistered place, from hour to hour, month to month, and year to year, is completely dictated by these stultifying rituals, the meanings of which (presuming that they ever actually had any) have long since been lost to time.

For an age nothing new at all has occurred within the walls of Gormenghast, but in the opening pages of *Titus Groan* the castle is shaken by not one but two dramatic developments. The Earl and Lady Gertrude have at last produced a son, Titus, who is destined to one day assume his hereditary title and rule over this gloomy land. With the birth of an heir it seems that the crucial stability and continuity of life in this stagnant domain is ensured, but something else now transpires which throws this into terrible jeopardy. This is the appearance of Steerpike, a supremely devious young man consumed by a vengeful desire to overthrow the Groan household once and forever. No sooner has Steerpike emerged from the lowest depths of the castle than he uses his abundant charm and ruthless intelligence to set in motion his scheme to secretly usurp control of Gormenghast. A brief summary cannot convey the intricacy of Peake's plotting, but in the first two books of the sequence he chronicles the deceptions, manipulations, and murders which Steerpike commits in order to advance his position within the castle's hierarchy and the brutal struggle to prevent him from fulfilling his plan.

Perhaps the best way to commence this examination of the *Gormenghast* sequence is to return to the accusation still occasionally made against Peake's books, specifically that they are spectacular examples of overwriting. Graham Greene has certainly not been alone in condemning Peake as a writer too much in love with the magic of words and lacking the skill and restraint to use them effectively.[14] Indeed, readers new to the author are likely to find themselves daunted by his sometimes page-long passages of description and his tendency to fixate lavishly on what might seem to be minor aspects of his secondary world. However, all of this Baroque extravagance is not so much a part of Peake's world-building technique as the very key to it. To depict an alternate reality buckling under the weight of centuries of ruination and clogged to capacity with obscure rites and obsolete customs, Peake deliberately utilizes this vast accumulation of detail. What this intentionally stifling excess of adjectives generates in the reader is the sense that they too, like the inhabitants of the castle, are powerless prisoners in this strange world whose Byzantine workings are now largely unfathomable.

Verisimilitude, or imbuing the unreal with the appearance of authenticity through the inclusion of plausible detail, is of course an intrinsic aspect of all fiction, and one arguably even more vital to works of the fantastic. In the *Gormenghast* sequence, Peake pushes this literary technique to its absolute extreme. As Peake's biographer G. Peter Winnington has written, these books contain such an extraordinary "proliferation of images"[15] that the difficulty "lies not so much in interpreting them, as in choosing among the plethora of possible meanings".[16] By cramming his narrative with a quantity of detail far greater than their mind is accustomed to processing, Peake leaves the reader so overwhelmed that they have little choice but to accept the reality of his imaginary world and all that it contains.

Farah Mendlesohn has rightfully cited the *Gormenghast* sequence as a prime instance of what she terms an "*immersive*" work of fantasy, one which is "set in a world built so that it functions on all levels as a complete world".[17] She writes that an immersive fantasy solicits belief by acting as if we "must share the assumptions of the world"[18]: in this kind of work the reader "must sit in the heads of the protagonists, accepting what they know as the world, interpreting it through what they notice, and through what they do not".[19] Surrounded by a multitude of details whose significance we don't even half understand, we nonetheless gradually find ourselves regarding this constructed place as normal just like the denizens of the castle do.

As Mendlesohn points out, in the *Gormenghast* sequence "the fantastic is embedded in the linguistic excesses of the text"[20] and this is how it compels the reader to believe in it. One of the most impressive examples of Peake's use of this technique occurs early on in *Titus Groan* when Steerpike escapes confinement and inches his way agonizingly across a rooftop before he finally beholds Gormenghast in all its vast, ruinous glory. Piece by piece, the enormous cityscape unfolds, and Steerpike's awestruck reaction to this panorama is much the same as that of the reader. Peake's feat of description is one of his finest:

> Steerpike, when he had reached the spine of the roof, sat astride it and regained his breath for the second time. He was surrounded by lakes of fading daylight.
>
> He could see how the ridge on which he sat led in a wide curve to where in the west it was broken by the first of four towers. Beyond them the swoop of a roof continued to complete a half circle far to his right. This was ended by a high lateral wall. Stone steps led from the ridge to the top of the wall, from which might be approached, along a cat-walk, an area the size of a field, surrounding which, though at a lower level, were the heavy, rotting structures of adjacent roofs and towers, and between these could be seen other roofs far away, and other towers.
>
> Steerpike's eyes, following the rooftops, came at last to the parapet surrounding this area. He could not, of course, from where he was guess at the stone sky-field itself, lying as it did a league away and well above his eye level, but as the main massing of Gormenghast arose to the west, he began to crawl in that direction along the sweep of the ridge.
>
> It was over an hour before Steerpike came to where only the surrounding parapet obstructed his view of the stone sky-field. As he climbed this parapet with tired, tenacious limbs he was unaware that only a few seconds of time and a few blocks of vertical stone divided him from seeing what had not been seen for over four hundred years. Scrabbling one knee over the topmost stones he heaved himself over the rough wall. When he lifted his head wearily to see what his next obstacle might be, he saw before him, spreading over an area of four square acres, a desert of grey stone slabs. The parapet on which he was now sitting bolt upright surrounded the whole area, and swinging his legs over he dropped the four odd feet to the ground. As he dropped and then leaned back to support himself against the wall, a crane arose at a far corner of the stone field and, with a slow beating of its wings, drifted over the distant battlements and dropped out of sight. The sun was beginning to set in a violet haze and the stone field, save for the tiny figure of Steerpike, spread out emptily, the cold slabs catching the prevailing tint of the sky. Between the slabs there was dark moss and the long, coarse necks of seedling grasses. Steerpike's greedy eyes devoured the arena. What use could it be put to?[21]

This dizzying, dazzling image of a patchwork of glittering rooftops stretching to the very limits of perception perfectly demonstrates Peake's astonishing ability to depict something utterly wondrous and yet entirely credible. So meticulous and dynamic are his descriptions that it never even occurs to the reader to consider whether these things could actually exist. Once again, the source of their power lies in the denseness of their detail. As China Miéville has observed, "Asserting the specificity of a part, [Peake] better takes as given the whole — of which, of course, we are in awe".[22] Although what he describes may be fantastic and outrageously exaggerated, the absolute precision he applies to its representation makes its reality seem incontestable. In the words of Miéville, "Peake acts as if the totality of his invented place could not be in dispute. The dislocation and fascination we feel, the intoxication, is testimony to the success of his simple certainty".[23]

The stunning visuality of Peake's prose is certainly one of its most remarkable qualities. John Clute and John Grant overstate nothing when they make the claim that the *Gormenghast* sequence is "perhaps the most intensely visual fantasy ever written"[24] and that its author stands as "the most potent visionary the field has yet witnessed".[25] The vivid people and vistas which emerge from the pages of these books inhabit the imagination with a force which makes them unforgettable. It is therefore easy to believe that the man who created them was also the most acclaimed and sought-after British illustrator of his generation. Peake was already producing superb drawings by the age of ten, and he later became equally adept as an oil painter. His accomplishment as a draughtsman brought him work as a teacher at the Westminster School of Art, but Peake also turned his versatile hand to theater costume designs, commercial graphics (his famous logo for Pan Books was used for decades), and even cartoons for magazines. As a book illustrator he scored major triumphs with his exquisite pen and ink drawings for editions of *Alice's Adventures in Wonderland* (1865) (widely considered as even more exuberant and true to the manic spirit of Lewis Carroll than Tenniel's) and Samuel Taylor Coleridge's "The Rime of the Ancient Mariner" (1798), which surpass those of Doré in their ghastly, numinous beauty.

As much as he excelled at it, Peake was never content with simply providing visual interpretations of other author's worlds. From his earliest years he produced skillful combinations of drawings and narrative, in which the pictures and text complimented one another and formed a unified whole. As an adult, Peake's literary experiments were often accompanied by sketches of their various characters, scenes and settings, and these helped him to form a better understanding of what he was creating. The *Gormenghast* sequence was conceived in this fashion. While the original editions of these novels regrettably featured only a handful of his drawings, Peake was constantly fleshing out his secondary world and its denizens in sketch pads, on canvas, and even in the margins of his manuscripts. In 2011, to mark the centenary of his birth, a lavish new edition of the *Gormenghast* sequence containing all of the artwork relating to the story was published, allowing readers to finally experience these texts in the way that Peake himself had probably always envisaged.

In his own modest way, Peake saw himself as following in the tradition of unclassifiable figures like William Blake, Dante Gabriel Rossetti and William Morris, whose drawings and oils are inseparable from their writings. Just as Peake considered his visual art and fiction as two aspects of a single creative endeavor, the *Gormenghast* books are informed as much by his artistic influences as his literary ones. What Winnington describes as his "richly figurative language [. . .] his wide range of vocabulary, including unusual and obsolete words, and his use of self-consciously 'poetic' terms"[26] must be perceived as his attempt to devise a prose style as opulent and vibrant as the imagery of El Greco, Velasquez, Goya and Van Gogh, the painters whom Peake cited as his most enduring inspirations. The collection of writers he credited as contributing to *Gormenghast*'s heady brew was no less diverse and illustrious: Christopher Marlowe, John Bunyan, the Brothers Grimm, Robert Louis Stevenson and above all Charles Dickens remained favorites from his childhood until the very end of his life.

What primarily distinguishes Peake's art, both visual and literary, is what Winnington terms his "eye for the grotesque".[27] Whether it was the unusual profile of a stranger who passed him on the street or some strikingly incongruous tableaux he stumbled upon, his memory recorded these things exactly and they became the raw material for his art. He possessed an innate appreciation of the bizarre and the *outré*, as well as an extraordinary gift for exaggerating and distorting natural phenomena. As with Coleridge, Poe, and Wilde (other authors who brought out the best in him as an artist), Peake's extravagant and decadent aesthetic seems not to have been the result of conscious choice. Instead, it derived purely from his way of seeing things.

Peake's use of the grotesque is particularly noteworthy for its tendency to deconstruct the subject into a set of components which share an uneasy co-existence but also seem to have independent lives of their own. Rather than providing general images of his characters, he fragments them to the point where a definite overall impression is difficult to obtain. In this regard, none of his descriptions are more memorable than those devoted to Mr. Swelter, the enormously gross and bloodthirsty head chef of Gormenghast's Great Kitchen and the arch-nemesis of Lord Sepulchrave's spindly and cadaverous manservant Mr. Flay. When we are introduced to the loquacious Swelter in his hellish lair, Peake describes him thus:

> The long beams of sunlight, which were reflected from the moist walls in a shimmering haze, had pranked the chef's body with patches of ghost-light. The effect from below was that of a dappled volume of warm vague whiteness and of a grey that dissolved into swamps of midnight — of a volume that towered and dissolved among the rafters. As occasion merited he supported himself against the stone pillar at his side and as he did so patches of light shifted across the degraded whiteness of the stretched

uniform he wore. When Mr Flay had first eyed him, the cook's head had been entirely in shadow. Upon it the tall cap of office rose coldly, a vague topsail half lost in a fitful sky. In the total effect there was indeed something of the galleon.[28]

At the ceremonial breakfast to celebrate the birth of Titus, Swelter peers through a door to inspect his gastronomic handiwork, and Peake reemphasizes this suggestion of a corporeal bulk so obscenely massive it cannot be considered by itself, only as a mass of individually animated constituent parts;

> Doubling his body he opens the door the merest fraction of an inch and applies his eye to the fissure. As he bends, the shimmering folds of the silk about his belly hiss and whisper like the voice of far and sinister waters or like some vast, earthless ghost-cat sucking its own breath. His eye, moving around the panel of the door, is like something detached, self-sufficient, and having no need of the voluminous head that follows it nor for that matter of the mountainous masses undulating to the crutch, and the soft, trunk-like legs. So alive is it, this eye, quick as an adder, veined like a blood-alley. What need is there for all the cumulus of dull, surrounding clay — the slow white hinterland that weighs behind it as it swivels among the doughy, circumscribing wodges like a marble of raddled ice?[29]

What is immediately noticeable from these passages is the gorgeously elegant manner in which Peake portrays this intensely loathsome figure. He sees fit to imbue the repellent Swelter with a curious variety of majesty and splendor, and this same ambiguity is evident in his descriptions of all of the inhabitants of Gormenghast. Even the more outwardly attractive of them are marked by some kind of oddness or peculiarity, while those who are monstrously ugly are so to such a complete and total degree that this quality in itself becomes something strangely exquisite. In other words, the real brilliance of Peake's *grotesquerie* lies in the way he constantly traverses the line which traditionally divides the beautiful from the hideous, blurring it to the extent that we are no longer certain that anything truly separates them at all. In his fantastically ornate vision of things, these aesthetic categories are inverted to the point where they have no actual value: there is only what exists and how it appears to us at any one moment.

As a writer and an artist, Peake's sensibility veered instinctively toward the weird and disturbing, which could make publishers wary of employing him. His first set of illustrations for a treasury of nursery rhymes entitled *Ride-a-Cock-Horse* (1940), produced at the age of 29, were criticized for being "nightmarish",[30] with one reviewer insisting that even though they possessed "a certain sort of horrible beauty"[31] they were definitely not for children. The poet Walter de la Mare more astutely characterized Peake's work as exhibiting "a rare layer of imagination, and a touch now and then, and more than a touch, of the genuinely sinister",[32] and he half-jokingly warned his friend that the parents of traumatized children would start sending him their psychiatrist's bills. However, this darkness is the very essence of Peake's creative talent and the quality which elevates the *Gormenghast* sequence to the status of a true work of art.

In setting out to write what he called the "Titus" books, Peake explained that it was his ambition "to create between two covers a world, the movements of which — in action, atmosphere and speech — enthral and excite the imagination".[33] However, one of the great ironies of these novels is that Peake invests such energy and visionary intensity in depicting a fictional world which has succumbed to paralysis and ossification long ago. Within Gormenghast's labyrinth of dank and shadowy passageways, winding staircases, and candlelit corridors, time, insofar as we understand it, does not exist. There is only the ceaseless repetition of set patterns of behavior, which recur over and over again, differing only in what would seem to be the most inconsequential of their details. Peake's imaginary world is an ageless mixture of ancient and modern. At various points in the sequence, it seems to be home to a medieval society, a late 18th-century one, a mid-19th-century one, and is even enlarged to incorporate elements of the 20th century. Nevertheless, it is a place without any concept of development or growth, only mindless and remorseless continuation.

At the heart of the *Gormenghast* sequence is a paradox which also constitutes an intriguing artistic challenge: how is it possible to represent life in a realm caught in stasis, a land where change of any kind is not just feared with a kind of paranoid mania but where the inhabitants struggle to even imagine the intrusion of anything unexpected? One of the reasons Peake's imaginary world seems so strange lies in the reader's difficulty in finding significance in the behavior of his characters. This is because Gormenghast is not merely the setting of his story; it is the very foundation of their identities.[34] They have no notion of *belonging* to this place because they cannot conceive the idea of ever belonging anywhere else. The very concept of existence outside of its environs is simply devoid of all meaning.[35] Even when the superannuated Mr. Flay is banished from court and Titus boldly ventures into the unknown places beyond his home, Gormenghast is still the vital center of their beings and continues to define their every thought and action. In this way, it makes perfect sense that Peake's central characters are known as "Castles" since each of them is a living component of this place, as integral a part of its fabric as its bricks, beams, and flagstones, and their fates are inextricably bound up with the endurance of its routines and rituals.

If the "Castles'" unthinking obedience to the inviolable traditions of Gormenghast has any real literary antecedent, it can be found in Charles Dickens's *Bleak House* (1853). In this work (which Peake knew well and for which he once produced an unpublished series of illustrations), all of Dickens's extensive cast of characters are enmired to varying degrees in the crushingly tedious and seemingly unending court case of Jarndyce and Jarndyce. Their free will is subservient to the maddening convolutions of this fantastically complex legal dispute, and like Peake's characters many of them are now demented or even insane. The ghoulish, twilight world Dickens conjures up in this great work is one which has become hopelessly moribund as a result of mankind's twisted machinations, its vitality and creativity wasted away to nothing long ago. The exhausted, crumbling world of the *Gormenghast* sequence is fundamentally the same. The "Castles" are so preoccupied with maintaining the Earldom's ludicrous laws and customs they are unaware that everything that surrounds them has grown rotten and verges upon collapse. This is what the calculating Steerpike is quick to recognize, and turn to his advantage.

Most critical and biographical studies of Peake and his work have assumed that the sprawling, dreamlike landscape of the *Gormenghast* sequence was heavily inspired by his childhood experiences of life in China. There is much truth in this: the son of an intrepid missionary doctor, Peake was born among the hills of Kuling, Kiang-Hsi Province, in Central Southern China in 1911, but his home for a large portion of his first 12 years was Tientsin, a Treaty Port in Northern China to the south-east of Peking. Better known today as Tianjin, the city of Tientsin was occupied by a shifting conglomeration of British, Japanese, Russian, French, German, and Austro-Hungarian forces. An unruly architectural mishmash marked by a myriad cultural influences, in this respect Tientsin closely reflected the bewildering heterogeneous quality Peake would later bring to his descriptions of the citadel of Gormenghast. Encircling Tientsin was, to quote Clute and Grant, "a territory as alien to [Peake's] world as the land surrounding Gormenghast seems alien"[36] to the Groan family and their courtiers. During his formative years Peake made occasional journeys into these regions, and his imagination was set alight by such magnificent sights as the Old Chinese Road and its royal guard of giant sculpted warriors, a colossal stone path named "The Thousand Steps", the massive expanse of the Yangtze River, and the sublime palaces of Kublai Khan's Forbidden City.

None of these left an impression quite as indelible as the country's elaborate traditions, which formed an inescapable part of everyday life. Discussing his father's memories of China, Peake's son Sebastian observed how he was captivated by the role these complicated rituals played. What particularly fascinated him was the fact that in all of them "[t]here was a historical numerical order, [and] that for example things had to be performed in the tenth month after the previous emperor had died, for the sustaining of the momentum of the historical progress of China".[37] Strictly observed by everyone from the aristocratic elite to the most lowly peasant menial workers, Peake came to realize that these rituals "were very much part of the upper-class Chinese imperative, to seek discipline and order within historical facts".[38] As he would later recreate in his own fictional land, in Tientsin the meaning of each thing was entirely contingent on the meaning of everything else, forming one huge semantic mosaic. The great tomes of Gormenghast's rituals include a "list of the activities to be performed hour by hour during the day by his Lordship"[39] as well as the archaic regulations stipulating the "exact times; the garments to be worn for each occasion and the symbolic gestures to be used",[40] and together these amount to a "complex system"[41] which cannot be deviated from.

At the same time, tradition might never have acquired the specific role it plays in the *Gormenghast* sequence had it not been for Peake's return to Britain in 1923. Winnington has argued that the writer's sudden uprooting from China and its ancient culture gave rise to "a sense of dissociation"[42] which lasted for the rest of his life. As an adult, Peake was conscious that he had occupied these two distant worlds, but found he could establish "no thread, no link between them",[43] and as a result "[h]is memories seemed not to be part of him".[44] China's mysterious, age-old way of life appeared even more fabulous compared to the grimness and mundanity of Interwar Britain. Nevertheless, in the *Gormenghast* sequence the exotic codes of conduct he encountered in China are reconfigured to reflect the very British preoccupations with preserving the heredity caste system and maintaining self-control. Transplanted into Peake's imaginary realm, these rituals no longer constitute a precious, orderly link to a glorious past but a pointless and irrational system which no-one can break free from. Just like the corrupt Court of Chancery in the London of *Bleak House*, this is an insane world where madness has become so all-pervasive it has assumed the form of law.

In his introduction to *Titus Groan*, which remains one of the most illuminating pieces of criticism ever written on Peake's fiction and was instrumental in reviving his reputation, Anthony Burgess identifies the distinctive qualities of Peake's approach to world-building. He argues that the secondary reality Peake created differs from that of other authors insofar as it was never his intention to construct a utopia or dystopia. Instead, the world we enter "is neither better nor worse than this one: it is merely different".[45] Rather than offering the reader "a central sermon or warning"[46] which will drastically transform their view of the reality they inhabit, Burgess contends that the *Gormenghast* sequence is "essentially a work of the closed imagination".[47] By this he means that Peake presents us with "a world parallel to ours"[48] which shares many similarities with our own, but it is one which "has absorbed our history, culture, rituals and then stopped dead, refusing to move, self-feeding, self-motivating, [and] self-enclosed".[49] Gormenghast is a myopic realm which has lost sight of all the meaningful things that history and tradition are supposed to preserve and yet cannot envisage any form of future without ritual. Like a once-magnificent machine which keeps operating long after it has outlived its purpose, this is a world perpetually doomed to continue going absolutely nowhere.

Burgess observes that for all its exuberant strangeness Peake's secondary reality is a place in which "[n]obody flies from a centre of normality"[50] and "everybody belongs to a system built on very rigid rules".[51] At the heart of this system is the foreboding structure of Gormenghast Castle itself. Several critics[52] have made the argument that Peake gives the castle such a distinct presence and personality that it can be considered the central character of the narrative. He certainly describes the rhythms of its sterile activity as one would the shifting moods of a deeply complex individual. It also requires little imagination to go about mapping a psycho-physiological structure onto the castle: the library housing Lord Groan's collection of precious tomes forms its brain, while the Hall of Bright Carvings (the attic in which the most magnificent pieces created over the centuries by the foremost craftsmen of Gormenghast lie all but forgotten) can be read as its unconscious; the infernal Great Kitchen, perpetually in a state of feverish and needless overproduction, forms Gormenghast's stomach and genitals, while the countless narrow stone lanes which riddle the entire edifice are akin to veins and arteries. Peake himself deliberately represents the castle in terms of some collapsed or even decomposing corporeal form many times throughout the books, most directly in the first paragraph of *Titus Groan*, where its topmost pinnacle the Tower of Flints (home to a parliament of vicious, flesh-eating owls) is described as rising upward "like a mutilated finger from among the fists of knuckled masonry".[53]

If Gormenghast's inhabitants are akin to tiny insects crawling around the innards of a gigantic festering cadaver, the need to escape from the horror of their predicament is the reason why they must create realms of their own: Sepulchrave lives more in the world of his beloved books than in waking reality, and the Master of Ritual Sourdust and his almost equally ancient and wizened son Barquentine are similarly obsessed with the minutia of the traditions they enforce; the Countess spends most of her time in a room full of cats and birds with whom she shares a more intimate bond than she does with her own children, while her sisters-in-law Clarice and Cora lie motionless dreaming of a great power they wouldn't know what to do with even if they possessed it. As we have seen, Flay and Swelter are consumed by their pathological hatred for one another, which culminates in a duel that is both gruesome and ludicrous; the marvelously jovial and valiant court physician Dr. Prunesquallor delights in linguistic absurdities, conundrums, and verbal play, while his nearly blind and chronically neurotic sister Irma is besotted with romantic fantasies about men she scarcely knows. As much as they are necessary, Peake portrays these fragile imaginary worlds as points of vulnerability each of which Steerpike exploits, in turn.

It is this rich interior life and desire for a private domain to avoid the harshness and frustrations of reality, which makes Peake's creations so compelling. Since the *Gormenghast* books are very often magnificently funny,[54] critics have tended to reinforce the impression that their characters are the sort of over-the-top and cartoonish eccentrics found in the novels of P. G. Wodehouse or even in *Monty Python* sketches. However, it is a complete misconception to think of them as mere comic figures. For all of their exaggerated qualities and beguiling oddnesses, they remain real people with natural reactions, thoughts, and feelings and Peake successfully encourages us to share his interest in their fates. We feel for them far more often than we laugh at them. Compared to the grandiose mythic archetypes of Tolkien or the broadly Judeo-Christian analogs of C. S. Lewis, Peake can be credited with inventing characters who are much more fully realized and whose often tragic plights are genuinely affecting. Among its many interpretations, the *Gormenghast* sequence can be read as a brilliant study of how people try, and fail, to maintain their identities in an unbearably overfamiliar environment which is progressively destroying their sanity.

Anyone who doubts Peake's ability to create enigmatic characters need only consider his depiction of his most disturbing creation, Steerpike. Like so many of Peake's characters Steerpike seems to owe a debt to earlier figures from literature, and yet on reflection the reader discovers that they have never encountered anyone quite like him elsewhere in the history of fiction. Embodying the text's perpetual openness, Steerpike can be read as any one of a range of vastly different figures, from an aspiring totalitarian dictator, a radical political ideologue bent on bringing down the old order they hate so that they can take control, a conniving Machiavellian who plots to seize power from within using any and all means to achieve this end, and an Iago-like malefactor who does terrible things simply because they can. Indeed, for much of the first novel he is more like an actor adopting a series of guises (an image Peake reinforces by describing him as having a face that is "pale like clay and, save for his eyes, masklike"[55]) than an actual person,[56] and it is only as the second volume unfolds that we are made aware of the true extent of his malignancy. What makes Steerpike so dangerous and yet so alluring is the ease with which Peake could have turned him into the hero of his narrative rather than its villain. After all, he is proud, charismatic, resourceful, and relentless in his pursuit of his goal and has many other traits we would consider admirable if only they were used to further good and not evil ends.

Like many of the finest villains in literature, Steerpike is all the more fascinating because he has no clearly stated origins. When we originally encounter him he is merely the wretched kitchen scullion Swelter singles out for special cruelty and abuse because he refuses to flatter the bloated chef's vanity, but we never learn anything of his past prior to this. He simply seems to have come into being, almost as though self-created. Peake deliberately portrays Steerpike as sympathetic in the early pages of the sequence, a victim of its draconian organizational structure, and this makes it all the more unsettling when his diabolical true nature is gradually revealed to us. One of the major strengths of the first two books is the consummate skill with which Peake juxtaposes the dual narratives of Steerpike and Titus. The kitchen urchin escapes his servitude to Swelter the same day that Titus is born and uses the gatherings which mark his transition from infancy to maturity to stage his grabs for greater and greater glory. Steerpike is at his most self-assured and unstoppable while Titus remains vague and unformed as a person, but his dreams of total mastery begin to fall apart as Titus develops an identity of his own and becomes conscious of his duty to protect his homeland. It is no coincidence that, in the end, it is Titus who dispatches Steerpike, finally ridding Gormenghast of the influence of his malevolent shadow-self.

So much about Peake's text cries out for interpretation that it is easy to over-look a pivotal question: what is Steerpike's ultimate goal? Although he makes a show of expressing his outrage on behalf of the castle's lowly and downtrodden, Steerpike's concerns about inequality are mostly superficial. He is a fiendish trickster who eliminates those who stand in his way by means of lethal practical jokes, but he seems to derive no great personal pleasure from what he does. Instead, he sees himself as an arch-rationalist and supreme pragmatist, the only one capable of re-organizing Gormenghast along what he sees as sane and effi-cient lines. Asked what he aspires to be by Dr. Prunesquallor, he responds that "In my less ambitious moments it is as a research scientist that I see myself".[57] This is precisely what he becomes, with all of Gormenghast for his experimen-tal subject. He is animated not by any genuine desire to improve things but by a fanatical mania to reshape the world around him into the grim, mechanized system he believes it should be. In this respect, the most profound statement which arises from the *Gormenghast* sequence is that we must be very wary of our longing for change since the new age we create may prove to be far worse than the ones which went before it. After all, as Steerpike conjectures, "haven't all ambitious people something of the monstrous about them?"[58]

Steerpike despises the antiquated farce of tradition, but in another of Peake's brilliant ironies he has enough cunning to know that the most effective way of making Gormenghast bend to his will is to assume the role of Master of Ritual himself. Rather than a liberating force to sweep away the injustices and oppressions of the past, the regime Steerpike introduces is even more repressive and tyrannical. In an episode which evokes the Nazi book burnings of the early 1930s, he uses fire to decimate Lord Groan's magnificent library and purge the castle of any ideas which do not fit with his worldview. Steerpike's obsession with order and perfection is so all-consuming that he becomes deluded into believing that emotions are unnecessary and people must be made to act like automata. He is too much the unfeeling intellectual to understand that human behavior is fundamentally messy and chaotic and can never be otherwise. In this way, in spite of his fixation with logic and reason in actuality Steerpike is the most completely deranged of all of Peake's characters.

Steerpike is defeated at the climax of *Gormenghast*, but it transpires that the modern world he was determined to bring about already exists outside of the castle. Having forsaken his ancestral home, in the third volume of the sequence, *Titus Alone* (1959), the young Earl enters into wild, unmapped regions which could not be further removed from the ones he has known all his life. This book, published after a hiatus of almost ten years, has generated some remarkably ambivalent attitudes, ranging from enchanted bemusement to outright dismissal. Many critics favorably inclined toward *Titus Groan* and *Gormenghast* regard it as a muddled failure and a steep decline from the majestic heights of those works.[59] Even some of the most ardent enthusiasts of Peake's fiction admit to its inferiority, and have attempted to excuse its perceived weaknesses on the grounds that the author was already being overtaken by symptoms of the neurodegenerative disease[60] that would eventually rob him of his talent and his mind, and end his life several decades prematurely in 1968. As ever with Peake's work, the reality is an altogether different story.

There is no denying that *Titus Alone* is a very strange beast, a great deal stranger in many respects than the books which preceded it. Other than its impetuous protagonist, it seems to share no fundamental connection with the earlier novels in the sequence. Whereas their action was confined to a single, horribly suffocating space, *Titus Alone* has a picaresque narrative which rambles with what appears to be erratic abandon through a variety of surreal and hallucinatory landscapes. Gone is Peake's grand, stately orchestration of plot and incident. So is his phenomenal attention to detail. In their place we have situations and characters sketched out only in their essential outlines, and a storyline which follows no single trajectory but undergoes constant metamorphosis. The entire work is less than half the length of its predecessors, with chapters running to an average of two pages. It is therefore understandable why many critics have concluded that, either due to illness or not, in the intervening years Peake had grown unsure of his abilities and possibly lacked any clear design for the book he was writing.

On the basis of its stylistic and structural differences, *Titus Alone* would obviously seem to support these assumptions. A more careful assessment of the text suggests that Peake knew exactly what he was doing, and that he made these artistic choices for specific reasons. For a start, the novel is set not in Gormenghast but in remote realms Titus has never seen before. They appear so alien to him that Peake quite rightly cannot find words for them, and the brief descriptions he does provide can be interpreted as representing the young traveler's total uncertainty about where he is and where he may be headed. Second, Titus is now cut off from the controlling influence of ritual and free to experience life at its most random and unpredictable. We receive only the most fleeting glimpses of the people and places he encounters, and it can be argued that it was Peake's deliberate intention to present the reader with a much more impressionistic view of reality than the one we had become accustomed to from his earlier books. It is as if we too are on this disorientating, kaleidoscopic journey with Titus, and no more able to make sense of it all than he is.

Peake's minimalist, episodic approach does not make *Titus Alone* any less of an achievement than his previous books. Although smaller, the novel's cast

of characters is equally as bizarre and colorful. During the course of his wan-
derings Titus becomes entangled with such richly imaginative figures as the
mercurial zookeeper Muzzlehatch, his beautiful former lover Juno, and the
seductive but deadly Cheeta. In terms of theme, it can be argued that *Titus
Alone* deals with even weightier subjects than its predecessors and confronts the
reader with a much darker vision of things. Its core images were undoubtedly
formed during one of the most significant episodes of Peake's life. Shortly after
the end of World War II[61] he accepted an assignment to travel to the devastated
ruins of Germany and record what he found there. After visiting a succession
of bombed-out cities, Peake entered the recently liberated Bergen–Belsen concentration camp. There he sketched the former prisoners as they lay dying as
well as some of their captors who were awaiting execution, and the harrowing
drawings he produced are easily his most important artworks. What Peake
witnessed in Bergen–Belsen never left him, and those who knew him felt that
the trauma of it robbed him of his simple joy in being alive.[62]

The specter of the Holocaust hangs over *Titus Alone*, and the book is per-
vaded by the sense that terrible violence is happening everywhere only just
out of sight. Titus's journey from innocence to experience is a transmogrified
version of Peake's own pilgrimage through a world in ruins, but it is also a
more universal exploration of how the very worst aspects of human nature have
followed mankind into modernity. Titus discovers an unnamed city whose impossibly vast glass and steel towers are the antithesis of Gormenghast's degraded
masonry, and its architecture summons to mind the futuristic metropolises
which the Third Reich had vowed to build. Then there are the haunting chapters where Cheeta tries to impress Titus by bringing him to see a huge modern
factory. Like the death-camp Peake visited, this sinister structure has slender
chimneys continually belching foul smoke and the surrounding area reeks of a
vile sickly smell. As he approaches the building Titus hears a dreadful, inhuman
sound emanating from within, and in each of its windows he sees identical
human faces which stare back at him helplessly before disappearing at the blast
of a whistle. Earlier on Titus meets the inhabitants of the Under-River, a sub-
terranean space where the city's vagabonds, nonconformists and refugees have
been banished, and these figures closely resemble the social outcasts the Nazis
had rounded up for extermination.

As well as trying to find meaning in the horrors of the Holocaust, in *Titus
Alone* Peake once again plays upon the fear of the future and speculates whether
there will be any room for human freedom in it. The great city is a frighten-
ingly credible dystopia: it has no government or individual rights, and there
is also no art, music, entertainment, or any other kind of self-expression. A
cabal of scientists has established an all-powerful technocracy, and those who
interfere with their plans are hunted down and disposed of by faceless secret
police. So far, the scientist's most prized inventions are a death ray (which they
callously test on Muzzlehatch's beloved zoo animals) and a floating surveillance

device (Peake had clearly envisaged the drone half a century before its invention) which can think for itself, but the heartless Cheeta (who is the chief scientist's daughter) suggests that the outcome of whatever unthinkable experiments are being conducted in the factory will be their greatest achievement. It is exactly the sort of world Steerpike would have marveled at and felt at home in.

The conclusion of *Titus Alone*, a work which reads like the offspring of Orwell's *Nineteen Eighty-Four* (1949) and the Beatle's *Yellow Submarine* (1968), is certainly proof that even at this late stage Peake's imagination was anything but exhausted and that he had further adventures in mind for his young exile. Realizing that he has accidentally arrived home in the novel's final pages, Titus boldly decides not to return to the safety of Gormenghast but to set off in another direction and discover what lies in wait for him there. Tragically Peake's health had soon deteriorated beyond the point where he could continue to tell his story, but his legacy is a sequence of books which demonstrate in every possible way the boundless potential of fiction. His everlasting gift to readers is a world of dreams and nightmares that is entirely and magnificently his own.

Notes

The essay's title, "Suckled on Shadows" comes from Mervyn Peake, *Gormenghast* in *The Gormenghast Trilogy*, London, England: Vintage, 1999, p. 373.

1 Quoted in Estelle Daniel, *The Art of Gormenghast: The Making of a Television Fantasy*, London, England: HarperCollins, 2000, page 41.
2 Quoted in G. Peter Winnington, *Vast Alchemies: The Life and Work of Mervyn Peake*, London, England: Peter Owen Publishers, 2000, page 168.
3 Ibid.
4 Ibid.
5 Ibid.
6 Ibid.
7 Ibid, page 185.
8 Ibid, page 186.
9 Ibid.
10 Ibid.
11 Ibid.
12 In August 2019 it was announced that Neil Gaiman would be one of the executive producers of a major new adaptation of all five Gormenghast texts to be made by the American television network Showtime.
13 Originally published alongside novellas by William Golding and John Wyndham in the anthology Sometime, *Never: Three Tales of Imagination*, London, England: Eyre and Spottiswoode, 1956.
14 Kingsley Amis was most disparaging about Peake's work. In his critical monograph *New Maps of Hell: A Survey of Science Fiction*, London, England: Penguin, 2012, page 153, he dismisses him in his typically pugnacious and unsupported fashion as "a bad fantasy writer of maverick status".
15 G. Peter Winnington, "Inside the Mind of Mervyn Peake" in *Etudes de Lettres*, Lausanne, Switzerland: University of Lausanne Press, Series VI, Vol. 2, No. 1, January–March, 1979, page 3.

16 Ibid.
17 Mendlesohn, Farah, *Rhetorics of Fantasy,* Middletown, Connecticut: Wesleyan University Press, 2008, page 59.
18 Ibid.
19 Ibid.
20 Ibid, page xxi.
21 Mervyn Peake, *Titus Groan* in *The Gormenghast Trilogy,* page 91.
22 Miéville, China, *Introduction to The Illustrated Gormenghast Trilogy,* London, England: Vintage, 2011, page ix.
23 Ibid.
24 John Clute and John Grant, editors, *The Encyclopaedia of Fantasy,* available at http://sf-encyclopedia.uk/fe.php?nm=peake_mervyn.
25 Ibid.
26 *Vast Alchemies,* page 98.
27 Ibid, page 59.
28 *The Gormenghast Trilogy,* page 20.
29 Ibid, page 262.
30 Quoted in John Watney, *Mervyn Peake,* London, England: Michael Joseph, 1976, page 106.
31 Ibid.
32 Ibid.
33 Quoted in *The Art of Gormenghast,* page 42.
34 Peake also observed how human identity could be interconnected with a sense of place when he lived as part of an artists' colony on the Channel Island of Sark for three years. The island's tiny population, which had almost no interaction with the outside world, resembles the isolated existence of the inhabitants of Gormenghast. Peake's years on the island, spent amidst the rugged, windswept majesty of its landscape, were some of the happiest of his life.
35 Peake provides a terrific metaphor for the Groan's peculiar form of attachment to Gormenghast in *Titus Groan,* when the Earl ponders the question "How could he love this place? He was part of it. He could not imagine a world outside it; and the idea of loving Gormenghast would have shocked him. To have asked him of his feelings for his hereditary home would be like asking a man what his feelings were towards his own hand or his own throat", *The Gormenghast Trilogy,* page 42.
36 *The Encyclopaedia of Fantasy.*
37 Quoted in *The Art of Gormenghast,* page 29.
38 Ibid.
39 *The Gormenghast Trilogy,* page 44.
40 Ibid.
41 Ibid, page 45.
42 *Vast Alchemies,* page 43.
43 Ibid.
44 Ibid.
45 Anthony Burgess, Introduction to *Titus Groan,* London, England: Penguin, 1968, page 9. Burgess's reverence for Peake's novel remained undiminished since he included it in his personal selection of the most important works of fiction in English of the past half century almost 20 years later in his book *99 Novels: The Best in English Since 1939,* London, England: Summit Books, 1985.
46 Ibid.
47 Ibid, page 13.
48 Ibid.
49 Ibid, page 9.
50 Ibid, page 11.

51 Ibid.

52 Among them Miéville, Mendlesohn, and Winnington, who all propose that Gormenghast Castle has so many distinctive qualities that it rightfully constitutes the main character of the sequence.

53 *The Gormenghast Trilogy*, page 7.

54 Peake's novels abound with wicked black humor. Especially hilarious are the chapters of *Gormenghast* set in the academy run by the benevolent but ineffectual Professor Bellgrove and his cadre of freakish oddballs. In this school, Titus meets such characters as the ancient Headmaster Deadyawn, who is catapulted to his demise from his own mobile high chair, and the venerable Idealist philosopher "The Leader", whose Berkeleyan theory that material reality and physical sensations are illusory is disproven when his beard goes up in flames and he perishes. The comedic highlight of the sequence, however, is Bellgrove's courtship of Irma Prunesquallor at her disastrous garden party.

55 *The Gormenghast Trilogy*, page 89.

56 This chameleonic aspect of the character was captured tremendously in actor Jonathan Rhys Meyer's performance in the BBC miniseries based on Peake's novels broadcast in 2000. His startling physical resemblance to Peake's drawings of Steerpike was also uncanny.

57 *The Gormenghast Trilogy*, page 127.

58 Ibid.

59 Fortunately, if belatedly, this view has begun to alter in recent years. Roger Luckhurst in *Science Fiction* (Cambridge: Polity Press, 2005), David Louis Edelman in his Introduction to *Titus Alone* (New York: The Overlook Press, Peter Mayer Publishers, 2011) and Michael Moorcock in "*Breaking Free: An Introduction to Mervyn Peake's Titus Alone*" in Michael Moorcock and Allan Kausch, editors, *London Peculiar and Other Nonfiction* (London: PM Press, 2012) offer much more perceptive and sympathetic readings of this text.

60 The exact nature of the medical condition which killed Peake over ten years and left the *Gormenghast* sequence incomplete remains the subject of speculation. It has variously been diagnosed as Alzheimer's disease, Parkinson's disease, and different forms of encephalitis, but contemporary research has postulated that Peake may have suffered from dementia with Lewy bodies, an extreme form of premature aging. His mental and physical deterioration was only accelerated by the medications, electroconvulsive therapy, and brain surgery he was prescribed. Peake was 57 when he died, but the last photographs of him show a man who looks thirty years older. Maeve Gilmore wrote a poignant account of her last years with her husband's entitled *A World Away* (London: Gollancz, 1970).

61 At the outbreak of the conflict Peake volunteered his services as a war artist. Despite being refused, he developed a project of his own, *The Works of Adolf Hitler*, a series of intensely horrific paintings supposedly by the Nazi leader showing scenes of carnage, misery, and anguish. These were purchased by the Ministry of Information for propaganda purposes but, no doubt due to their macabre content, were never used.

62 Winnington states that although there were 30,000 living prisoners of various nationalities in Bergen-Belsen when it was liberated by British troops on April 15, 1945, approximately one hundred survivors were still dying each day from typhus and the effects of starvation when Peake reached the camp a month later; see *Vast Alchemies*, page 179. Peake's son Sebastian movingly summed up the effect of this experience on his father when he eloquently wrote that he "suffered and later died as a result of seeing manifest the antithesis of joy, love, and beauty. How can his experience of the camp not have created an eternal helplessness of the soul?" Quoted in *The Art of Gormenghast*, page 28.

7

THE GOTHIC WORLD-BUILDING OF *DARK SHADOWS*

Andrew Higgins

In 1966, American television saw the birth of two very different worlds. The more well-known of these was first seen on September 6, 1966 when the episode "The Man Trap" of the original series of *Star Trek* (1966–1968) appeared on the NBC television network; introducing a world that has grown into one of the most popular transmedial science fiction franchises. However, slightly earlier that summer — on June 27, 1966 — daytime television was introduced to a very different world with the first episode of the gothic soap opera *Dark Shadows* (1966–1971). Like its science fiction counterpart, the unique story-world of *Dark Shadows* was initially created through over one thousand daily television episodes and then added to and expanded by several motion pictures, novelizations, comic books, games, original music compositions, television and film reboots, audio dramas, and even bubble gum trading cards. All of these texts, in their broadest sense, were received, interacted with and, in some cases, creatively developed by a multi-generational group of viewers and an active fan base. Therefore, the gothic world-building of *Dark Shadows* typifies Henry Jenkins's concept of transmedia storytelling as "narrative material spread across works appearing in different media, resulting in a narrative that spans multiple media" (2006, pp. 95–96). In this essay, I will explore how the gothic story-world of *Dark Shadows* came and continues to exist, by focusing on three key phases of its development, concluding with how this world, like the *Star Trek* story-world, continues to endure and grow today over 55 years after its first broadcast.

Phase 1: The Birth of the *Dark Shadows* Story-world

In 1965, a young TV executive named Dan Curtis, who was up to then best known for producing sports shows like *CBS Golf Classics,* awoke one night after having a very vivid dream about a young woman on a train. Curtis would later recount the details of this dream:

> She was about 19, and she was on a train reading a letter that stopped in a dark, isolated town. She got off the train and started walking and walking. Finally, she came to a huge, forbidding house. She turned and slowly walked up the long path towards the house. At the door, she lifted a huge brass knocker and gently tapped it three times. I heard a dog howl, then just as the door creaked open — I woke up!
>
> *(Benshoff, 2011, p. 11)*

The following day, Curtis told his wife Norma about the dream and she thought it would make a good basis for a new television show pointing out that it had a gothic feeling — "something eerie and threatening" (Thompson, 2009, p. 56). Curtis pitched the idea as a television series to ABC Network officials who green-lit it for production. At the time, the ABC Network was considered the third network in terms of ratings and perceived quality of shows (Benshoff, 2011, p. 8). This network was looking for interesting shows that would attract new and different audiences from the two rival networks of CBS and NBC. One strategy that ABC development executive Harve Bennett, who would later go on to write and produce several of the *Star Trek* franchise films, employed was to commission and develop television shows with supernatural themes such as *One Step Beyond* (1959–1961) and *The Outer Limits* (1963–1965) and especially one of their biggest hits of this era, *Bewitched* (1964–1972), a comedy in which a mortal man marries a good witch played by Elizabeth Montgomery. Another commissioning success by ABC at this time was *Batman* (1966–1968), featuring Adam West and Burt Ward as the dynamic duo fighting a host of celebrity criminals. Therefore, ABC's green-lighting of Curtis's eerie show concept was in line with Bennett's strategy. Curtis assembled a group of writers led by Art Wallace, Sam Hall, and Gordon Russell to come up with a narrative outline for this new television show which was initially to be called "Shadows on the Wall" (Scott, 2000, p. 18). For the narrative, Wallace drew heavily from a teleplay he had worked on entitled *The House* which had appeared as an episode in the television anthology show *GoodYear Playhouse* in 1957. *The House* was about a reclusive woman living in an old house set in New England fishing village (ibid). The name of this new show went through several phases, with other suggested names of "The House on Widow's Hill" and "Terror at Collinwood", until Curtis stumbled upon the name "Dark Shadows" when he told a technician developing the lighting for the show to "go out to a museum and film some dark shadows" (44).

The show would be set in the fictional seaside village of Collinsport in the real state of Maine. The main focal point of this town was the brooding mansion high a top Widow's Hill (Curtis's huge forbidding house), which was initially called "Collins House" but was changed to the more gothic-sounding name of "Collinwood", ancestral home to the Collins family.

Unlike *Batman* and *Bewitched*, *Dark Shadows* was conceived and broadcast as a daytime soap opera. The "soap opera" television format had been introduced to this new medium in the 1950s; coming from the radio soap operas of the 1930s and 1940s (Benshoff, 2011, p. 10). These early radio dramas were actually produced and owned by soap manufactures (hence the name "soap opera"), such as Lux and Proctor & Gamble, and were used to sell soap and washing products to the housewives who would tune into the shows on a daily basis while doing the housework. At the start of its development, *Dark Shadows* was very much targeted to a similar audience but, as will be explored, as the tone of the narrative changed from just eerie and suggestive of the gothic to actual supernatural and horror, the audience target would change to younger viewers (including students and the counterculture hippies of the late 1960s and early 1970s). A characteristic of the narrative structure of the soap opera (or daytime drama) that makes it an important candidate for in-depth world-building is the opportunity to offer open-ended diegetically braided narratives developed over a long period of time. For the viewer, the overall story-world unfolds almost in real-time on a daily basis and therefore the depth and complexity of the narrative arc of key storylines are enriched through the actual time the narrative is given to develop and grow. For the *Dark Shadows* story-world, this narrative richness would be enhanced with the eventual introduction of such fantastic elements as time travel (to the past and the future of the then-present time) and, later in the series, parallel time (in the past, present, and future of alternative *Dark Shadow* worlds). This combination of the traditional daytime drama narrative structure as well as the addition of fantastical and supernatural elements into the story-world resulted in "a unique diegetic world, one that allowed for gothic and romantic frissons as well as more specialized meta-textual pleasures based on performance, character, and narrative" (Benshoff, 2011, p. 68).

Collinwood and its collection of gothic characters was introduced to television audiences through the eyes of an orphaned young woman inspired by Curtis's initial dream vision as well as such characters from traditional gothic literature as Jane Eyre. In the first episode, we learn that the reason this character is on a train is due to her being invited to Collinwood from the orphanage she had been left in as child in New York City. This invitation has come from the reclusive matriarch of Collinwood, Elizabeth Collins Stoddard (played by the Hollywood screen actress Joan Bennett) to work as a governess for young David Collins, son of Elizabeth's brother Roger Collins. An early storyline of the show, never resolved in the original television series, was whether Elizabeth was really the estranged mother of the young governess. In the original "Shadows on the Wall" treatment, the name of the governesses was Sheila March but this was changed to the much more regal and older sounding name of Victoria Winters (Scott, 1995, p. 15).

Starting with the first episode, Curtis subverted the traditional opening narration of past radio and television soap operas in which the voice of the sponsor would attempt to sell the soap or cleaning product to the listeners before the episode began. In the case of *Dark Shadows,* an actor from the episode would deliver a voice-over narration as a teaser for the episode to follow. This would position the *Dark Shadows* world-building narrative as a tale being told — the television equivalent of the Gothic text trope of the entry into a journal or chronicle; as in the entries made by Jonathan Harker in his journal at the beginning of Bram Stoker's *Dracula* (1897). For the first years of the show, the opening narrator would be spoken by the focalizing portal character of the governess Victoria Winters who, like the viewing audience, was being introduced to this strange eerie world of the Collins family. This opening narration from the first episode typifies what Benshoff characterizes as "set[ting] the gothic [*sic*] mood, as she often describes ongoing events in sinister and foreboding terms" (2011, p. 38).

> My name is Victoria Winters. My journey is beginning, a journey that I hope will open the doors of life to me. . . a journey to link my past with my future. . . to darkness and strangeness. . . A journey to people I've never met, who, tonight are still only shadows in my mind, but who will soon fill the days and nights of my tomorrows.
> (Dark Shadows, *Episode 1 (1966))*

As introduced above, the story-world of *Dark Shadows* was located in a fictional place, Collinsport. Wolf (2012) states that in order to qualify something as a secondary world it requires a fictional place (that is, one that does not appear in the Primary World) (25). Wolf further notes that the term "world", as applied to world-building, is not "simply geographical but experiential, that is, everything that is experienced by the characters involved" (ibid). "A single city or town can qualify as a world unto itself if it is secluded enough from its own surroundings so as to contain most of its inhabitant's experiences" (26). However, Collinsport itself was set in the real-world state of Maine, and therefore like other similar towns — such as Stephen King's Castle Rock, John Updike's Eastwick, and Sunnydale California of the Buffyverse — it is much closer to the Primary World geographically and conceptually.

However, from the start there was a sense that this "world" was separate from the real world. For example, the overall narrative, which initially was set in contemporary time, did not overtly engage with any of the current political, social, or cultural issues of the turbulent era of the late 1960s and early 1970s in America. Down at the local Blue Whale tavern in Collinsport, people danced to modern music from a jukebox and some characters, such as Elizabeth's daughter Carolyn Stoddard's reprobate (and thankfully short-lived) biker boyfriend Buzz, used the lingo of the hippies of the late 1960s. However, the conversation at the Blue Whale never overtly mentioned such current topics as the Civil Rights movement or the Vietnam War, which was raging during the time of the original broadcast of the show. This sense that the world of *Dark Shadows* was a world onto itself was noted by Dan Curtis himself in an interview he gave looking back on the show, "Dark Shadows is its own unique fairyland. It doesn't exist in the reality of today, and it doesn't care about war and other problems. *Dark Shadows* is like nothing else" (Thompson, 2009, p. 11). Further to this, one of the actors on the show, evoking another fantasy world, called it "a dark Brigadoon, because the world outside of Collinsport did not seem to exist" (ibid).

In terms of Wolf's spectrum of the "secondariness" of a world (2012, pp. 26–27), the initial story-world of *Dark Shadows* was very much like the example Wolf gives of "overlaid worlds" in which there are fictional elements overlaid into a real-world setting (28). However, as the texture of the story's narratives started to change, the world of *Dark Shadows* would move further along Wolf's spectrum of "secondariness". This transition occurred several months into the show when in the face of plummeting daytime ratings Curtis and his writers decided to turn the narrative focus of the story-world from being just eerie and suggestive of the gothic to becoming one that would include the intrusion of supernatural and ultimately horror elements. There were three key storylines in the early history of the television show that marked this change and caused the story-world of *Dark Shadows* to become much more "secondary" through the introduction into the world of the first (of many!) ghosts, a supernatural being and finally, and most significantly, a vampire.

- **Ghost** — At the end of Episode 70 (broadcast on September 30, 1966) viewers saw the ghost of a long-dead relative, Josette Collins, clearly emerge from her portrait, and dance around the grounds of the great estate. This ghost was played by the actress Kathryn Leigh Scott, who in addition to playing Maggie Evans on the show, would later play the real-life Josette Du Pres (Collins) in a prequel sequence discussed below.
- **The Phoenix** — In Episode 123, a new character was introduced who was to be David Collins's estranged mother Laura Murdoch Collins (played by Diana Millay). In the original plans, Laura was to be Roger Collins's alcoholic wife who came back to Collinwood to get custody of David and was to die in mysterious circumstances leading Victoria Winters to be tried for her murder. However, this was changed to Laura being slowly revealed to be a supernatural creature called "The Phoenix" who, like the mythical bird, was reborn through being consumed in fire every hundred years. With a twist to the original plot, the storyline now focused on Laura attempting to get David to join her in the consuming fire that would give her and her son eternal life. Thanks to Victoria Winters, she does not succeed and ultimately Laura is consumed by flames. Later in the series, when

the plot point of time travel was introduced, Laura would reappear (played again by Diana Millay) in different time periods in the Collins history again as the Phoenix reborn.

- **Vampire** — The ultimate intrusion of the supernatural into the *Dark Shadows* story-world, which would become the element that would turn the show's low ratings around and make it one of the most watched daytime dramas of all time, was the introduction of a vampire, Barnabas Collins. At the end of Episode 207 (broadcast on April 17, 1967), viewers witnessed the grave robber Willie Loomis, attracted by the potential of finding the legendary Collins family jewels, discover a secret room in the Collins mausoleum in Eagle Hill Cemetery and in it a chained coffin. Thinking that the jewels must be in the coffin, Willie opens it and immediately a hand with a black onyx ring reaches out and grabs him by the throat as the episode ends. In the next episode a new character appears at Collinwood, bearing an incredible resemblance to a portrait that hangs in the entry foyer in Collinwood, of Barnabas Collins who lived in the 18th century. Surprisingly, this stranger introduces himself to the Collins family as the descendent of Barnabas Collins who has come from England. The inhabitants of Collinwood are shocked at how similar this Barnabas is to the portrait down to the black onyx ring on his hand. Of course, as viewers would learn first, and the characters later, there was only one Barnabas Collins — a vampire released from his chained coffin by Willie Loomis and now set to resume his "life"; in the late 1960s. The use of the portrait as a plot device in this storyline suggests inspiration from the 19th-century penny-dreadful *Varney the Vampire or The Feast of Blood* attributed to James Malcom Rymer and Thomas Pickett Priest (published from 1845 to 1847) in which a portrait of Marmaduke Bannerworth hanging in the family's mansion betrays the true identity of Francis Varney the Vampire.

Originally, the writers only intended for this character to be on the show for a couple of months and wreak havoc as an evil vampire. However, given the focused acting of Canadian stage actor Jonathan Frid who played Barnabas throughout the series, viewers became intrigued by him. Frid was a Shakespearean trained actor who was not used to acting on television. This caused him to appear nervous and he at times had problems remembering his lines and reading from the teleprompter. This nervousness played right into the character of Barnabas who was a man out of his time hiding a great secret. Frid also played Barnabas as one of the first in a now-long line of reluctant vampires — cursed to live this life and hating himself for what he had to do to exist.

The introduction and success in the ratings of the vampire Barnabas would open the door for Curtis and the writers to introduce other tropes from the horror genre into the plots of the show. In addition, the show moved further along the spectrum of Wolf's "secondariness" with the introduction of the science fiction theme of time-travel. Given the popularity of the Barnabas character, viewers eventually wanted to know how he had become a vampire and been chained in that coffin. In order to answer this, the writers developed a fantastic storyline that had Victoria Winters, through a séance, be sent back into the past to relive an extended prequel sequence set in 1795 that showed how Barnabas become a vampire. At the start of this narrative sequence, Barnabas is human, and due to a night of indiscretion during his time in Martinique, he becomes involved in a love triangle with his fiancé Josette DuPres (later to be Josette Collins, who appeared as the first ghost played both times by Kathryn Leigh Scott) and her scheming maid and practicing witch Angelique Bouchard (played by Lara Parker). In the time transference, Victoria Winters takes the place of the original governess at Collinwood in 1795, Phyllis Wick (who is transported to the present) and again serves as the focalizing point-of-view character for the events that led to Barnabas being doomed with the vampire curse by the scorned witch Angelique. Given the always-limited budget of the show, characters for the 1795 storyline were played by the actors and actresses from the modern story (so, for example, in this sequence Joan Bennett played Barnabas's ill-fated mother Naomi Collins). This gave viewers a familiar feeling to the show but now set in a different time with the actors in period costumes. To create a stronger sense of this strangeness for the viewer, the writers initially had Victoria react to the new characters in the past as if they were the characters she knew from the present. For example, Victoria meets a good friend from the present Joe Haskell (played by Joel Crothers) but now he is the villain and rake Lieutenant Nathan Forbes. Victoria's confusion would match the viewers' confusion as they became reoriented to the same company of actors, for the first of several times, playing different roles in this new element of the *Dark Shadows* story-world. However, Victoria would not just be an observer in this prequel sequence, she also became an active character in the past, and became convicted of being a witch herself by the evil witch-finder Reverend Trask (modeled on real-world witch-finders such as Matthew Hopkins). When Victoria is hanged as a witch the writers ended this story sequence by having Victoria transferred back to the present, with Phyllis Wick transferred to the gallows.

For the narratives that followed, the writers used the characters and storylines they developed from the 1795 sequence as new storylines in the present. Angelique comes to the present day in the guise of the aptly named Cassandra Collins to torment Barnabas (who was temporarily cured of vampirism by a mad doctor engaged in creating his own Frankenstein-like monster). When she comes into the present, the blonde-haired witch Angelique disguises herself as Cassandra with a black wig; a similar device that Elizabeth Montgomery used on *Bewitched* when she wanted to portray Samantha's mischievous sister Serena (and to hide the actress' identity; the role of Serena was credited as being played by Pandora Spocks!). Time travel was used again, this time through the use of ancient Chinese I-Ching wands that allowed Barnabas this time to astral project back to 1895 to learn the history of the second-most popular character on the show, Quentin Collins (played by David Selby) who had been introduced in the present as a Henry James *Turn of the Screw*-like ghost (his name comes from James's "ghost", Peter Quint) who terrorizes David Collins. The way the I-Ching wands are used in the story sequence strongly suggests that in addition to drawing from classic horror tropes, the writers of the show also found inspiration in the supernatural fiction published in such pulp magazines as *Weird Fiction* and *Amazing Stories*. The use of "Yai Ching" wands to go back into time through a door is a key plot point in Seabury Quinn's "The Door Without A Key", first published in *Weird Tales* in September 1939. The dialog in this short story almost matches what the learned Professor Stokes says to Barnabas Collins on how to use the I-Ching sticks to travel back in time by throwing them on a table, forming a hexagram and visualizing a door with this marking that opens into the past.

> "And now observe", Professor Hulling continued. "One lays the six wands parallel and brings them close together. Then he sees, formed by the markings on their sides interspersed with blanks, one of the sixty-four possible Chinese geometric hexagrams." Drawing the flattened wands together he pointed to the figure they described.... To get the best result one makes his mind a perfect blank, and concentrating on the door which has no lock or key or latch, and opens only of its own accord.
>
> *(Quinn, 1939, p. 36)*[1]

Another example of the writer's use of supernatural fiction was the sudden intrusion at the end of the 1895 time-travel sequence of a race of supernatural creatures called "Leviathans"; evil beings who ruled the earth before humans came into existence. In this sequence, the Leviathans seize the mind of Barnabas Collins in the past and put him under their power, so that he travels back to the present with the "naga box" which contains the essence of a new Leviathan creature who will be born in the present and through rapid growth become a new leader for the Leviathans. Their ultimate goal is to repopulate the world with new Leviathan creatures. This creature has two essences, one a horrific monster that is never seen on camera — presented to the viewers as very heavy evil breathing — and the other a human boy who quickly grows through several manifestations into the Leviathan leader Jeb Hawkes. Jeb Hawkes is to marry and have a child with Elizabeth Collins's daughter Carolyn Stoddard, whose estranged father pledged her to the Leviathans in the past. The Leviathans are clearly based on the works of the writer H. P. Lovecraft (1890–1937), especially his tale *The Dunwich Horror* (1929) which also first appeared in *Weird Tales* and forms part of the cycle of Lovecraft's Chthulu mythos. *The Dunwich Horror* is set in the fictional town of Dunwich, Massachusetts (not far from Maine) and tells how the Old One cosmic entity Yog-Sothoth invaded earth through a portal and impregnated a woman, Lavinia Whateley. From this unnatural union, she gives birth to twins, one of whom is William Whateley, who looks human but grows at an astonishing rate. The other is an invisible monster who is kept hidden in the Whateley farmhouse. In the *Dark Shadows* world, the character of Jeb Hawkes was modeled on both these sons with the writers meshing the human and monster state into one character.

While inventive with lots of twists and turns, the "Leviathan" sequence was not all together popular with *Dark Shadows* fans and when ratings started to slip, the storyline was quickly modified to a new sequence that moved the world of Collinwood even further along the spectrum of Wolf's "secondariness". In his attempt to escape the vengeance of the Leviathans, Barnabas Collins finds a room in the abandoned East Wing of Collinwood that at times through a time warp would become a portal to another alternate time-band (actually multiple time-bands) where familiar characters living in the present and past had made different choices in their lives and thus led different lives than the ones they had in the "Primary" one.

The concept of "parallel time" and "alternative universes" had been depicted in science fiction starting with the works of Francis Stevens (1883–1948) and Murray Leinster (1896–1975); especially in his short story "Sidewise in Time" which first appeared in the pulp publication *Astounding Stories* in June 1934 and continued to be depicted in stories by such authors as L. Sprague de Camp, Larry Niven, and Frederik Pohl. Although a more probable influence may have come from *Star Trek* (1966–1968) with the broadcast in October 1967 of the now-iconic episode "Mirror Mirror", in which, through a transporter malfunction, the crew of the Enterprise are switched with their evil counterparts from a parallel universe (a storyline that continues into the *more* recent *Star Trek* text, *Star Trek: Discovery* (2017-present) with the Terran World). In the case of *Dark Shadows*, it is now Barnabas Collins who becomes the focalizing character and first sees these counterparts in this parallel version of Collinwood and then eventually becomes a part of it. This new narrative device opened up *Dark Shadows* narratives to new storylines and formed new relationships among the familiar characters. Parallel-time storylines would include a recasting of Daphne du Maurier's *Rebecca* (1938) with the witch Angelique cast in the role of the first Mrs. de Winter, Stevenson's *Strange Case of Dr. Jekyll and Mr. Hyde* (1886), Shirley Jackson's *The Lottery* (1948), and for the last six months of the show, set in a parallel 19th century, Emily Bronte's *Wuthering Heights* (1847). This would be the only sequence in which Jonathan Frid would play a different character than Barnabas Collins. In this ending sequence of the original television series, Frid would play the Heathcliff-like character of Bramwell Collins, the son of a parallel-time Barnabas Collins, who in this time-band never became a vampire, married Josette, and had a son played by Frid himself.

While the narrative texts of the 1,225 episodes established the core of the first phase of the *Dark Shadows* story-world, the world gestalt was also built through a series of paratextual elements over several types of media. One of the earliest of these was a series of thirty-three *Dark Shadows* novelizations written by William Edward Daniel Ross under the female pen-name Marilyn Ross. These gothic texts were published by the Paperback Library starting several months after the premiere of the television show in December, 1966 through to 1972. Almost all of these novels were part of a shared continuity separate from the history supplied in the original television series, offering the reader a combination of known places and characters and new ones. Given the popularity of Barnabas Collins on the television show, a majority of these novels became focused on him (with images from the show of Jonathan Frid appearing on the covers) and several of them followed the formula of a heroine arriving at Collinwood and falling in love with Barnabas not realizing he is a vampire. The heroine is plunged into some supernatural danger (usually evident from the title of each novel) from which Barnabas has to rescue her and is subsequently forced to leave her due to his vampire curse. Quentin Collins was introduced in *Barnabas Collins and Quentin's Demon* (published in February 1970). Like the television show, Ross used Gothic and horror tropes for some of these stories. In *Barnabas Collins vs The Warlock* (1969), Ross also drew upon Henry James's *Turn of the Screw* (1898), as the writers of the television show did to introduce Quentin Collins. In *Barnabas, Quentin and The Mummy's Curse* (April 1970), Ross drew upon the horror mummy trope which had not been used in the television show. Edgar Allan Poe's short story *The Premature Burial* (1844) was re-told in *Barnabas, Quentin and The Crystal Coffin* (July 1970). In *Barnabas, Quentin and the Body Snatchers* (February 1971), Ross paid homage to Jack Finney's science fiction novel *The Body Snatchers* (1955). The last volume in this series, *Barnabas, Quentin and the Vampire Beauty* (March 1972), was about a woman wanting to become a vampire to keep her beauty; suggesting shades of the 15th-century Hungarian noblewoman and serial killer Elizabeth Bathory.

The story-world was also extended through a line of comics. From 1969 to 1976, Gold Key comics released a series of thirty-five comics which were later republished in 2010 as collections through Hermes Press. Like the books, many of these early comics focused on the popular character of Barnabas Collins (with, again, a picture of Jonathan Frid as Barnabas on the cover). In May 1971, Issue 9, "Creatures in Torment", the other popular character of Quentin Collins, who suffered the curse of the werewolf, was added. In the June 1973 issue "Quentin the Vampire" (Issue 20), Quentin Collins mistakenly takes a serum that turns him into a vampire (which never happened on the television show). As with the Ross novelizations, the writers of the comic series took the characters and story situations into new scenarios, thus expanding the story-world of *Dark Shadows* through these imaginative texts. Probably one of the most interesting of these is Issue 31, "The Doom of Hellgi Kolnisson" (April 1975), in which Barnabas becomes part of a Norse saga and fights fiendish wizards.

The cover art for this issue shows a large wizard zapping Barnabas with some mystical force and Viking warriors attacking him.

There were also two board games that invited interaction and participation with the world of *Dark Shadows*. The first one of these came out in 1966, the first year of the television show and was a fairly typical board game with players drawing cards from two coffin spaces to move around the board made up of a drawn image of the exterior of Collinwood. While the board and the pieces suggest Gothic and horror elements from the *Dark Shadows* world (e.g., bats, wolves, spiders, gravestones), there are no images of characters from the show in the game. Therefore this game recreates some of the narrative elements of the world without any specific reference to characters (or actors) from the television show. The second game, brought out by Milton Bradley in 1968, was much more focused on the character of Barnabas Collins with a picture of Jonathan Frid on the cover. To promote this game, Milton Bradley produced a special television commercial (https://youtu.be/rvzwVpV8yRM) featuring Frid with a group of kids playing this game in the drawing room set. The goal of this game is to assemble glow-in-the-dark pieces of a skeleton on a gallows. Included with the game was a very early example of how fans could interact with the *Dark Shadows* world — a set of glow-in-the-dark Barnabas vampire fangs. The inside box of the game cautioned "the toy fangs are not part of the game. They are placed over the teeth of a player to play the role of Barnabas Collins. They should be washed before a player uses them" (cited from Benshoff, 2011, p. 87). The television commercial also featured a boy becoming a vampire like Barnabas with these fangs.

Another key aural world-building element that became very popular during the show's original run was its music and the themes that came out of Robert Cobert's haunting scores. An album *Original Music from Dark Shadows* was released in 1969 and made it to number 18 on the Billboard record charts (Benshoff, 2011, p. 89). Included in this collection was the instrumental piece known as "Quentin's Theme" — first heard in the diegetic world to signify the appearance of Quentin as a ghost and would go on in the show to become his leitmotiv. This theme became a hit single reaching number 13 on Billboard's "Hot One Hundred Singles" chart (ibid). Later, this theme was re-released with a haunting, sexually charged narration by the actor David Selby as Quentin ("Shadows of the night / Falling silently / Echoes of the past / Calling me to you"). A similar instrumental with narrative, "I Barnabas", was released soon after with Jonathan Frid's narration of Barnabas from his coffin opining "I feel your yearning, I know that you want me, I know that you need me" (Benshoff, 2011, p. 89). In both these cases, the theme of the narration was an invitation for the listener to engage with the Gothic romantic characters of Quentin and Barnabas, a paratext that not only helped build the story-world but also invited interaction and engagement with its listeners.

Other paratextual items that added to the world gestalt of the first phase of the *Dark Shadows* world included lunch boxes with images from the television show and two lines of *Dark Shadows* bubble gum trading cards. These cards were first manufactured in 1968 by the Philadelphia Gum Corporation and featured all the actors and actresses from the show, sometimes with an autograph from them, and on the backs of the cards, pieces of a puzzle picture from the show that encouraged users to find the other pieces to make the overall image.

While the television show was still on the air, MGM produced the first major motion picture set in the story-world of *Dark Shadows*. *House of Dark Shadows* directed by Dan Curtis was released in September 1970 and revisited the introduction of the Barnabas Collins storyline, this time in a more self-contained form with Barnabas being very much the evil vampire who after turning practically everyone in the cast into vampires (including Roger Collins) is killed off at the end of the film. Although, in the final moment of the film, a bat suddenly appears in the shot and flies away (*HODS* script, p. 118), thus keeping the door open for another cinematic appearance by Barnabas. Victoria Winters does not appear, as she had been written out of the television show, and certain actors, such as Laura Parker as Angelique, did not appear as she was busy at the time the movie was being shot with her own storylines for the television show. Indeed, the writers had to come up with a way to have Barnabas re-chained in his coffin in parallel time on the television show so Jonathan Frid could be free to do the filming for the movie. The follow-up to *House of Dark Shadows* was *Night of Dark Shadows* (1971), which is more of an original self-contained story featuring the characters of Quentin and Angelique (Frid did not want to appear in the second film as Barnabas and by this time was portraying his non-vampire son Bramwell). Like the television series, the storyline draws from some key Gothic sources including *Rebecca* and Poe's *The Fall of the House of Usher* (1839). Other actors from the television series appeared in new roles, so, like the use of time travel and parallel time on the television show, viewers would be familiar with the faces on the screen in new character roles set in the story-world. The plot around the possession of Quentin by the ghost of the witch Angelique was, unfortunately, heavily edited by MGM from Curtis's original version (Curtis was forced to excise 32 minutes of footage from the original 129 minutes and then another 4 minutes of graphic scenes for the film to be given a PG rating) and there have been efforts over the years by the *Dark Shadows* fandom to find and restore the original "director's cut" of this film.

Phase 2: Re-runs, Reboots, and the Importance of Fans

On April 2, 1971 the original series of *Dark Shadows* came to an end. The final show would be the only time a voiceover narrator would be used, for the last haunting words heard on the television series: "And for as long as they lived, the dark shadows at Collinwood were but a memory of the distant past"

(*Dark Shadows,* Episode 1245 (season 12, episode 45) (1971)). Dan Curtis very shrewdly had insured that he, through the ubiquitous extra-diegetic "Dark Shadows is a Dan Curtis Production", seen and announced on the end credits of every show, would be the sole owner of the original prints of each episode and therefore could syndicate them for re-runs. Shortly after the end of the series, he had episodes dubbed into Spanish and broadcast in South America. To promote this run, Jonathan Frid went on a promotional tour of South America. In 1975, the first syndicated reruns were shown in the United States, starting with the introduction of Barnabas Collins, and continued to be shown in through the 1980s and 1990s — with a full run on the Sci-Fi Channel starting in 1992.

The popularity of the original broadcast, and an even wider viewership in re-runs, developed a strong fan base for the world of *Dark Shadows*, as well as opportunities for fans to interact and build the story-world through fan-produced materials and conventions. In *Textual Poachers: Television Fans and Participatory Culture* (1992), Henry Jenkins maintains that fandom allows for "the translation of program material into new texts that more perfectly serve fan interests, the sense of possession that the fan feels towards favored media products, and the celebration of intense emotional commitments" (53). This interaction was clear in the growth of *Dark Shadows* fandom and how fans interacted with and built the story-world through fan fiction in fanzines, cosplay, and at conventions. In 1975, as re-runs started being broadcast, the first fanzine, *The World of Dark Shadows*, was published which included interviews, artwork, articles about the world including "The Collinsport Debating Society", and original fan fiction such as the long-running fiction serial *Journey through the Shadows* and *The Stranger in the Mirror*. A key element of this fan work was the development of *Dark Shadows* Concordances which outlined each episode in incredible detail (the forerunner of today's Dark Shadows Wiki Powered by Fans, at https://darkshadows.fandom.com/wiki/Dark_Shadows_Wiki). As Jenkins further states, "The fan, while recognizing the story's connectedness, treats it as if its narrative world were a real place that can be inhabited and explored as if the characters maintained a life beyond what was represented on the screen; fans draw close to that world in order to enjoy more fully the pleasures it offers them" (53). The world-building impulse of fans is characterized by Kathleen Resch in *Dark Shadows in the Afternoon* (1991);

> Back in the 1960s, for 30 minutes a day, we [fans] had the chance to share the lives of the Collins family and their friends and enemies. Those small, daily segments of time infiltrated our minds. Characters and situations seeped into our consciousness, giving us insights which developed into fan-written stories and novels, that filled blanks, answered questions, rationalized plot discrepancies, and created back-stories concerning major and often minor characters in the Dark Shadows universe. (54)

In 1983 the first fan-organized *Dark Shadows* festival was held in Newark, New Jersey, which included panels and Q&A with members of the original cast and production team. These annual festivals would continue (to this present day) in Los Angeles and New York City. In 1988, a stage play based on the 1795 timeline of *Dark Shadows* was presented by Dance Theatre Workshop in New York City. In 1989, MPI Home Video started releasing the television episodes on VHS followed in 2002 with their release on DVD which included for the first time the pre-Barnabas episodes not seen since the first broadcasts in 1966–1967. These releases also included new footage of interviews with the actors and teams who put together the original series offering new insights into the creation of the first phase of the world of *Dark Shadows* and an introduction to a new generation of the shows' original storylines.

In 1990, NBC, one of the original rival networks of ABC, produced the first reboot to *Dark Shadows* again directed by Dan Curtis. This was a slicker re-telling of the Barnabas storyline, now played by English actor Ben Cross, for a prime-time audience used to dramas like *Dallas* (1978–1991) and *Dynasty* (1981–1989). It again used the character of Victoria Winters as the focalizing point and followed the original television storyline fairly loyally — although the character of the witch Angelique was introduced a lot earlier as the story of the curse of Barnabas Collins was now known (as opposed to in the original series, when it was being developed through the creation of the Barnabas/Josette/Angelique 1795 storyline). The timing of the revival series (as it came to become known) was not ideal as the events of the First Gulf War caused constant interruptions and rescheduling. Twelve episodes of the show were aired and then it was canceled. There were plans to introduce the character of Quentin Collins in the second season. In conjunction with this reboot, a new series of comics were published by Innovation for eight issues from 1992 to 1993, which used the familiar "My name is Victoria Winters" introductory opening in the first panel of each issue.

Phase 3: The Return to Collinwood

In 2004, there was another attempt to reboot *Dark Shadows* for prime-time television on the WB Network, and a one-hour pilot featuring Alec Newman, as Barnabas was commissioned and shot. However, the pilot was not picked up and the show was never publicly broadcast.

More significantly for the actual world-building of *Dark Shadows*, in that same year, a dozen of the original actors for the television series performed a new audio sequel, *Return to Collinwood* (2004) onstage at the Dark Shadows Festival in Brooklyn, New York, and then agreed to record it for distribution. The script was written by Jamison Selby, the son of David Selby (Quentin Collins) who himself was named from a character in *Dark Shadows*. This was released by MPI Video and, instead of rebooting old storylines, added a new narrative layer to the story-world; resuming the television show's narrative after the death of Elisabeth Collins Stoddard (the actress Joan Bennett passed away in 1990) with the main focus of the story being characters coming back to Collinwood to hear the reading of her last will and testament. It was only in *Return to Collinwood* that we learn that Victoria Winters was indeed Elizabeth's estranged daughter out of wedlock. The success of the sales of this audio recording suggested there was a market for new *Dark Shadows* stories which could be acted out by original members of the cast. After working with Dan Curtis Productions on the copyright and licensing in 2006, Big Finish Productions in the United Kingdom (known for their continuing line of Dr. Who audio dramas using some of this extended story-world's original actors) started producing these audio dramas featuring original and new cast members in new stories set in the world of *Dark Shadows*. With the drama *The House of Despair*, an entire new storyline set after the television series began. Two sequences were produced from 2004 to 2010, and then in 2016 to celebrate the 50th anniversary of the show, a third full audio drama ("Blood and Fire") was issued again using many members of the original cast and the revival series. Concurrent to this another series of "Dramatic Readings" were issued that usually involved two to three cast members (either actors from the original series with new ones) in one-off dramas around some of main storylines of the original show (e.g., The Leviathans, the Trask story arc, etc.). In 2010, Jonathan Frid was persuaded to reprise his role as Barnabas Collins in a special audio drama *The Night Whispers,* where he teamed up with John Karlen as his servant Willie Loomis. These audio dramas which continue to expand the *Dark Shadows* world also feature the pairing of characters in new situations. For example, starting with episode "The Vodoo Amulet", the private detective Tony Peterson joins forces with the witch Cassandra Collins to solve a murder mystery in New Orleans. This *X-Files*-like pairing would be repeated in "The Phantom Bride" (May 2013, where they posed as husband and wife!) and "The Devil Cat" (May 2014, set in England) and has gone on to create three seasons of *The Tony and Cassandra Mysteries* with 12 episodes so far. Two characters, practically adversaries in the original series, have now come together in new roles in the story-world. There has also been a 13-part original series called *Bloodlust*, which introduced a new story arc to Collinwood and will be followed up in 2019 with another series called *Bloodline*. *Dark Shadows* fans have worked to join all these narratives braids together in a world-building *Dark Shadows* consistent chronology on the Dark Shadows Fandom Wiki, at https://darkshadows.fandom.com/wiki/Chronology_(audio_dramas).

In addition to performing in the *Dark Shadows* Big Finish audio dramas, Lara Parker, who played the witch Angelique on the original television series, has gone on to expand the world through another series of novels published first by HarperCollins and then Tor Books set in the story-world. In *Angelique's Descent* (1998), she told her own character's backstory and added more narrative depth and insight into Angelique's initial relationship with Barnabas Collins. We learn that Angelique was raised in the mysterious world of voodoo witchcraft and pledged her soul to the devil to become immortal. There is also a stunning story twist about who Angelique's parents were, which changes the dynamic between her and her rival for Barnabas's love Josette. In *The Salem Branch* (2006), Parker returns to the present of the end of the television series, 1971, when Barnabas has been cured of his vampirism and is about to marry his curer, Dr. Julia Hoffman. A mysterious woman comes to Collinwood with a daughter who proves to be a reincarnation of the form Angelique took in Salem during the notorious witch trials. Like the television series, this novel uses time travel as one of its key plot devices. In *Wolf Moon Rising* (2013), Parker added more depth and story elements to the Quentin Collins narrative and again set part of it in the late 1920s, expanding the timeline for the story-world. In her most recent novel, *Heiress of Collinwood* (2016), Parker adds more narrative depth to the story of Victoria Winters and her true link to the Collins family. In addition to Lara Parker, authors Steven Mark Rainey and Elizabeth Massie wrote *Dreams of the Dark* (1999), another original story which introduced a rival vampire Thomas Rathburn who was made a vampire during the American Civil War and comes to Collinwood and becomes attracted to Victoria Winters, making him the enemy of Barnabas Collins. Another veteran actress of the show, Kathryn Leigh Scott, is both an author and publisher, and in addition to writing books about the history of the *Dark Shadows* broadcasts, also wrote the intertextual novel *Dark Passages* (2012) about a female vampire who comes to New York in the 1960s to become an actress on the cult television series *Dark Passages*, only to face her nemesis, a three-hundred-year-old witch bent on destroying her. In addition to being a brilliant inventive story, Scott also used it to relay her experience with some of the actors and actresses on the original television show through the lens of fictional characters.

From 2011 to 2013, Dynamite Comics began publishing a new line of *Dark Shadows* using continuity from the original series for twenty-three issues. As before, these stories focused on the Barnabas character who in this narrative becomes a very dark, evil character, who amasses a vampire army to take over Collinwood and in the last issue, causes the residents of Collinwood to flee forever. In 2012, Dynamite started a second line of comics, this time with a crossover with the "Vampirella" franchise. Vampirella is a super-heroine created by Forrest J. Ackerman and costume designer Trina Robins. In this narrative, Barnabas goes to New York and meets the sexy Vampirella in a seedy underworld of clubs. Barnabas and Vampirella join forces to find the "Big Apple Butcher" who turns out to be the interestingly named Lady Bathory, who herself has teamed up with Jack the Ripper to wreak havoc on New York City. In issue 2 of this series, Quentin Collins, still suffering the werewolf curse, joins in on the search. In 2013, Dynamite published a new series focusing on the origins of Barnabas Collins and revisiting the 1795 storyline from the show — marketed as "a retelling of the classic Dark Shadows history".

In 2012, two dedicated fans of the original television series — the actor Johnny Depp and film director Tim Burton — set out to tell the story of *Dark Shadows* reimagined again for the big screen. While this new highly anticipated cinematic adaptation was not all together favorably received and tended to treat the familiar Barnabas being unchained now in the 21st century for laughs (more *Love at First Bite* (1979) than *Dark Shadows*!) it did pay homage to the original series by having four of the original cast, including the last appearance of Jonathan Frid, appear with Depp in Collinwood as cameos in the film. On the set at Pinewood Studios, Johnny Depp turned to Frid and said "We would not be here without you" (Scott, 2012, p. 30).

Conclusion

In the documentary *Master of Shadows: The Gothic World of Dan Curtis* (2019) by MPI Video, the actress Whoopi Goldberg, one of the many fans who grew up with the show, characterized the *Dark Shadows* story-world narrative as "it wasn't your Mom's gothic romance, it was your gothic romance". Through its imaginative re-use of tropes drawn from Gothic and horror stories as well as weird literature and pulp fiction, *Dark Shadows* created an engaging and inter-active story-world that appeared on many different media platforms, and was consumed by a multi-generational fan base with a desire to both learn more and engage in their own building of the world through fan interaction and original story-making. Current *Dark Shadows* writer Stuart Maning believes that it is the strength of the narratives in concert with the continuing soap opera format that has built, and continues to expand, this story-world;

> *Dark Shadows* has endured because of its characters and that original, brilliant cast of actors. The soap opera format will always be about worlds without end, and with the right stories, any character's journey can be infinite. Five decades on, those personalities still burn brightly, and it's a privilege to guide them through new adventures.
>
> *(Scott, 2012, p. 195)*

And like the *Star Trek* universe that was created in the same year, the world-building of *Dark Shadows* continues with more planned audio dramas from Big Finish, a new line of unabridged audio books from Audible of the original Marilyn Ross novelizations read by Kathryn Leigh Scott and through social media and the dedication of a fan base that continues to actively engage with this world and introduce new people into it — over fifty years after Dan Curtis had his dream of a young woman on a train heading to a huge, forbidding house — into the eerie and gothic world of *Dark Shadows*.

Note

1 The author is grateful to writer and scholar Douglas A. Anderson for finding this Weird Tale for him.

Bibliography

Benshoff, Harry M (2011), *Dark Shadows: TV Milestone Series*. Detroit, Michigan: Wayne State University Press.

Hall, Sam and Russell Gordon (1970), *House of Dark Shadows HODS* (Shooting Script).

Hamrick, Craig (2003), *Barnabas and Company: The Cast of the TV Classic Dark Shadows*. New York: I Universe Star.

Jenkins, Henry (1992), *Textural Poachers: Television Fans and Participatory Culture*. New York: Routledge

Jenkins, Henry (2006), *Convergence Culture: When Old and Media Collide*. New York: New York University Press.

Quinn, Seabury, "The Door Without a Key", *Weird Tales*, September 1939, pages 33–54.

Resch, Kathleen (1991), *Dark Shadows in the Afternoon*. New York: Image Pub.

Scott, Kathryn Leigh (1986), *My Scrapbook Memories of Dark Shadows*. Los Angeles, California: Pomegranate Press.

Scott, Kathryn Leigh (ed.) (1990), *The Dark Shadows Companion*. Universal City, California: Pomegranate Press.

Scott, Kathryn Leigh and Pierson, Jim (2000), *The Dark Shadows Almanac*. Beverly Hills, California: Pomegranate Press.

Scott, Kathryn Leigh and Pierson, Jim (2012), *Dark Shadows: Return to Collinwood*. Beverly Hills, California: Pomegranate Press.

Thompson, Jeff (2009), *The Television Horrors of Dan Curtis*. Jefferson, North Carolina: McFarland.

Wolf, Mark J.P. (2012), *Building Imaginary Worlds: The Theory and History of Subcreation*. New York: Routledge.

8

DAVENTRY AND THE WORLDS OF KING'S QUEST

Christopher Hanson

First indirectly introduced in the On-Line Systems's early graphical adventure game *Wizard and the Princess* (1980), the mythical world of Daventry is perhaps best known as the place in which the original *King's Quest* (1984) (later titled *King's Quest: Quest for the Crown* in a 1987 re-release) and its subsequent series were set. As discussed below, the name "Daventry" is not used in *Wizard and the Princess*, but the game takes place in Serenia, a land that later becomes part of the world of Daventry. Daventry was constructed by Roberta Williams and is populated by original elements and familiar fairy-tale characters alike, weaving a rich and charming tapestry that transcends simple pastiche. Since 1980, it has served as the location for eight games in the original *King's Quest* series, as well as in its 2015 reboot as an episodic adventure game series by the Odd Gentlemen.

Daventry has also served as the setting for a number of spin-offs. These include the appearance of Daventry's world in other Sierra games and the re-imagining of Daventry numerous fan-produced games. These fan games are comprised of straight remakes with enhanced graphics, re-imagined versions of games. Multiple published novels and other works have also taken place in the imaginary world of Daventry, in addition to new numerous accompanying paratexts and other written content created by authorized authors and dedicated fans alike. At various times, "Daventry" has functioned as shorthand for several bounded areas in this fictional world: from the entire world to a continent to a kingdom to a town to a castle.

In this essay, I explore the world of Daventry through a number of its iterations to better understand its construction. I examine the complexities of its development through multiple versions and its expansion by multiple authors. Daventry exists across numerous articulations, including the games designed by Roberta Williams, the paratextual materials released in conjunction with these games, fan works, and the reboot of the game in 2015. As I reveal, this collective authorship reveals the fissures of a singular and coherent notion of "Daventry" by laying bare contradictions and inconsistencies. Building from its remediation and combination of a variety of fables, myths, and fairy tales, I argue that while Daventry's multiple authors help to build and enrich its imaginary world, they also simultaneously reveal the limits of canonicity.

Roberta Williams, Sierra, and *King's Quest*

Raised in LaVerne, California, Roberta Williams recollects being an avid teller of tales from an early age. She recalls that as a child, she was, "interested in anything that had to do with magic, or fantasy, like the *Wizard of Oz* or *Alice in Wonderland*. I always read a lot and fantasized a lot. I was always a story-teller. I used to tell my friends and my cousins stories, and I used to get in trouble for it".[1] In high school, she met Ken Williams, whom she married.

Roberta Williams then co-founded Sierra On-Line (founded as On-Line Systems, and later commonly known as Sierra) with Ken in 1979. According to their recollections, Ken was programming an income-tax program in that year from home on a mainframe computer. He stumbled across a program called *Adventure,* which quickly captured his and Roberta's imagination: "Within minutes I was calling over to Roberta to show her my discovery. No work got done that night".[2] The game to which Ken refers is the influential *Adventure* or *ADVENT*, released in 1977 after Don Woods expanded upon Will Crowther's *Colossal Cave Adventure* (1976). In Ken's account, he recalls his and Roberta's fascination with the game, which led them to more text adventure games developed by Scott and Alexis Adams and released by their company Adventure, International.[3] He recalls that, "Roberta loved the games but wondered if they wouldn't be better if, instead of a textual description, there would be a picture".[4] They subsequently purchased an Apple II in late 1979 and began working on Roberta's vision for an adventure game which added graphics set in a mansion in which a murderer lurks among seven other guests.

In 1980, On-Line Systems released *Hi-Res Adventure #1: Mystery House* (commonly known just as *Mystery House*). The game proved popular and sold over 10,000 copies, and the company made several more games in the *Hi-Res Adventure* series, including *Wizard and the Princess*.[5] However, On-Line Systems floundered somewhat before it partnered with IBM as that company launched its IBM PCjr, a version of its popular business computer designed for the home. IBM sought a game to showcase the technical abilities of the PCjr, and helped to fund the development of Roberta Williams's vision of *King's Quest* as an animated graphic adventure game that was released as a launch title for the PCjr in 1984.

While the IBM PCjr proved to be unsuccessful, *King's Quest* was enormously popular — thanks to it being ported to multiple other home computers at the time including the Apple II, Amiga, and the Macintosh. The game spawned numerous sequels through the 1980s and 1990s and Sierra concurrently released other graphic adventure games which also eventually became their own series including the *Space Quest*, *Police Quest*, and *Leisure Suit Larry* series. As a result of these and other titles, Sierra became a highly successful game software company during the 1980s and the early 1990s and was sold in 1996 for around $1.5 billion (USD). In the year or two following its sale, however, both Roberta and Ken Williams left the company. Sierra was downsized and restructured multiple times and eventually dissolved in 2004, before resurfacing first as a Vivendi brand in 2005 and then later as an Activision brand in 2014.

The *King's Quest* games take place in the world of Daventry, a mythical world that compiles elements from fairy tales, folklore, mythology, and popular culture. In the first *King's Quest*, the player guides the animated avatar of the knight Sir Graham, who has been tasked with locating and recovering three treasures critical to the kingdom of Daventry and its ruler, King Edward. Graham becomes king at the conclusion of the first game after recovering the treasures and the sudden death of King Edward. The next game in the series, *King's Quest II: Romancing the Throne* (1985) follows King Graham as he travels in search of a bride to Kolyma, located on another continent in the world of Daventry. Subsequent games expand upon Graham's family and further build out their imaginary world, or both.

The world of Daventry is constituted of multiple fictional lands, which grow, shift, and morph across the series and paratexts such as accompanying materials packaged with the games, related games, and works published separately from the games. Even within the main games themselves, certain ambiguities and apparent inconsistencies complicate getting a clear idea of the boundaries and dimensions of Daventry. For example, the manual for *King's Quest: Mask of Eternity* (1998) describes the seven "Lands" of the game, which include physical locations such as the "Kingdom of Daventry" and "The Swamp" but also mystical realms such as "The Dimension of Death" and "The Realm of the Sun".[6] This is compounded by paratextual materials which add to the world of Daventry while also introducing internal contradictions.

Serenia and "Daventry"

Strangely enough, Daventry was introduced in an earlier Roberta Williams game but was not actually called Daventry at the time. As noted above, the imaginary world of Serenia was first introduced in *Wizard and the Princess* (1980), the second in the On-Line Systems's *Hi-Res Adventures* series.[7] Later in the *King's Quest* games, it is revealed that Serenia is part of the world of Daventry.

However, the packaging and instruction manual for *Wizard and the Princess* offer scant initial description of Serenia, setting up the player as a "happy wanderer passing through a village in the land of Serenia" who learns that kingdom's King George is offering half of his lands to anyone who can rescue his daughter, Princess Priscilla, from the evil wizard Harlin.[8] Priscilla is said to be held captive "beyond the great mountains" that are so distant that they are not visible, but lie north of this village, beyond a "vast desert that seems never to end".[9] The game starts in the village described in the packaging, with a static color image of the town and a text description at the bottom of the screen (Figure 8.1).

As is common in text adventures, the player enters one- or two-word phrases via the text parser at the bottom of the screen to navigate and interact with the game space. Movement is in discrete steps, with each location presenting another image in the top of the screen and a text description at the bottom. As the player must venture into the desert and other subsequent locations, these images may repeat with only minor variation and emulate the repetitive features of the area. This can be disorienting for the player and effect a maze-like experience which all but requires the player to draw a map as they play to help navigate the game world — a standard game mechanic in text adventures.

As the player explores Serenia, they discover numerous items and puzzles which must be solved in order to explore further. For example, the player encounters multiple instances of snakes with which must be dealt in different manners. The first snake that blocks the way must be killed by throwing a rock found elsewhere in the desert. The player may then encounter rattlesnakes which require a stick to scatter. Finally, aiding another snake trapped

FIGURE 8.1 Start screen of *Wizard and the Princess* (1980).

by a rock will reward the player with the means to transform themselves into a snake to traverse a small opening found later. As Henry Jenkins has argued, the "narrative architecture" of the adventure game is designed around spatial navigation in that solving puzzles opens up more areas to explore and reveals more narrative — and more puzzles.[10]

The imaginary world of Serenia expands far beyond the village and desert of the opening screens. Past the desert lies a chasm which can only be traversed using a magic word, allowing access to a house on the other side and labyrinthine woods inhabited by mischievous gnome, a parrot, and a lion. At the edge of the woods lies an ocean which must be navigated via rowboat to locate a desert island to explore, complete with jungle, a pirate, and buried treasure. Using more magic, the player flies to a distant mainland and finally reaches foothills that lead to the mountains which must be successfully navigated. In the foothills on the other side of the mountains, the player reaches the evil wizard's castle, which is encircled by a crocodile-infested moat.

Inside the castle, the player then must negotiate an actual maze, beyond which lies the titular wizard and princess — albeit in animal forms. Upon transforming the princess, the player can then magically transport both of them back to the starting village with its familiar accompanying graphic. Curiously, this is identified in the game's text as "YOU ARE TRANSPORTED TO SERENIA. . . .YOU ARE IN THE VILLAGE OF SERENIA". This final text suggests that only the initial portion of the game involves the actual kingdom of Serenia, with the other areas belonging to some other realm.

Wizard and the Princess is acknowledged in a 1994 article in Sierra's magazine *InterAction* as a "prequel" to *King's Quest* games.[11] However, the events of *Wizard and the Princess* were later established to take place sometime before the events of 1990's *King's Quest V: Absence Makes the Heart Go Yonder!*, and both games take place in Serenia. The Serenia in *Absence Makes* shares some similar geographical features with the Serenia represented in *Wizard and the Princess*, and the later game even recycles some puzzles from the earlier game.

World of Daventry & *The Companion*

The "world of Daventry" is generally used by fans to describe the imaginary world in which the games and canonical paratexts take place. One essential work in this process is Peter Spear's *The King's Quest Companion* (1989). This book performs critical work in world-building for the game series beyond the short stories that it offers based on each of the games in the series. First published in 1989, *The Companion* initially included material for the series up to *King's Quest IV: The Perils of Rosella* (1988). Four editions of *The Companion* were released, with each subsequent iteration including material from the most recently released game in the series. The fourth edition, published in 1997, covers the series up to *King's Quest VII: The Princeless Bride* (1994).

However, only the first and second (1991) editions of the book include the "Encyclopedia of Daventry (Abridged)" section, which collects information from the games and other sources on key characters and other elements and links them to myths and fairy tales. For example, the entry for the beanstalk found in the first *King's Quest* notes that, "In our world, we have the story of 'Jack and the Beanstalk'", and provides a synopsis of the fairy tale as well as the story "Jack the Giant-Killer".[12] *The Companion* functions primarily as an authorized hint book to the series, and content from the "Encyclopedia" serves to provide greater context to in-game elements, such as in the entry for "Castle Daventry", which references elements from multiple games in the series.[13] The disparate influences for the games are made apparent in this encyclopedia, which includes entries for "Castle Dracula", "chicken soup", "Cupid", "Merlin's Mirror", "Riding Hood", and "Seven Dwarfs".[14]

The *Companion*'s encyclopedia supplies information about the different kingdoms and continents of the world of Daventry while also evincing the sometimes-confusing and contradictory nature of such information. For example, the entry on Serenia notes that the name refers to "three distinct places", namely that of a continent, kingdom, and also a town.[15] The entry for Daventry states that the name is given to a kingdom and a continent, but also that, "the name is sometimes used as a generic name for the universe that contains [the] kingdom", before noting the existence of multiple towns named Daventry in the real world.[16]

Earlier in *The Companion*, it is explicitly stated that Serenia is actually a continent, in which the Kingdom of Daventry is located.[17] The continent was named for the "Sovereignty of Serenia", another area which borders Daventry.[18] But further compounding this confusion is that the Daventry encyclopedia entry states that this is "the name of the continent of which the kingdom [of Daventry] is part".[19] However, the entry for Serenia declares that the continent of Serenia, "is broken up into many kingdoms and principalities, with two of the most significant ones being the Kingdom of Daventry and the Sovereignty of Serenia".[20] The Kingdom of Daventry thus is identified as being in two different continents. Contradictions and inconsistencies can thus be found between texts which contribute to this imaginary world, but even within single texts such as the *Companion*. Fan culture notes that the continent of Daventry is "also known as Serenia at times", indicating a recognition and tacit acceptance of such variability.[21]

Size, Mapping, & "Wrap Around"

After establishing the diegetic world of Daventry in the first couple of games, subsequent games gradually expanded its fictional boundaries, sometimes in quite literal fashion. As technological and storage capacities increased, so did the scope of the games. Larger-capacity storage media such as higher-density floppy disks and then CD-ROMs facilitated the capability to grow the games and allowed for larger maps. Roberta Williams had previously pushed the pro-verbial (disk) envelope in creating large games that spanned a number of disks. For example, her earlier *Time Zone* (1982) featured over 1,400 color images and shipped on six double-sided floppy disks (the equivalent of 12 single-sided floppy disks) for the Apple II.[22] Games were almost exclusively shipped on a single disk at the time, including larger-scale games such as role-playing games (RPGs).[23] The size of *Time Zone* was highlighted in the game's promotional materials.[24]

Correspondingly, Daventry's geography shifts and grows throughout the *King's Quest* series. With the exception of the 3D *Mask of Eternity*, players tra-verse the game by navigating an animated avatar through a series of "screens". Each screen represents a distinct location in the game and tends to connect logically and visually to adjoining screens. For example, the first *King's Quest* begins the player outside of Castle Daventry, located on one side of the front of the castle (see Figure 8.2, top). By moving the avatar across the bridge of the crocodile-infested moat and exiting to the left on this screen, the player's avatar moves to the next screen. Here, the player appears on the right side of a screen depicting the continued front side of the castle and its front door (see Figure 8.2, center). There, the player can exit via the side of the screen or gain access to the castle by approaching the door and typing "open door" into the text parser. Entering the castle leads to a depiction of an interior hallway of the castle, rendered in a linear perspective that shows the hallway leading away from this front door (see Figure 8.2, bottom). Each "screen" is connected to other screens, with some screens limiting navigation in particular directions via impassable barriers. The perspective of the standard screen of outdoor spaces in the *King's Quest* games generally corresponds to the compass in that the edges of the screen correlate to directions so that the left side of the screen is west and the right side is east, while the top and bottom are equivalent to north and south respectively.

This construction facilitates coherently mapping the space using paper, a practice which the game manuals explicitly encourage and even visually model. The manual for the first *King's Quest* suggests that the player, "Create a map showing objects and landmarks you see along the way. You'll want to note dan-gerous areas, in particular".[25] The manual then provides a sample map of how different screens connect. Hintbooks and guides for the games often emphasize this mapping and provide maps of each game. Donald B. Trivette's *The Official Book of King's Quest: Daventry and Beyond* (1988) supplies maps and hints for sev-eral games in the series. This book divides the first game's map into quadrants and describes its layout: "The Kingdom of Daventry is small and compact; it is just eight screens from east to west (left to right) and six screens from north to south (top to bottom)".[26] As Trivette explains in his book, each quadrant of Daventry in his book is composed of four screens east to west and three north

FIGURE 8.2 Start screen of *King's Quest* (top); screen to left of the other side of the castle with the front door (center); and screen of interior hall of castle (bottom).

to south. Maps for each quadrant can thus be clearly rendered on a page and hints for the different quadrants are described in subsections. As technology progressed in subsequent games in the series, the size of these virtual worlds would grow substantially over time; for example, the main area of *King's Quest II: Romancing the Throne* (1985) expands to a map of seven screens by seven screens and later games grow to dozens of screens.

Trivette describes a curious way in which the totality of Daventry is modeled in the first *King's Quest* game. He states, "In almost every case, Daventry, like the real world, wraps around itself: If you go east (right) from Edward's Castle, which appears [in the top right] on the northeast [quadrant] map, you'll end up at the beautiful lake shown [in the top left] of the northwest [quadrant] map".[27] In other words, it is possible to move in one direction long enough (i.e., six screens north or south) that one will eventually return to the same screen at which one started. Some barriers in the world such as a river or the castle's moat may require one to circumnavigate the obstacles or solve puzzles, but the underlying circularly connected grid-like structure remains. Daventry, then, mimics a globe in that it is possible to travel in one direction far enough to return to the starting point. Echoing *The Official Book*, this effect is also described in *The Companion* as "wrap around".[28] Players of earlier arcade games such as *Asteroids* (1979) and *Pac-Man* (1980), or even the pioneering computer game *Spacewar!* (1962), which utilize a single-screen wraparound mechanism, would already be familiar with it.

This "wrap around" game mechanic is directly addressed in the manual for the original 1984 release for the first game, which suggests that the world of Daventry is actually shaped in this way. The IBM PCJr manual states "Daventry's world has a three-dimensional quality about it. Places 'wrap around' like countries on a globe. Imagine Daventry as a country so large that it bends around the world. Remember this when drawing your map".[29] This manual then provides two suggested methods of mapping the game, one of which places a grid of locations around a three-dimensional globe.[30]

Within the tales of Daventry found in *The Companion*, the "wrap around" is explained by a narrative conceit. This is referred to as a magical law of "containment", wherein kingdoms in the world of Daventry (e.g., the settings for the first four games in the series) loop in peculiar ways. *King's Quest II* transports King Graham to the continent of Tanalore and begins in the kingdom of Kolyma on a beach on the western shores. In the *Companion*'s narrativizing of these events, it is stated that, "the magical law of 'containment' operated in this western part of the continent. For reasons now forgotten — or perhaps it was whimsey on the part of the multiverse — movement to both the north and south in this part of Kolyma eventually turned back upon itself, contained as if inside some transparent cosmic doughnut".[31] This diegetic principle apparently operates in describing significant parts of game worlds as in the Daventry found in the earlier games in the series before *King's Quest V: Absence Makes the Heart Go Yonder!* (1990).[32]

Adding to confusion about this imaginary world are questions about where Daventry is actually located. In the instruction manual for the first *King's Quest*, it is suggested that the kingdom of Daventry existed "a long, long time ago, when unicorns still roamed in the forests and the merfolk still dwelt in the shallow waters frequented by men".[33] And in the manual for *King's Quest II: Romancing the Throne*, the manual is more explicit in describing the location of Daventry as being on Earth: "A long, long time ago, when creatures of myth and magic walked the earth openly with lesser mortals, there dwelt in the kingdom of Daventry a King named Graham".[34] It should be noted, however, that this mention of "earth" in the instruction manual is complicated by the fact that the story in which it is mentioned is attributed to Annette Childs. Even relatively early in series, the complicated function of paratexts created by other authors — in this case, an introductory story written in the game's instruction manual — is clearly indicated. However, other references to Daventry's location on earth can be found in the games and have been confirmed by Roberta Williams herself. In a 1998 interview, she describes Daventry as being "somewhere on Earth", and that Daventry is a "very old, very old city. . . from a long time ago".[35] Her tongue-in-cheek claim that Daventry is located on Earth in an unknown location intimates that Daventry exists in a mythical past rather than an actual past.

Multiples of Daventry

It is difficult to construct a definitive and singular map of Daventry, due to the inconsistencies in, and resulting incoherence of, the various versions of it. One reason for this is a result of Sierra's own practices in updating its games. Several titles within the original *King's Quest* series were released in multiple versions. These iterations extend beyond ports to different platforms, and include versions which incorporated newer technologies. Both the systems used by the game developers and the capabilities of the platforms themselves changed significantly over the course of the game series. And, as the success of the series grew, interest in the earlier games was rekindled. As a result of these and other factors, there exist multiple versions of the earlier games, with varying differences between each in their representations of Daventry.

Sierra's earlier adventure games were made using a development tool called AGI, the acronym for Adventure Game Interpreter. AGI was developed in conjunction with IBM in creating the 1984 IBM PCJr version of the original *King's Quest* game, and it facilitated the porting of the game to similar platforms of the time such as the Apple II, the Amiga, the Atari ST, the Macintosh, and other IBM PCs. Used by Sierra from 1984 to 1989, AGI-based versions of each of the games appeared in the series up to *King's Quest IV: The Perils of Rosella* (1988). However, as newer computers, higher resolution graphics, and improved sound capabilities emerged during the 1980s, the limitations of

AGI's underlying technologies (such as its absence of mouse support) became increasingly apparent. Sierra developed SCI, the Sierra Creative Interpreter, as a replacement for AGI. SCI allowed for games with significantly increased graphical resolution and the use of other emergent multimedia technologies such as sound cards. Two versions of *King's Quest IV* were developed, one in AGI for older machines and one in SCI which featured significant visual and aural improvements.

The original *King's Quest* has been released multiple times with notable differences between some versions. In the original 1984 version, the game manual spells the protagonist's name as "Grahame" and provides a cartoonish representation of this protagonist and other characters in the game.[36] Sierra released multiple versions of this game between 1984 and 1987, and then released a new version of the game made using SCI in 1990 called *King's Quest: Quest for the Crown*. This later version changed aspects of the game including puzzles, character dialog, and some layout aspects of in-game elements.

Different versions of these games range from minor improvements to graphics and sounds to the development of more complex backstory and other narrative alterations. The changes made to 1990 SCI remake of the first game were substantial enough to the point that fans do not necessarily consider it part of the world of Daventry's canon.[37] Fans have also remade this first game as Tierra Entertainment's *King's Quest I: Quest for the Crown VGA* (2001). This unofficial remake was then improved upon and re-released in a licensed version in 2009 by AGD Interactive (formerly Tierra), adding *Enhanced Edition* to the title. Notably, these fan remakes also update the graphics, sound, and other elements but stay closer to the original game than Sierra's 1990 SCI remake. Other fan games such as AGD Interactive's *King's Quest II: Romancing the Stones* (2002) and *King's Quest III Redux: To Heir is Human* (2011) are based on the original games, but are positioned as "retelling" and re-imagining the events of the original games while also updating them to use a graphical interface.

Daventry's Author(s)

Among the numerous complexities in mapping the space of the fictional world(s) of *King's Quest* are those that relate to issues of authorship and ownership. On the one hand, Roberta Williams can clearly be considered the primary creator of these imaginary worlds. Her *King's Quest* games established the world of Daventry and its characters, just as her earlier *Wizard and the Princess* created the world of Serenia. On the other hand, however, numerous others are involved in building the world of Daventry, including those associated with the development of the main series games, the writers of supplementary materials that accompanied the games, authors of commissioned "official" paratexts such as game guides, and fans who play roles in the compiling of these sources and the building of Daventry.

Beyond these fictional worlds, the early original *King's Quest* games established other key components for the franchise and broader adventure game genre, including thematic tendencies, and the interrelated domains of play mechanics and the incorporation of technological advancements.[38] That is, while the characters and settings spawn multiple games and transmedia articulations, the various texts that build and expand upon these worlds also share narrational tropes and themes, and even occasionally recycle puzzles from earlier Sierra games. Furthermore, games within the series iteratively build upon the first games' text parser interface to integrate technologies such as color, sound, higher-definition graphics, and mouse-driven control schemes. In a sense, these games build their imaginary worlds both in content and in form.

Although Roberta Williams can be considered the primary designer of the *King's Quest* series, several industrial and cultural factors must be recognized in the authorship of these games and the world of Daventry. As with the vast majority of digital games, the creation of any single title in the *King's Quest* series was the result of a collaborative process between multiple people. Roberta Williams is unmistakably the driving force behind the series, but the actual implementation of each game inevitably required multiple developers to supplement Williams's design, including programmers, artists, and so on. Furthermore, technological capacities of personal computers developed rapidly in the series' initial years of development (1980–1998), spanning from the "prequel" *Wizard and the Princess* to the ninth game, *King's Quest: Mask of Eternity*, evolving from monochrome terminals to multimedia computers capable of playing complex sound effects, music, and video. Attendant to these expanding expressive capabilities was the growth of development teams, adding composers, animators, and actors.

The closest to single authorship in the series may well be the earliest game, *Wizard and the Princess*, in which only Roberta and Ken Williams are credited. In describing the development process for *Hi-Res Adventure #1: Mystery House* (1980), Ken Williams recounts, "Roberta wanted pictures of every room in the house and would write the story and draw the pictures, write the program".[39] Using an Apple II with a monochrome monitor, the Williamses created the first text adventure to include supplemental graphics.[40] *Wizard and the Princess*, the second game in the *Hi-Res Adventure* series, had the same development team of two, but added color to the in-game illustrations. The development team size would grow considerably by the first official game of *King's Quest I* for the IBM PCJr, which features a development team of five identified in the in-game credits: Roberta Williams, Charles Tingley and Ken MacNeill (programming), and Doug MacNeill and Greg Rowland (artwork). These development teams would grow considerably over time and eventually, mushrooming to dozens of people in the credits for *Mask of Eternity*.

Furthermore, multiple designers and writers were involved in the creation of some of the games. While *King's Quest V: Absence Makes the Heart Go Yonder!*

(1990) credits only Roberta Williams as its designer, later games in the series list multiple designers and writers.[41] *King's Quest VI: Heir Today, Gone Tomorrow* (1992) credits Roberta Williams and Jane Jensen as writing and designing the game.[42] Furthering this trend, *King's Quest VII: The Princeless Bride* (1994) lists Lorelei Shannon before Roberta Williams under "Designed [b]y", and credits only Shannon as its writer.[43] The final official sequel in this series, *King's Quest: Mask of Eternity* (1998) once again credits Roberta Williams first, under "Designer/Writer", but next lists Mark Seibert as "Producer/Director/Co-Designer".[44]

The original games were supplemented by other paratexts, including materials supplied with the games and guides such as *The Official Book of King's Quest* and *The King's Quest Companion*, as discussed above. Three "official" novels were also released from 1995 to 1996, ostensibly taking place within the world of Daventry: *The Floating Castle* (1995) by Craig Mills, and *The Kingdom of Sorrow* (1996) and *See No Weevil* (1996), both by Kenyon Morr. However, Roberta Williams was not directly involved in these licensed works, which take place in between the events of the games but also introduce confusing elements to the world of Daventry.

In 2015, the series was "rebooted" by game developers The Odd Gentlemen as *King's Quest: Adventures of Graham*. The reboot was initially released episodically, with separate six separate "Chapters", concluding in 2016. These games take many elements such as characters and settings from the original games' world of Daventry, but stray considerably from the original series. Fans thus refer to this iteration of Daventry as "reboot canon" or "TOG canon" (an acronym for the development team)."

Fan Works

There is clear evidence that fan engagement with Daventry began shortly after the original games reached players' hands. Sierra On-Line published its own magazine, which began as the *Sierra Newsletter* and changed its name upon the acquisition of Dynamix, Inc., before eventually being renamed *InterAction*. Fan art inspired by the *King's Quest* games can be found in the earliest issues of the newsletter, in particular in the "Sierra Cartoon Corner", which invited readers to submit cartoons about Sierra products. This includes a cartoon by a fan in which a television is shut off in favor of *King's Quest* in the second issue of the *Newsletter*. Active fan engagement in the imaginary worlds of *King's Quest* can be found in the next issue, in which a cartoon by Adam Paul depicts Gwydion, the player-controlled protagonist of *King's Quest III: To Heir is Human* (1986), and jokingly imagines the hero contemplating the game's "flying spell" puzzle after brushing away a dead fly.[45] Fan re-imaginings of the characters and settings of *King's Quest* became regular features in the pages of later issues of the *Newsletter*.

Fan participation in Daventry has expanded far beyond these contributions, however. In addition to fan-driven remakes and re-imaginings of the original games by Tierra Entertainment/AGD Interactive above, fans have produced wholly original games such as Interactive Fantasies *King's Quest ZZT* (1997). These fan engagements illustrate multiple aspects of the world-building that these games perform, and clearly demonstrate the existence of a committed fanbase eager to participate in the worlds of Daventry, Serenia, and the other fictional lands of *King's Quest* beyond merely the games themselves. The fan cartoons and art also riff off the *King's Quest* games' uses of characters from fables, fairy tales, and other works of literature, as well as the tendency of other Sierra games to utilize characters from the *King's Quest* games via cameos or joking references. Such playful intertextual references play a critical part in this aspect of world-building, as they provide numerous points of entry for fans to re-imagine and build upon the worlds of the games.

Parallel Universes

The multiplicities of Daventry may be contradictory, but they also mesh well with the suggestions made in the original games and paratexts that Daventry operates in a "parallel universe". This positioning of Daventry acknowledges its function within a "multiverse" of numerous parallel universes, which intersect with and inform one another. This suggestion is posited by *The Companion*, which offers "novelizations" (actually more the length of book chapters or short stories) of the games of the series and further builds out the fictional backgrounds of the games' imaginary worlds. These stories are dramatic accounts of the events of the games and themselves are positioned as artifacts from the diegetic world of the games.

The story "The Eye Between the Worlds" introduces "Derek Karlavaegen", the fictional narrator of this and other stories in *The Companion*. The epigraph suggests that the story was "Compiled from Messages to this World from the World of Daventry, as Sent by Derek Karlavaegen".[46] Karlavaegen describes himself as "a writer here [in Daventry], scribing stories about the current events of the day, which are then published for the information and amusement of whoever cares to read them".[47] The character of Karlavaegen was introduced in the paratext of the *Companion*, but then becomes a character in *King's Quest VI: Heir Today, Gone Tomorrow* (1992) and also the fictional narrator of the short book *Guidebook to the Land of the Green Isles*, which was written by Jane Jensen and packaged with the game. While some of the included materials packaged with the games and other licensed material stray from the world of Daventry represented in the games, other materials such as Jensen's *Guidebook* function to bridge the game between paratexts and the games themselves.

In *The Companion,* Karlavaegen explains how he discovered the "Eye Between the Worlds", which allows him to communicate directly to the reader, outside of Daventry and in the real world. Karlavaegen notes that the world of Daventry intersects with the real world through a structure of "multiverses", in which Daventry exists as a "fantasy adventure — a made-up story intended as entertainment for people".[48] The implication is that the magical imaginary world of Daventry is akin to a dream in the real world but is actually a real place. Furthermore, Daventry is realized in the real world via imagination and other mechanisms. Karlavaegen states, "our worlds touch together in a place shared by the head in this study and in certain of your machines", obliquely referring to the computers upon which the *King's Quest* games run.[49]

As in many Sierra games, *King's Quest* would also break the fourth wall with some frequency. Intertextual references are abundant in Sierra games, with characters, locations, and other elements from what might appear to be entirely separate worlds intersecting. For example, a Daventry-themed virtual pinball board can be found in Dynamix's *Take a Break! Pinball* (1993).[50] In some versions of *King's Quest II*, looking into a hole in a rock would let the avatar see elements from either the *Space Quest* games or a preview of *King's Quest III.* Al Lowe, the designer of Sierra's *Leisure Suit Larry* series also conducts a fictional interview with Daventy's character of Rosella in *The Official Book of Leisure Suit Larry.*[51] Such intertextual references support the fan theory of a Sierra multiverse, which allows for character crossovers (often in the form of hidden Easter eggs).[52]

Conclusion

While the *King's Quest* series unmistakably draws from a number of influences in myth and popular culture, Roberta Williams has acknowledged Andrew Lang's *Fairy Book* series as being among the most prominent.[53] Lang was a literary critic and pioneer in cultural anthropology, helped to legitimize folklore studies as a discipline, and is credited with compiling a number of folklore works.[54] Among the most influential works of his oeuvre are a subset of a dozen volumes of these which became known as the "Color[ed]" *Fairy Books,* as each were named for a different color, and were published between 1889 and 1910. These books collected folk tales and myths from a myriad of sources, publishing many for the first time in the English language. While the books clearly sought to profit from the contemporary British interest in fairy tales, they simultaneously helped to concretize the cultural function of fairy tales and folklore.[55]

Notably, Lang's books were largely compiled from other sources, taking their source material from the myths of a number of different countries. Furthermore, as Andrea Day demonstrates, most of the work of collecting, editing, and translating the majority of *Fairy Books* was actually performed by his wife, Leonora Blanche "Nora" (Alleyne) Lang, but were instead attributed to Andrew Lang himself.[56] Day observes that while Andrew Lang acknowledges that much of the series was "wholly" the result of Lang's wife's labor in the preface to *The Lilac Fairy Book* (1910), Lang endeavored to minimize Nora's work as being done under his supervision, "subordinating his wife's intellect to his own".[57]

It seems fitting that Roberta Williams was influenced so heavily by these books in her storytelling, and in the recombinant nature of the world of Daventry. As Molly Clark Hillard argues in her analysis of Lang's work, "All authorship is, of course, a collective endeavor between forms and across time".[58] The remediation of these fairy tales is evident across all of the *King's Quest* games, and is apparent in the ways in which players were encouraged to play. The instruction manual for one of the 1984 versions commands the player to "Look to the fables and fairy tales of yore for clues".[59] When recounting the influence of Lang's *Fairy Books* on her, Roberta Williams responds to a question about whether these stories and books were written by different authors: "I don't even remember. Probably a lot of them are the same old fairy tales, just rewritten".[60] Like the fairy tales from which it draws, the palimpsestic world of Daventry is one which has been — and remains — prone to revision.

Notes

1 DeWitt, "Wizard and the Princess: Computer Fantasy Comes True," 23.
2 Williams, "Introduction," 3.
3 Williams, 4.
4 Williams, 4.
5 Trivette, *The Official Book of King's Quest: Daventry and Beyond*, 6.
6 *King's Quest: Mask of Eternity Instruction Manual*, 28, 29.
7 In a subsequent 1982 port for the IBM PC, the game was retitled *Adventure in Serenia*.
8 Williams and Williams, *Wizard and the Princess: Hi-Res Adventure #2 Instruction Manual*, 4.
9 Williams and Williams, 4.
10 Jenkins, "Game Design as Narrative Architecture," 121, 122.
11 "Then and Now (Sierra's 15th Anniversary)," 45.
12 Spear, *The King's Quest Companion*, 1991, 442, 443.
13 Spear, 448.
14 Spear, 435–524.
15 Spear, 506.
16 Spear, 455, 456.
17 Spear, *The King's Quest Companion*, 1997, 32.
18 Spear, 33.
19 Spear, *The King's Quest Companion*, 1991, 455.
20 Spear, 506.
21 "Daventry Continent".
22 Clark and Williams, "The Coinless Arcade — Rediscovered," 87.
23 Jimmy Maher notes this includes games such as *Ultima* (Richard Garriott/Origin Systems, 1981) and *Wizardy: Proving Grounds of the Mad Overlord* (Sir-Tech, 1981),

which began to use the second side of a double-sided floppy disk. For more, see Maher, "Time Zone The Digital Antiquarian".

24 These advertised the game as "Multi-Disk Hi-Res Adventure by On-Line Productions" and aped the style of film poster down to the rating of "UA: Ultimate Adventure" several decades before the Entertainment Software Ratings Board (ESRB) instituted game ratings in the United States.

25 *King's Quest Instruction Manual*, 11.

26 Trivette, *The Official Book of King's Quest: Daventry and Beyond*, 41.

27 Trivette, 41.

28 Spear, *The King's Quest Companion*, 1991, 324.

29 *King's Quest IBM PCJr Instruction Manual*, 22.

30 It should be noted that this four-directional wraparound would actually not be a globe, but would actually be more akin to a non-Euclidean shape. See Wolf, "Theorizing Navigable Space in Video Games".

31 Spear, *The King's Quest Companion*, 1991, 62, 63.

32 Spear, 400.

33 *King's Quest Instruction Manual*, 1.

34 Childs, *King's Quest II: Romancing the Throne Instruction Manual*, 1.

35 Wilson, Roberta Williams interview.

36 *King's Quest IBM PCJr Instruction Manual*.

37 "King's Quest I".

38 Anastasia Salter has argued for the consideration of adventure games in relationship to interactive books: see Salter, *What Is Your Quest?* Laine Nooney, however, has suggested the utility removing the notion of "genre" in analyzing Sierra's adventure games; see Nooney, "Let's Begin Again: Sierra On-Line and the Origins of the Graphical Adventure Game".

39 Williams, "Introduction," 5.

40 At the time, the development team and the staff of On-Line Systems consisted of the same two people. The Williamses thus also served as their own distributors, personally delivering copies of the game, packaged in plastic bags, to software stores on US West Coast.

41 *King's Quest V: Absence Makes the Heart Go Yonder! Instruction Manual*, 1.

42 Jensen, *Guidebook to the Land of the Green Isles*, 52.

43 *King's Quest VII: The Princeless Bride Instruction Manual*, 11.

44 *King's Quest: Mask of Eternity Instruction Manual*, 39.

45 "Sierra Cartoon Contest".

46 Spear, *The King's Quest Companion*, 1997, 1.

47 Spear, 2.

48 Spear, 5.

49 Spear, 5.

50 Sierra acquired Dynamix in 1990, so this game was released under Sierra's ownership.

51 Roberts and Lowe, *The Official Book of Leisure Suit Larry*.

52 "Multiverse".

53 DeWitt, "Wizard and the Princess: Computer Fantasy Comes True," 23.

54 Hensley, "What Is a Network? (And Who Is Andrew Lang?)," 8.

55 Hillard, "Trysting Genres: Andrew Lang's Fairy Tale Methodologies," 9–13.

56 Day, "'Almost Wholly the Work of Mrs. Lang': Nora Lang, Literary Labour, and the Fairy Books".

57 Day, 401.

58 Hillard, "Trysting Genres: Andrew Lang's Fairy Tale Methodologies," 7.

59 *King's Quest Instruction Manual*, 10.

60 DeWitt, "Wizard and the Princess: Computer Fantasy Comes True," 23.

Bibliography

Childs, Annette, *King's Quest II: Romancing the Throne Instruction Manual*, Coarsegold, CA: Sierra On-Line, 1985.

Clark, Pamela, and Gregg Williams, "The Coinless Arcade – Rediscovered", *Byte Magazine*, December 1982.

"Daventry Continent" in *King's Quest Omnipedia*. Fandom/Wikia, March 5, 2019, available at https://kingsquest.fandom.com/wiki/Daventry_continent.

Day, Andrea. "'Almost Wholly the Work of Mrs. Lang': Nora Lang, Literary Labour, and the Fairy Books", *Women's Writing*, 26, No. 4 (2019), pages 400–420, available at https://doi.org/10.1080/09699082.2017.1371938.

DeWitt, Robert. "Wizard and the Princess: Computer Fantasy Comes True", *Antic*, Vol 9, No. 2 (November 1983) pages 23–25.

Hensley, Nathan. "What Is A Network? (And Who Is Andrew Lang?)." *Romanticism and Victorianism on the Net*, No. 64 (2013), available at https://doi.org/10.7202/1025668ar.

Hillard, Molly Clark. "Trysting Genres: Andrew Lang's Fairy Tale Methodologies", *Romanticism and Victorianism on the Net*, No. 64 (2013), available at https://doi.org/10.7202/1025670ar.

Jenkins, Henry. "Game Design as Narrative Architecture" in *First Person: New Media as Story, Performance, and Game*, edited by Noah Wardrip-Fruin and Pat Harrigan, pages 118–30. Cambridge, MA: MIT Press, 2004.

Jensen, Jane. *Guidebook to the Land of the Green Isles*. Coarsegold, CA: Sierra On-Line, 1992.

"King's Quest I: Quest for the Crown" in *King's Quest Omnipedia*. Fandom/Wikia, April 18, 2019, available at https://kingsquest.fandom.com/wiki/King%27s_Quest_I:_Quest_for_the_Crown.

King's Quest IBM PCJr Instruction Manual. Boca Raton, FL: IBM Corporation, 1984.

King's Quest Instruction Manual. Coarsegold, CA: Sierra On-Line, 1984.

King's Quest: Mask of Eternity Instruction Manual. Sierra Studios, 1998.

King's Quest V: Absence Makes the Heart Go Yonder! Instruction Manual. Coarsegold, CA: Sierra On-Line, 1990.

King's Quest VII: The Princeless Bride Instruction Manual. Bellevue, WA: Sierra On-Line, 1994.

Maher, Jimmy. "Time Zone." *The Digital Antiquarian*, available at https://www.filfre.net/2012/06/time-zone/.

"Multiverse" in *King's Quest Omnipedia*. Fandom/Wikia, June 30, 2019, available at https://kingsquest.fandom.com/wiki/Multiverse.

Nooney, Laine. "Let's Begin Again: Sierra On-Line and the Origins of the Graphical Adventure Game." *American Journal of Play*, 10, No. 1 (Fall 2017), pages 71–98.

Roberts, Ralph, and Al Lowe. *The Official Book of Leisure Suit Larry*. Radnor, PA: Compute! Books, 1990.

Salter, Anastasia Marie. *What Is Your Quest?: From Adventure Games to Interactive Books*. Iowa City: University of Iowa Press, 2014.

"Sierra Cartoon Contest." *Sierra Newsletter*, Spring 1988.

Spear, Peter. *The King's Quest Companion*. Second Edition. Berkeley, CA: Osborne McGraw-Hill, 1991.

Spear, Peter. *The King's Quest Companion*. Fourth Edition. Berkeley, CA: Osborne McGraw-Hill, 1997.

"Then and Now (Sierra's 15th Anniversary)." *InterAction*, 1994.

Trivette, Donald B. *The Official Book of King's Quest: Daventry and Beyond.* Greensboro, NC: Compute! Books, 1988.

Williams, Ken. "Introduction" in *The Roberta Williams Anthology Manual*, pages 3–8. Sierra On-Line, 1996.

Williams, Ken, and Roberta Williams. *Wizard and the Princess: Hi-Res Adventure #2 Instruction Manual.* Coarsegold, CA: On-Line Systems, 1980.

Wilson, Johnny. Roberta Williams interview. TalkSpot, December 6, 1998, available at http://sierrahelp.com/Assets/RealMedia/Roberta_on_TalkSpot_1-3.rm.

Wolf, Mark J. P. "Theorizing Navigable Space in Video Games" in *DIGAREC Keynote-Lectures 2009/10*, edited by Stephan Günzel, Michael Liebe, and Dieter Mersch, pages 18–48. Potsdam, Germany: Potsdam University Press, 2011.

Transmedia Worlds

9

THE SOFTER SIDE OF *DUNE*

The Impact of the Social Sciences on World-Building

Kara Kennedy

The success of Frank Herbert's *Dune* (1965) as a world-building novel challenges the idea that there is a preferable type of science fiction within the much-debated "hard" to "soft" spectrum. Instead, it suggests that a variety of sciences can be blended to become the bedrock for an interesting and believable world. Science fiction scholar James Gunn postulates that *Dune* is difficult for the reader to categorize because it is a mixture of hard and soft sciences — "the ecology is hard, the anthropology and the psychic abilities are soft" — but that "[t]his may be the reason for its success" because readers can enjoy different kinds of richness (Gunn, 1986, p. 79). Yet the relative lack of criticism on the novel's world-building features has left the complexities of its categorization largely unexplored. The breadth of sciences present in the novel attests to an extended process of study on the part of the author, who, according to his biographers Timothy O'Reilly and son Brian Herbert, spent years researching "works of history [. . .], religion, psychology, ESP, dry land ecology, geology, linguistics, anthropology, botany, [and] navigation" (Herbert, 2003, p. 164). Unlike science fiction writers who focus on exploring a single science in detail, Herbert brings a wide range "together in one consistent and entertaining fictional world" while still pursuing a high level of verisimilitude (O'Reilly, 1981, p. 13). Although he uses a mixture of sciences, Herbert relies heavily on the social sciences to create a world focused on the development of the human mind and body rather than technology. He positions the fictional historical context of the Butlerian Jihad — when humans revolted against machines after having been enslaved by them — as justification for the necessity of new orders of enhanced humans. Such orders include the Spacing Guild, with its navigators who guide spaceships; Mentats, with their logical, computer-like functions; and the Bene Gesserit, with its women skilled in perception, nerve and muscle control, and hand-to-hand combat. Herbert draws on real-world history to help maintain plausibility, placing all of these orders in a familiar feudal governing structure with emperors and family clans. Ultimately, by extrapolating from contemporary understandings of various social sciences to develop the world in *Dune*, Herbert proves that a focus on the human offers a tremendous opportunity for building an interesting and believable universe.

The classification of science fiction as either "hard" or "soft" can be a point of contention, but these categories represent a useful way in which to view *Dune* as a bridge between them that showcases the value in focusing on sciences concerned with the human. The terms "hard" and "soft" reflect a division in the real-world scientific community, which then appears in criticism and valuation of texts in the science fiction genre as well. Although the value judgments regarding these categories may vary, on the whole, the so-called hard-pure knowledge in fields like physics "tends to carry high prestige" and have more privileged status than the soft or applied knowledge in the social sciences and humanities, which are more concerned with human society and culture (Becher and Trowler, 2001, pp. 177, 192). In Gunn's definition, hard science fiction involves a story turning "around a change in the environment that can be understood only scientifically and generally through what are known as the hard sciences, usually the laboratory sciences such as chemistry, physics, and biology, and the observational sciences such as astronomy, geology, and geography" (Gunn, 1986, p. 74). In *The Encyclopedia of Science Fiction* (1999), Peter Nicholls includes computers, physics, space flight, spaceships, and technology in the category of hard science fiction, noting that it should not ignore known scientific principles but that leeway is given for some aspects like ESP and faster-than-light travel ("Hard SF"). He classifies soft science fiction as stories that deal primarily with social sciences including anthropology, ecology, linguistics, perception, psychology, and sociology ("Hard SF", "Soft Sciences"). In *Dune*, there are noticeable aspects of hard science, particularly the attempt to realistically portray a desert planet and the creatures that might live there, as well as the adaptations humans might undergo for it to be inhabitable. Spaceships and space flight are also features of this universe, along with smaller pieces of technology like the stillsuit, though they are not explained in great detail. However, the backdrop is a ban on thinking machines and similar advanced technology, which gives Herbert the space to focus on social sciences like psychology, linguistics, and sociology in relation to how the human mind and body might develop in such a world.

The contribution that the social sciences make is crucial to *Dune*'s success as a world-building novel. As Mark J. P. Wolf explains in *Imaginary Worlds: The Theory and History of Subcreation* (2012), constructing an imaginary world requires making changes to the real world, or Primary World, in one or more distinct realms: nominal, cultural, natural, and ontological (pp. 35–36). But most changes appear in the cultural realm, "which consists of all things made by humans (or other creatures), and in which new objects, artifacts, technologies, customs, institutions, ideas, and so forth appear" (Wolf, 2012, p. 35). This realm also includes "new countries and cultures, [and] new institutions and orders", and Wolf specifically cites the Jedi and Bene Gesserit as examples of such invented orders (Wolf, 2012, p. 35). What is key to making a world interesting and believable, though, is making changes while avoiding implausibilities: "Even though audiences know something is not real, Secondary Belief is easier to generate if the proposed inventions fit in with what the audience knows (or does not know) about the Primary World" (Wolf, 2012, pp. 37–38). If an author can make changes that the reader will readily accept based on the reader's current knowledge, the reader is more likely to accept the "world logic" that governs these changes and stay immersed in the imaginary world (Wolf, 2012, p. 53). In *Dune*, Herbert makes use of his audience's knowledge by drawing on 20th-century scientific explorations into concepts in both established and emerging social science fields, especially psychology. He also subtly justifies a focus on such sciences by hinting at a past revolt against technological advancement which would lead people to turn toward the development of the human mind and body. In this way, the focus on the human rather than technology is able to contribute to successful world-building by making new orders such as the Spacing Guild, Mentats, and Bene Gesserit and their enhancements seem not only necessary but natural. It facilitates the believability of a science fictional world wherein characters possess extraordinary skills without requiring technological assistance.

The novel sets up the justification for characters having a suspicious attitude toward technology by developing a historical background of a war against thinking machines that resulted in an edict against their creation. Rather than include a lengthy history lesson, though, the novel establishes the historical context through several lines of dialog between the young protagonist, Paul Atreides, and one of the senior members of the Bene Gesserit, Reverend Mother Mohiam, after he has survived the test to determine whether or not he is human — that is, if he can override his instincts:

"Why do you test for humans?" he asked.

"To set you free."

"Free?"

"Once men turned their thinking over to machines in the hope that this would set them free. But that only permitted other men with machines to enslave them."

"'Thou shalt not make a machine in the likeness of a man's mind,'" Paul quoted.

"Right out of the Butlerian Jihad and the Orange Catholic Bible," she said. "But what the O. C. Bible should've said is: 'Thou shalt not make a

machine to counterfeit a *human* mind.' Have you studied the Mentat in
your service?"

"I've studied *with* Thufir Hawat."

"The Great Revolt took away a crutch," she said. "It forced *human*
minds to develop. Schools were started to train *human* talents." (*Dune*,
pp. 11–12)

Within the space of a mere few lines, the novel sets out several important aspects of the universe: there was some kind of holy war related to a commandment against certain machines, this engendered a focus on developing humans,
there exist training schools with this focus, and Mentats represent an example
of trained humans. Though terms are left unexplained, the name Great Revolt
immediately suggests a reaction against something that was strong enough to
cause humans to no longer value machines so highly. By presenting Mohiam's
responses as matter-of-fact and logical, the novel prompts the reader to absorb
the brief history lesson as an adequate explanation for why a universe would
have both space travel and an injunction on advanced machinery. Since there
is no reason given to doubt the information, it quickly becomes part of the
history of this universe (even though a discerning reader might question the
extent to which Mohiam's bias as a member of the Bene Gesserit affects her
understanding of the order's origins).

The inclusion of further information about the Butlerian Jihad and the
Great Revolt only in the appendices adds to the sense that this historical context is factual data that can sit outside of the main narrative. If the reader
wishes to know more about the struggle between humans and machines that
Mohiam alludes to, they are required to consult the appendices and use their
imagination to expand upon the limited information given there. The placing
of this information in the appendices can constitute a technique of effective
world-building, since "[s]uch additional information can change the audience's experience, understanding, and immersion in a story, giving a deeper
significance to characters, events, and details" (Wolf, 2012, p. 2). In "Appendix II: The Religion of Dune", the Butlerian Jihad is described as two generations of chaos and violence during which the "god of machine-logic was
overthrown among the masses and a new concept was raised: 'Man may not
be replaced'" (*Dune*, p. 502). In Terminology of the Imperium, it is defined
as "the crusade against computers, thinking machines, and conscious robots",
also known as the Great Revolt, and its chief commandment is the one found
in the Orange Catholic Bible: "Thou shalt not make a machine in the likeness
of a human mind" (*Dune*, p. 521). Based on these descriptions, the Butlerian
Jihad and the Great Revolt appear to be synonymous terms for a campaign of
at least several decades against anything that replicated the workings of the
human mind. The presentation of the material in a short, encyclopedic-like
format gives the illusion of it consisting of historical facts and prompts the

reader to imagine what the crusade involved and how advanced societies had become before destroying their technology. In addition, for the reader familiar with Samuel Butler's *Erewhon* (1872), the name "Butlerian Jihad" itself hints at an intertextual connection between the destruction of inventions in Butler's satirical novel and similar occurrences in *Dune*. Yet none of this information interrupts the main storyline, as if it consists of facts that only the reader needs to be educated about. There is no need for characters to discuss it, because it is part of the fabric of their lives. In this way, the lack of emphasis on the history plays a role in normalizing historical events and enables the reader to immerse themselves in an alternative universe.

The fictional historical context is critical to setting up one of the foundational themes underlying the novel: that humans should be prioritized over machines and other technologies. Mohiam's explanation clearly connects the aversion to machines with the development of groups that specialize in training humans to gain extraordinary abilities. Her insistence on the importance of the human, emphasized by the continual italicization of the word in this scene, justifies why so many characters are "highly trained", as C. N. Manlove notes (p. 87). It appears that humans would rather rely on their own enhancements than risk going down the path of enslavement, chaos, and death again. Just as when someone loses or damages one of their five senses and the others must adapt and strengthen, so too the characters in this universe have compensated for the loss of thinking machines by strengthening their own abilities. Mohiam later notes that the training schools that survive are those of the Bene Gesserit and the Spacing Guild, implying that their ranks are composed of humans with extra-developed minds and special talents. This establishes these groups as both long-lived and the ones most concerned with developing human potential. This pro-human, anti-technology theme gives Herbert space to extrapolate from the social sciences in order to develop new orders whose skills are plausible without technological assistance.

The lack of advanced technology makes the Spacing Guild a necessary part of the Imperium as the only means by which travel between planets is possible. Based on Mohiam's limited descriptions of the Guild, the reader knows that it is a "secretive" group that "emphasizes pure mathematics" and maintains a "monopoly on interstellar transport" (*Dune*, pp. 12, 23). It appears to have focused on training humans to pilot ships and enable planetary travel without computational assistance. This is logical and understandable given the historical context provided, for without interstellar travel humans would be cut off from one another. The implication is that the Guild has capitalized on a gap left by the war against machines, which is supported by the appendix's description of it as "the second mental-physical training school [. . . .] after the Butlerian Jihad" whose "monopoly on space travel and transport and upon international banking is taken as the beginning point of the Imperial Calendar" (*Dune*, p. 520). Specially trained pilots constitute a necessity in a universe averse to auto-pilot capabilities, and it is likely that they would leverage the demand for their services to extend their control to other areas as well.

Although the enhancements that the Guild cultivates are kept secret from other characters and thus the reader, the text implies that they are gained naturally through tapping into the potential of the human psyche with the aid of the spice known as melange. Melange is an addictive substance "chiefly noted for its geriatric properties" that can also provide access to new forms of consciousness and "prophetic powers" (*Dune*, p. 523). A conversation between Duke Leto and Paul reveals that a possible reason for the Guild's secrecy is that their navigators are more than ordinary pilots — that "they've mutated and don't look.... *human* anymore" (*Dune*, p. 46). As Paul himself begins to change and reach a higher plane of consciousness when exposed to higher concentrations of the spice on Dune, he realizes that his strangeness is like that of the navigators and prescience is indeed possible. Here the connection between piloting and mutations becomes clearer: Guild navigators appear able to guide spaceships due to prescient abilities unlocked by the spice, in essence a powerful drug. The reader is left to fill in the gaps while wondering how humans discovered these abilities and how they were able to become skilled enough to safely pilot entire ships through space.

The indication that a drug is an integral part of the Guildsmen's operations signals that access to expanded consciousness may one day lead the human psyche to new, previously unbelievable achievements. Herbert was writing at the beginning of a period that would become known for a heightened interest and experimentation in drugs. As discussed in Robert C. Cottrell's *Sex, Drugs, and Rock 'n' Roll: The Rise of America's 1960s Counterculture* (2015), college students were leaving school to join LSD cults, Timothy Leary at the Harvard Psychedelic Project was studying whether psilocybin might be used for psychiatric disorder treatment, and the CIA was conducting experiments on hallucinogens in relation to gaining an advantage over foreign adversaries. Herbert himself had a few experiences with hallucinogenic drugs, and though he did not advocate their use, he was comfortable with using them in the novel as a means to heightened awareness and perception (O'Reilly, 1981, pp. 82–83). Without having to go into detail, Herbert relied on popular conceptions of drugs being a way to facilitate a person's access to different levels of consciousness in order to develop his world. Thus, he hints at an explanation for how Guild pilots can eschew technology and rely on themselves to guide spaceships through the universe by suggesting that it is part of the mysterious abilities related to the spice. In this way, the characterization of the Guild demonstrates how an aspect relating to psychological study can be utilized and enable an author to bypass the need to include hard scientific explanations.

The ban on thinking machines, computers, and robots makes the order of Mentats another necessary component of the Imperium, one that fulfills the need for the computational processing of data and other feats of logic. As with the Spacing Guild, Mohiam's brief mention of the Mentats serves to both introduce them and prompt the reader to imagine how they might have developed enough skills to fill the gap left in the wake of the Butlerian Jihad. Presumably, without the ability to rely on machines with data processing capabilities, humans had to learn how to memorize and process information in a way that resulted in useful, reliable predictions and calculations. With such skills, the Mentats would then be in a position to assist others with decision-making and other data-driven tasks. Indeed, the reader sees both the Atreides and Harkonnen families employing Mentats who can store seemingly large amounts of data and use it to make projections. Although Baron Harkonnen describes his Mentat, Piter de Vries, to his nephew in an almost dehumanizing way — "This is a Mentat, Feyd. It has been trained and conditioned to perform certain duties" — he still clearly values de Vries's skills (*Dune*, p. 18). After the Baron commands him to "[f]unction as a Mentat", de Vries outlines possible scenarios and probabilities relating to enemy movements and provides an analysis of the plan to displace the Atreides family (*Dune*, p. 18). Duke Leto is also shown consulting with his Mentat, Thufir Hawat, as they strategize about how to manage finances, outmaneuver their enemies, and consolidate their power. As David Miller writes, "All the major power brokers need a Mentat to guide their machinations" (p. 19). There is every indication that these leaders rely on this assistance and that it is normal that humans are performing the work of computers. Although little information is given about Mentat training or motivations, such detail is unnecessary because the reason why humans would need to adapt themselves to fulfill the role of a computer has already been established.

Viewed within the context of the so-called cognitive revolution begun in the 1950s, Mentats' abilities reflect an extrapolation of then-contemporary psychological research into the capabilities of the human brain. The 1950s saw an increasing interest in theories of the mind, with topics such as artificial intelligence, perception, and information theory being discussed by experimental psychologists who were dissatisfied with the limitations of behaviorism (Miller, 2003, p. 142). Earlier work was revived, such as the theories of perception developed by Gestalt psychologists, who had theorized that "the way the parts are seen is determined by the configuration of the whole, rather than vice versa" (Gardner, 1985, p. 112). In their view, people who could look at the whole picture and have the "capacity to grasp the basic fundamental relations" were partaking in more intelligent processes than those making piecemeal associations (Gardner, 1985, p. 113). The cognitive revolution led to cognitive scientists theorizing about the mind and how memory works. In part, this was spurred by advancements in computing. As Howard Gardner explains in *The Mind's New Science: A History of the Cognitive Revolution* (1985), "There is little doubt that the invention of computers in the 1930s and 1940s, and demonstrations of 'thinking' in the computer in the 1950s, were powerfully liberating to scholars concerned with explaining the human mind" (Gardner, 1985, p. 40).

The significance to psychology was that psychologists became more willing to consider how the mind processed and represented information, since the brain could be considered a powerful computer based on its operation via the principles of logic (Gardner, 1985, p. 19). This involved a recognition of the human mind as being more complex with more capabilities than had previously been thought. Such recognition, as it permeated into society's understanding of human potential, would serve to make the abilities of the Mentats seem potentially realizable.

Thus, rather than depict the outsourcing of logical functions, *Dune* keeps dominion over computational thinking in the minds of humans in a plausible way. Herbert's grandmother, Mary Herbert, apparently provided the inspiration for this type of human whiz with computation, being an uneducated woman who nevertheless had an aptitude for figures and a remarkable memory (O'Reilly, 1981, p. 12; Herbert, 2003, p. 34). Indeed, the original computers were people, with the term referring to a human who solved equations; it was only after 1945 that it began to refer to machines that could solve complex mathematical problems (Ceruzzi, 2003, p. 1). It should also be noted that not only were computers still in the early stages of development at the time Herbert was researching for and writing *Dune*, but there was an increasing level of exasperation in the United States regarding automation and the related alienation of workers consigned to attending machines (Lepore, 2018, pp. 558–559). It is significant, then, that the Mentats' skills highlight the strength of the mind and show that society can function without relying on external computers. Their characterization as being capable of great feats of logic flows on from the emphasis in the novel on human over technological development. They appear to have abilities that a human could develop in the future, allowing them to contribute to the reader's understanding of a world where cognitive development has improved to the point where humans are relied upon to act as computers.

However, in an environment full of skepticism about anything reminiscent of thinking machines, the Mentats are at times critiqued and even dehumanized for their logical thinking patterns. Both the Bene Gesserit and Baron Harkonnen harbor an attitude of caution toward Mentats, indicated by the language they use in dialog with and about Mentats. As shown in the passage above, Mohiam suggests to Paul that the Atreides' Mentat is an object worth studying — a human who fills some of the gap left by the destruction of computers. Another Bene Gesserit woman, Jessica, who is Paul's mother, tells Hawat directly that his "projections of logic onto all affairs is unnatural, but suffered to continue for its usefulness" (*Dune*, p. 153). Although she seems to question his very humanity with this choice of the words "suffered" and "unnatural", she clearly does see value in Mentat training because she has permitted Paul to undergo the training in the hope that he might gain an additional skill. The notion that Mentats are constrained by their adherence to logic also appears in the descriptions of the Baron's Mentat performing his duties. While functioning as a Mentat, de Vries proceeds to straighten his body and "assum[es] an odd attitude of dignity — as though it were another mask, but this time clothing his entire body" (*Dune*, p. 18). His posture and demonstration of detailed analysis signal that he is a special type of human — one trained to be more than a mere calculator. Yet he is shown disconnected from his body while in the Mentat trance, indicating that the Mentats embrace a mind-body split to the point that they lose some of their humanity. The clearest indication that a critical attitude toward Mentats is justifiable comes through the dramatic irony that Hawat is completely wrong about the identity of the traitor to the Atreides family, yet smugly believes until the very end of the novel that he knows best: "'I've always prided myself on seeing things the way they truly are,' Thufir Hawat said. 'That's the curse of being a Mentat. You can't stop analyzing your data'" (*Dune*, p. 207). More so than other enhanced groups, Mentats reflect the problems with technology insofar as they are similar to computers in their reliance on data and quantifiable measurements. The presence of this group both reinforces the fictional historical context and enables an examination of potential consequences of humans becoming more like machines.

The emphasis on the development of the human is also noticeably illustrated in the all-female order of the Bene Gesserit, whose members showcase an impressive array of abilities that seem to fill a natural void left in the absence of advanced technology. The Bene Gesserit are considerably better developed characters than those in the other enhanced groups, largely because Jessica is such a prominent figure with a wide skillset displayed throughout the novel. However, there is little elaboration on their training, prompting the reader to imagine the kind of intense education likely required for women to gain their abilities. Like the Mentats, the Bene Gesserit act as close advisors, but they also possess a special ability to truthsay, or detect whether or not people are lying based on their speech. Especially in a world without lie-detector technology, such truthsaying is a valuable skill, particularly in the realm of politics. Its effectiveness is shown through several examples of the Baron Harkonnen and others ensuring they do not take any action that would entail them being revealed as liars by a Truthsayer. Another role the Bene Gesserit hold is that of administrators of the test for humanness, which appears necessary to ensure that people can rise above their animal instincts as thinking creatures and never again be enslaved by machines. One of the most mysterious items in the novel is the black box that Mohiam uses for Paul's test: a box which stimulates nerves to feel pain but does no physical damage to the body. What might seem like an extreme measure — her holding a poisoned needle known as a gom jabbar at his neck and forcing him to endure the nerve pain or else die — fits within the reader's emerging understanding of the precautions humans must take against falling back into letting their instincts or machines override their own reasoning. Yet the Bene Gesserit themselves have exploited the existence of human weakness by mastering the ability to control others via two main mechanisms:

the religious propaganda of the Missionaria Protectiva and the controlling intonations of the Voice, which adds additional complexity to their characterization. The Bene Gesserit also have developed precise control over their bodily functions, to the point that they can manipulate reproduction, tap into the memories of their female ancestors, and engage in hand-to-hand combat on a level unparalleled in the Imperium. In an environment without artificial reproduction, computer memory, or advanced weaponry, women have taken it upon themselves to expand their abilities to excel at virtually everything they do.

The above examples demonstrate that the Bene Gesserit are primarily concerned with control: control of their own minds and bodies as well as those of others around them. What makes them function well as characters in the world of *Dune* is that this control seems achievable based on an extrapolation from contemporary explorations into the social sciences of psychology, linguistics, and sociology.

Dune is permeated by ideas and concepts from psychology, and the incorporation of elements from this field in the characterization of the Bene Gesserit facilitates the reader's belief in these women being able to perceive and respond to their environment in extraordinary ways. Psychology was a burgeoning field in the 20th century, containing a variety of theories about how the mind and body function and how much control a person can exercise over their thoughts and behaviors. In fact, Herbert took a keen interest in psychology and was influenced by his friendship with two psychologists, Ralph and Irene Slattery, "who gave a crucial boost to his thinking" regarding Freudian and Jungian psychoanalysis (O'Reilly, 1981, p. 18). Although psychology is considered a social science, more than other disciplines it "self-consciously modelled itself upon successful sciences such as physics, chemistry, and biology" (Greenwood, 2015, p. 6). In this way, psychologists attempted to gain legitimacy for their investigations into the often-subjective realm of human cognition, emotion, and behavior, including the study of "sensation, perception, emotion, memory, dreaming, learning, language, and thought" (Greenwood, 2015, p. 16). Looking at the Bene Gesserit, the reader sees a group that has created a whole training system to bring order to these seemingly instinctive and uncontrollable aspects.

The Bene Gesserit's training system and approach to life, known as the Bene Gesserit Way, is an amalgamation of elements from psychology and Eastern traditions as well as the Jesuit religious order, which their name signals (Kennedy, 2016, p. 101). The term "Way" signals a link with the Way in Taoism and a striving for balance in life. Following the Way involves the Bene Gesserit gaining skills in Gestalt psychology and the "minutiae of observation", to the point of being able to perceive the slightest details and analyze their significance as a whole (*Dune*, p. 5). Like the Mentats, the Bene Gesserit appear to be able to take a big-picture view based on their gathering of small bits of data. But they also learn to gain control of every muscle and nerve in the body through training in prana-bindu, prana standing for "prana-musculature" and bindu for "bindu-nervature" (*Dune*, pp. 526, 514). It is implied that this training is what enables Jessica to best the armed Fremen leader Stilgar in hand-to-hand combat, which makes her superior fighting abilities believable not only for herself as an individual, but also for the Bene Gesserit as the group who trained her. Use of the Sanskrit words *prana* and *bindu* reinforces the link with Eastern philosophic traditions and suggests the possibility that some of these abilities may already have been achieved in a land unfamiliar to the reader. There is also a link with Eastern traditions in the appearance of biofeedback, the technique whereby a person can self-regulate or control functions normally regulated by the body's autonomic nervous system at an unconscious level ("Biofeedback"). Although biofeedback was named and recognized in the United States in the 20th century, there are thousands of years of yogic practice that demonstrate a similar autonomic control (Peper and Shaffer, 2010, pp. 142–143). Biofeedback appears to be an important aspect of the Bene Gesserit's prana-bindu skillset, as demonstrated by Jessica when she is shown "*compos[ing] herself in bindu suspension to reduce her oxygen needs*" after being covered in a sandslide (*Dune*, p. 249). This establishes that a woman's control of her nerves and muscles extends to their unconscious movements as well and becomes significant to explaining how a woman is able to manipulate fertilization and choose whether to become pregnant and what the sex of her fetus will be. Thus, rather than the reader dismissing the Bene Gesserit's reproductive control (and breeding program) as fantastical, they are more likely to instead speculate about the details and make connections to advancements in reproductive control and technology in the real world.

A more obvious element from psychology in the characterization of the Bene Gesserit is that of the collective unconscious, a concept from Jungian psychology that provides at least a layer of plausibility to the presence of Other Memory. In a world without computer memory, it follows that humans must rely on themselves to remember their histories and pass on stories and ideas to their community, whether through oral or written means. But the Bene Gesserit have gone one step further and discovered a way to make a psychic connection with their ancestors and thus gain access to their own bank of ancestral memory. In *Dune*, this concept is described through Jessica's point of view when she ingests the Fremen's poisonous Water of Life as part of the ceremony to become a Reverend Mother. Somehow going inside her own psyche, she encounters the psyche of the dying Reverend Mother Ramallo, whom she is physically touching, and Ramallo transfers her memories and those of her Fremen ancestors into Jessica's mind: "The experiences poured in on Jessica — birth, life, death — important matters and unimportant, an outpouring of single-view time"; "And the memory-mind encapsulated within her opened itself to Jessica, permitting a view down a wide corridor to other Reverend Mothers until there seemed no end to them" (*Dune*, pp. 357–358).

Both individually and as a group, the Bene Gesserit benefit from the guidance of Reverend Mothers "who have, through poison, joined the collective memory of all their female ancestors" (Miller, 1980, p. 20). Although Herbert keeps the descriptions surrounding Other Memory opaque and at times inconsistent, there remains a clear parallel with the collective unconscious and the relevancy of genetics. In Jung's view, the collective unconscious is a part of the unconscious that contains memories, instincts, and experiences that are shared among humans (Colman, 2015). Such racial memory is distinct from the personal unconscious and presumably inherited through genetics (Kellerman, 2009, p. 9). By drawing on Jungian concepts in his characterization of Other Memory, Herbert places it on a psychoanalytical foundation such that even if readers disagree with the tenets, they are likely to be familiar with it as a potentially believable idea with some adherents.

The exercising of control over the unconscious is also a critical factor in the Bene Gesserit's roles as Truthsayers and users of the Voice, whose techniques combine ideas from psychology and linguistics into a conceivable way of influencing others. In an interview, Herbert once explained that a low level of vocal control was already possible by knowing a few details about someone and altering one's language and tone, so it was not too far of an extrapolation for him to show that greater vocal control might be achievable in the future (O'Reilly, 1981, p. 61). One of the key influences on Herbert was the pseudo-scientific field of general semantics, what O'Reilly describes as "a philosophy and training method developed in the 1930s by Alfred Korzybski" that revolves around problems with people's use of language and the unconscious assumptions built into it (O'Reilly, 1981, p. 59). By incorporating it into *Dune* through the Bene Gesserit's "technology of consciousness", Herbert speculates that people can train themselves into new linguistic habits and even use their new perception of verbal and nonverbal cues to influence others (O'Reilly, 1981, p. 62). The Bene Gesserit's truthsaying ability relies on their skill at perceiving a variety of small vocal cues in others' speech to determine whether others believe what they are saying. Any reader familiar with someone who is highly perceptive and hard to deceive can see this ability as realistic for a group with an advanced understanding of the psyche and its connections with language. The Bene Gesserit's ability to use the Voice is more complex, demanding that they first register others' speech patterns and then speak back to them in a customized tone that commands them to obey. The Voice appears to work on an unconscious level since most subjects are unaware when it is used on them and obey instinctively. Like Other Memory, the Voice is never fully explained, but there is enough detail to enable the reader to see that it is a kind of psychological trick that plays on the unconscious and would require a sophisticated level of linguistic skill. This leads to a measure of irony wherein the Bene Gesserit are administrators of the test for humanness, which rewards humans for rising above their instincts, yet also users of the Voice, which manipulates humans at a level below their conscious control.

The test for humanness illustrates an aspect of Herbert's concern with sociology, the study of societies and how they develop and function. This test appears to be a critical component of the world of the novel because it acts as a gatekeeper for people who are unable to control their bodily urges and instincts. Paul must endure intense pain in order to prove he is human: "It mounted slowly: heat upon heat upon heat. ... upon heat. [...] His world emptied of everything except that hand immersed in agony [...]. He thought he could feel skin curling black on that agonized hand, the flesh crisping and dropping away until only charred bones remained" (*Dune*, p. 9). Yet although the first key conflict in the novel revolves around this test, there is very little information given about how it functions in the society at large. Through Jessica's mentioning of it to Stilgar, the reader knows it is a part of the Fremen's society as well, but they are left to speculate beyond this about whether it is mandatory for everyone in the Imperium, how many people fail, and when the Bene Gesserit developed the nerve induction box. What is clear is that the Bene Gesserit use the test as part of their shaping of society. Both Jessica and Paul are shown as never forgetting their memories of that test, reminding the reader, in turn, why society has had to develop in such a way as to have a test for humanness, namely because of the Butlerian Jihad. Presumably, people who fail the test are more susceptible to letting themselves be enslaved by machines and therefore must be removed from society at an early age. Without this historical context present, the test might seem nonsensical or depraved; instead, it follows on from the reader's understanding of this world and appears to be a way of determining a person's likelihood of resisting their baser instincts should the need arise. The careful attention to crafting a society which could reasonably be expected to have accepted such a test as a necessary precaution enhances the world-building of *Dune* and demonstrates the usefulness of drawing on sociological understandings in such an endeavor.

Overall, the lack of emphasis on aspects from traditionally "hard" scientific fields such as physics and mathematics makes it believable that an all-female group that largely eschews technology could maintain such a powerful hold over society. As can be seen, the Bene Gesserit's control often is exerted behind the scenes. However, the portrayal of their wide-ranging influence and authority demonstrates that they possess a great deal of "soft" power, having responded to, and taken advantage of, the suspicion around technology to develop themselves into extraordinary humans. In part through their mastery of psychology and linguistics, they are shown having found a niche in manipulating politics, running a secret breeding program, acting as lie detectors and banks of ancestral memory, and engaging in hand-to-hand combat, without these abilities seeming fantastical or illogical in their world.

Complementary to the historical context of the Butlerian Jihad is the medieval, feudal-like setting, which reinforces that this world is one lacking in advanced technology. From the first few pages the reader becomes aware of the existence of the Padishah Emperor, Castle Caladan, Jessica as a Bene Gesserit Lady, and Duke Leto as the leader of one of the Great Houses of the Landsraad. These proper nouns provide a strong signal that the characters live under some kind of feudal regime with a hierarchy of rulers, titles for nobility, fiefs, and medieval castles as residences. Castle Caladan is described as an "ancient pile of stones" that has been in the Atreides family for twenty-six generations, evoking an image of a European fortress built on a hill whose ownership is safeguarded through long dynastic lineages (*Dune*, p. 3). When the term "faufreluches class system" appears, it also indicates that there is an old but familiar political system in play, rather than a heretofore unknown new one. Even without checking the appendices for the definition — "the rigid rule of class distinction enforced by the Imperium. 'A place for every man and every man in his place'" — the reader can imagine people being part of an imperial system where their role in the order is largely pre-determined (*Dune*, p. 518). Although such a system would not necessarily need to be lacking in technology, it makes for a more comfortable fit to have societies eschewing technology set in an environment reminiscent of a medieval period during which feudalism was prominent. The setting invokes a feeling of technological simplicity and court intrigue, as well as allowing all of the stereotypes about this historical period to surface. The Middle Ages are still popularly considered to be a period of "ignorance, superstition" and stifled development, despite challenges to this narrative by more recent historians (Power, 2006, p. 16). Therefore, the evocation of this period is important to the relatively quick establishment of a world in which it is believable that technological advancement has been halted and humans have had to develop themselves to have a functional society.

By placing all of these new orders — Spacing Guild, Mentats, Bene Gesserit — in this setting, Herbert successfully maintains a link with real-world institutions and enables the reader's expectations to adjust to a framework different from the futuristic, "hard", high-tech one available in other science fiction narratives. Skills valuable in popular conceptions of the period of feudalism are valuable in this world as well. The reader sees Paul being trained in sword-fighting and both Paul and Jessica defeating enemies in hand-to-hand combat with abilities gained through their prana-bindu training. Although body shield technology does exist, because of the potential for shields to attract sandworms or explode if they are hit by a lasgun, they are less useful on Dune and so those who can attack or defend themselves competently without them have a distinct advantage. At one point, Paul must defeat an assassination weapon, a hunter-seeker, by relying on his wits and honed reflexes when his shield is out of reach (*Dune*, pp. 67–68). Atomic weapons also exist and the major houses have their own personal stores, but there is an injunction against their use:

as Paul states, "The language of the Great Convention is clear enough: 'Use of atomics against humans shall be cause for planetary obliteration'" (*Dune*, p. 450). When Paul decides to use them against a planetary feature instead, the explosion is given little narrative description, which serves to deemphasize the technology. Indeed, after the explosion, the focus turns to the Fremen riding the sandworms, reminiscent of knights charging into battle: "Out of the sand haze came an orderly mass of flashing shapes — great rising curves with crystal spokes that resolved into the gaping mouths of sandworms, a massed wall of them, each with troops of Fremen riding to the attack. They came in a hissing wedge, robes whipping in the wind as they cut through the melee on the plain" (*Dune*, p. 464). The reader continually sees that it is the development and strengthening of humans' own abilities that are beneficial in this world, more so than even powerful technological instruments. The choice of this historic setting, then, as opposed to something based on more modern conceptions of federations of states or democratic structures, makes it more likely that readers will accept the novel's focus on the human.

References

Becher, Tony; and Paul R. Trowler, *Academic Tribes and Territories: Intellectual Enquiry and the Culture of Disciplines*, The Society for Research into Higher Education and Open University Press, 2001.

"Biofeedback" in Robert Hine and Elizabeth Martin, editors, *A Dictionary of Biology*, Oxford, England: Oxford University Press, 2015.

Butler, Samuel, *Erewhon: or, Over the Range*, London, England: Trübner & Co., 1872.

Ceruzzi, Paul, *A History of Modern Computers*, 2nd edition, Cambridge, Massachusetts: The MIT Press, 2003.

Colman, Andrew M., "Collective unconscious", *A Dictionary of Psychology*, 4th edition, Oxford, England: Oxford University Press, 2015.

Cottrell, Robert C., *Sex, Drugs, and Rock 'n' Roll: The Rise of America's 1960s Counterculture*, Lanham, Maryland: Rowman & Littlefield Publishers, 2015.

Gardner, Howard, *The Mind's New Science: A History of the Cognitive Revolution*, New York, New York: Basic Books, 1985.

Greenwood, John D., *A Conceptual History of Psychology*, Cambridge, England: Cambridge University Press, 2015.

Gunn, James, "The Readers of Hard Science Fiction" in George E. Slusser and Eric S. Rabkin, editors, *Hard Science Fiction*, Carbondale, Illinois: Southern Illinois University Press, 1986, pp. 70–81.

Herbert, Brian, *Dreamer of Dune: The Biography of Frank Herbert*, New York, New York: Tom Doherty Associates, 2003.

Herbert, Frank, *Dune*, 1965, New York, New York: Penguin Random House, 1984.

Kellerman, Henry, "Collective unconscious", *Dictionary of Psychopathology*, New York, New York: Columbia University Press, 2009.

Kennedy, Kara. "Epic World-Building: Names and Cultures in *Dune*", *Names*, Vol. 64, No. 2, 2016, pp. 99–108.

Lepore, Jill, *These Truths: A History of the United States*, New York, New York: W.W. Norton & Company, 2018.

Manlove, C. N., *Science Fiction: Ten Explorations*, Kent, Ohio: Kent State University Press, 1986.

Miller, David, *Frank Herbert*, Mercer Island, Washington: Starmont House, 1980.

Miller, George A., "The Cognitive Revolution: A Historical Perspective", *Trends in Cognitive Sciences*, Vol. 7, No. 3, 2003, pp. 141–144.

Nicholls, Peter, "Hard SF" in John Clute, David Langford, Peter Nicholls, and Graham Sleight, editors, *The Encyclopedia of Science Fiction*, London, England: Gollancz, 2015, available at http://www.sf-encyclopedia.com/entry/hard_sf.

Nicholls, Peter, "Soft Sciences" in John Clute, David Langford, Peter Nicholls, and Graham Sleight, editors, *The Encyclopedia of Science Fiction*, London, England: Gollancz, 2015, available at http://www.sf-encyclopedia.com/entry/soft_sciences.

O'Reilly, Timothy, *Frank Herbert*, New York, New York: Frederick Ungar Publishing, 1981.

Peper, Erik; and Fred Shaffer, "Biofeedback History: An Alternative View", *Biofeedback*, Vol. 38, No. 4, 2010, pp. 142–147.

Power, Daniel, *The Central Middle Ages: Europe 950–1320*, Oxford, England: Oxford University Press, 2006.

Wolf, Mark J. P., *Building Imaginary Worlds: The Theory and History of Subcreation*, New York, New York: Routledge, 2012.

10

EARTH, AIR, FIRE, AND WATER

Balance and Interconnectivity in the Fractured Worlds of Margaret Weis and Tracy Hickman's *The Death Gate Cycle*

Jennifer Harwood-Smith

Centuries ago, the Sartan thought to defeat our ambition by sundering the world that was ours by rights and throwing us into their prison. As you well know, the way out of the Labyrinth is long and tortuous. It took centuries to solve the twisting puzzle of our land. The old books say the Sartan devised this punishment in hopes that our bounding ambition and our cruel and selfish natures would be softened by time and suffering.

You must always remember their plan, Haplo. It will give you the strength you'll need to do what I ask of you. The Sartan had dared to assume that, when we emerged into this world, we would be fit to take our places in any of the four realms we chose to enter.

Something went wrong. Perhaps you'll discover what it was when you enter Death Gate. It seems from what I have been able to decipher in the old books, that the Sartan were to have monitored the Labyrinth and kept its magic in check. But, either through malicious intent or for some other reason, they forsook their responsibility as caretakers of our prison. The prison gained a life of its own - a life that knew only one thing, survival. And so, the Labyrinth, our prison, came to see us, its prisoners, as a threat. After the Sartan abandoned us, the Labyrinth, driven by its fear and hatred of us, turned deadly.

When at last I found my way out, I discovered the Nexus, this beautiful land the Sartan had established for our occupation. And I came across the books. Unable to read them at first, I worked and taught myself and soon learned their secrets. I read of the Sartan and their 'hopes' for us and I laughed aloud - the first and only time in my life I have ever laughed. You understand me, Haplo. There is no joy in the Labyrinth.

But I will laugh again, when my plans are complete. When the four separate worlds - Fire, Water, Stone, and Sky - are again one. Then I will laugh long and loudly.[1]

The opening prologue of Margaret Weis and Tracy Hickman's *Death Gate Cycle* series, published from 1990 to 1994, is entirely in the voice of an as-yet unnamed leader of an as-yet unnamed people, plotting to send a man named Haplo to the "Realm of the Sky", with orders to find their ancient enemies and not to betray their people.[2] There is a great deal to unpack in only three pages; the language suggests that the speaker is from a race that was imprisoned by ancient enemies, that the jailers —and, indeed, anyone who can confirm the prisoners' crimes— are long gone or dead, and perhaps most chilling of all, that vengeance will soon fall upon the other worlds. However, more questions are raised than answered, as is the case with the maps that precede the prologue,[3] which make sense only once the reader learns in Chapter One that Arianus, the Realm of the Sky, is a series of floating islands. It is this strange and mysterious beginning, with its difficult to interpret maps, that introduces the reader to the sundered worlds, the Sartan who created it, and the Patryn who are seeking their revenge. Over seven books,[4] the reader learns how a catastrophe on Earth sparked the appearance of elves, dwarves, and two races of demi-gods, first the Sartan and then the Patryn, the animosity between the demi-gods, the Sundering of the Earth into four elemental worlds by the Sartan to prevent the Patryn taking power, and the consequences that followed, including the near-extinction of the Sartan race and the trapping of the Patryn people in a semi-sentient prison gone mad. It is also a story of the Patryn Haplo and the Sartan Alfred forming a friendship as a direct result of exploring the various worlds and their own history, finding the balance between their peoples that could have prevented the Sundering. (Haplo is originally a spy sent by the Patryn leader Xar to learn about the other worlds, report back on the Sartan, and help Xar in his plan to recreate the Earth. He is accompanied for much of the narrative by a dog which is actually a portion of his soul he subconsciously partitioned to keep himself alive. Alfred is one of the Sartan who were sent to Arianus to guide the humans, elves, and dwarves who live there. He was the only survivor of a mysterious event that killed all other Sartan on Arianus, and so spent centuries pretending to be a clumsy human).

Running through the narrative is a deep interest in interconnectivity, balance, and the consequences of disrupting such a balance. In fact, interconnectivity is considered to be the foundation of the universe, as explained in the first Appendix of the series in *Dragon Wing* (1990), where reality is defined as the point where two waves of possibility meet.[5] The runic magic used by the Sartan and the Patryn is the manipulation of the waves of possibility to alter reality.[6] In *Elven Star* (1990), Patryn magic is further explained as the ability to understand an object, represent it with a rune, and how even poorly drawn runes will balance themselves (though not always behaving as expected), and the difficulty in exerting too much control through runic magic.[7] While both these Appendices are quite technical —as is fitting with documents which are meant to represent archival evidence, as will be discussed later— they can be ultimately understood to describe a system where a user of magic, understanding the structure of an item and its associated rune, can choose from all possibilities a new reality, and bring it into being for the duration of a spell. Consider the battle in *Serpent Mage* (1992), where Haplo's "steel chain still hung in the air. Haplo instantly rearranged the magic, altered the sigla's form into that of a spear, and hurled it straight at Samah's breast. A shield appeared in Samah's left hand. The spear struck the shield; the chain of Haplo's magic began to fall apart".[8] This battle shows both the extent and the limits of possibility magic; while Haplo can change a chain into a spear, he must rewrite the spell first. However, he cannot have the spear act any differently from a real spear, thus a shield is sufficient to stop it. This exchange further shows the balance between the performance of magic; for the Sartan, runes are sung or signed, where for the Patryn, they must be spoken and written, and so Samah can create a shield out of thin air, where Haplo's chain originally came from the runes tattooed all over his body.[9] However, despite their differences, both forms of rune magic are actually complementary, strengthening each other when used together, as seen when Haplo and Alfred finally use their magic together.[10] This is reinforced by the explanation of the Wave provided at the end of the series:

> 'All of us, drops in the ocean, forming the Wave. Usually we keep the Wave in balance - water lapping gently on the shoreline, hula girls swaying in the sand,' said Zifnab dreamily. 'But sometimes we throw the Wave out of kilter. Tsunami. Tidal disturbances. Hula girls washed out to sea. But the Wave will always act to correct itself. Unfortunately' - he sighed - 'that sometimes sends water foaming up in the opposite direction'.[11]

For the Death Gate universe, balance is not merely a desire but an inevitability, and chaos and order are mere tools to ensure this. The rise of the Sartan necessitated the rise of the Patryn, and, as will be seen throughout this essay, this secondary creation will not allow for imbalance or disconnection for long. The need for interconnectivity is also highlighted by the use of portals; the worlds of Air, Fire, Earth, and Water are reached by a portal called Death's Gate, which also reaches both the Nexus and the Labyrinth. In the Labyrinth, gates are not only physical structures for escaping, but also temporal markers, as they are used to tell time, albeit unevenly at first.[12] However, Weis and Hickman do not only use balance and interconnectivity in the narrative of *The Death Gate Cycle*, but also in their use of four discrete world-building techniques: textual world-building, footnotes, Appendices, and maps. To fully appreciate just how much balance permeates this subcreation, it is necessary to explore the balance Weis and Hickman have created in how the reader engages with the subcreation. However, it is first necessary to discuss the core of *The Death Gate Cycle*, the very thing that allows its various worlds to be explored, and that which both disrupts and restores balance: the portal.

When a speculative fiction text introduces a portal, that device often becomes the driving force of the subcreation. From the rabbit hole in Lewis Carroll's *Alice's Adventures in Wonderland* (1865) to the free standing portal doors in Stephen King's *The Dark Tower* series, the portal becomes the linchpin of the series, driving the narrative and either assisting or hindering the characters. In *The Dark Tower II: The Drawing of the Three* (1987), portal doors along a beach are used to find and extract the companions Roland Deschain will need on his quest to the Dark Tower, but they also serve as signifiers in other texts. In the *Haven* (2010–2015) episode "Lost and Found", the appearance of a free standing portal door acts as an indicator to an audience familiar with King's other works that *Haven* is not just a King text, but also a *Dark Tower* text.[13] Farah Mendlesohn describes the portal fantasy as being "about entry, transition, and exploration. . . it denies the taken for granted and positions both protagonist and reader as naïve".[14] Rarely is such denial of the reader's expectations of reality more extreme than in *The Death Gate Cycle*. The history of the Earth in the *Death Gate Cycle* already crosses into fantasy, as a world that, after a nuclear catastrophe, saw the rise (or return, as some claimed) of elves and dwarves, and the Sartan and the Patryn.[15] However, when Weis and Hickman introduced the series (with Lord Xar's words above), this Earth is long gone, sundered and replaced by four primary realms, along with the Patryns' prison the Labyrinth, and the Nexus. What each of these worlds shares is Death's Gate, designed to allow two-way travel between the various worlds (this differs from the one-way conduits in the series, which are intended for the transport of energy, supplies, and perhaps prisoners).[16]

Death's Gate itself is barred when the series begins, shut down by the Sartan leader Samah when he became afraid of the dragon-snakes which appeared on the world of water, Chelestra after the Sundering.[17] Passage through Death's Gate is an experience that is at first difficult to understand; in *Fire Sea* (1991), Haplo's journal entry informs the reader that, in each journey through Death's Gate, he has lost consciousness: "One moment I was awake, looking forward to entering the small dark hole that seemed far too tiny to contain my ship. The next moment I was safely in the Nexus".[18] Indeed, it is only when Haplo is accompanied by Alfred that he actually experiences the interior of Death's Gate. At the heart of the portal which links all the worlds, Weis and Hickman built in interconnectivity and balance; both Alfred the Sartan and Haplo the Patryn lose consciousness when travelling through Death's Gate alone, but together they remain awake, to experience the dichotomies of it together, from moving too slowly and too fast at once, to their bodies exploding and imploding at the same time, and hearing screams when deaf, among other experiences: "'Death's Gate. A place that exists and yet does not exist. It has substance and is ephemeral. Time is measured marching ahead going backward. Its light is so bright that I am plunged into darkness'".[19] Death's Gate, then, exists in a quantum state and appears to respond in some way to the animosity and polarity between the ancient enemies, as their journey through Death's Gate forces both men to swap consciousness for a short time, with each seeing the most traumatic event in the other's life.[20] While Death's Gate itself does not appear to be sentient, it would appear that it abhors extremes and sought to balance how each saw the other; from then on in the series, Haplo did not see Alfred merely as his jailor, and in *Serpent Mage*, Alfred gives a moving speech about the love and loyalty the Patryn have for each other.[21]

However, as with all elements in *The Death Gate Cycle*, Death's Gate is also balanced by the Seventh Gate, the physical/magical location which allowed the Sartan to cast the spells for the Sundering of the worlds. It is also the place where a higher power can be felt, the one which controls the Wave and brings balance where it is needed.[22] Where Death's Gate is a corridor where all possibilities exist at once, the Seventh Gate is room which is "a hole in the fabric of magic wherein the possibility exists that no possibilities exist".[23] Where Death's Gate is a maelstrom of chaos, the Seventh Gate is calm, "a room with seven marble walls, covered by a domed ceiling. A globe suspended from the ceiling cast a soft, white glow. . . the words of warning remained inscribed on the walls: *Any who bring violence into this chamber will find it visited upon themselves*".[24] The Seventh Gate is a null place, with doors leading to each of the worlds of Air, Water, Fire, and Stone, the Labyrinth, the Nexus, and finally, Death's Gate itself.[25] While Samah, the architect of the Sundering, claimed to have created Death's Gate, it could be surmised that he did not design the chaos of it, but that it was instead the Wave correcting itself; in this universe of balance, the null possibility of the Seventh Gate could not exist without its counterpart. However, these two portals created the greatest imbalance in the series, between the living and the dead, as the existence of Death's Gate prevents the souls of the dead from leaving. This led to the Kenkari elves of Arianus storing the souls of their dead, and the necromancy which trapped the Sartan dead on Abarrach. Indeed, the trapping of souls by Death's Gate could be seen as the counteraction to the Sartans' violence against Earth in the Seventh Gate, as the raising of the dead on Abarrach likely killed Sartan on all the other worlds. (Even Alfred is not sure that this was the cause of the death of his fellow Sartan on Arianus, but it seems a likely explanation). By closing Death's Gate at the end of the series, the gate to the afterlife is opened.[26] The sacrifice for this spiritual travel is that the four worlds of Air, Water, Fire, and Stone are no longer physically accessible; however, this too is a restoration of balance, as will be explored later in this essay.

Having understood the groundwork of how magic and movement work in *The Death Gate Cycle*, it is important to understand how Weis and Hickman use the techniques of world-building to facilitate the reader's understanding of this world. It is telling that much of the information on how magic and Death's Gate operate does not come from the text, but rather from the Appendices. This is related to the structure of the novels; in *The Seventh Gate* (1991), Appendix I reveals that the series has not been written for a human reader, but rather is a history for the Sartan and the Patryn who now live together in the Nexus and the Labyrinth.[27] The text is intended to be structured as an historical account, and so the means Weis and Hickman use to engage the reader become part of the subcreation itself, beginning with textual world-building.

Textual world-building is perhaps most common across all fiction which engages in world-building. The first line of Stephen King's *The Dark Tower I: The Gunslinger* reads: "The man in black fled across the desert, and the gunslinger followed".[28] This is narrative, but it is also the reader's first glimpse of End-world, of a desert and a world where gunslingers still existed. At this point, the reader is unaware of who the villains and heroes are, or why one is chasing the other. It is not until *The Dark Tower IV: Wizard and Glass* (1997) that the relationship is fully understood; in fact, King halts the quest narrative for an entire book to fully explain the nature of the man in black's betrayal of the gunslinger.[29] This is perhaps the greatest weakness of textual world-building; as Mark J. P. Wolf points out:

> One of the cardinal rules often given to new writers has to do with narrative economy; they are told to pare down their prose and remove anything that does not actively advance the story. World-building, however, often results in data, exposition, and digressions that provide information about a world, slowing down narrative or even bringing it to a halt temporarily, yet much of the excess detail and descriptive richness can be an important part of the audience's experience.[30]

It is the disruption of narrative pacing that is the greatest risk in textual world-building, particularly in the "infodump", defined by Jeff Prucher as "a large amount of background information inserted into a story all at once".[31] The long quote at the beginning of this essay is something of an infodump; it is explained away by Lord Xar of the Patryn claiming that he is rambling, which is likely the result of his sharing a drink with Haplo.[32] However, the reader cannot rely on the potentially tipsy ramblings of characters to describe these worlds, and although Haplo is the logical conduit for world-building as an Innocent Abroad, acting as the kind of guide Farah Mendlesohn describes,[33] Weis and Hickman do not introduce him again until Chapter 17, page 120, when he is rescued by the dwarf revolutionary leader, Limbeck. However, where Haplo differs from an Innocent Abroad is that his apprehension of Arianus is not overt; rather he listens in to the conversations around him before speaking up to join the revolution.[34] This denial of Haplo's role as a potential Innocent Abroad is in keeping with his intended role as the harbinger of Patryn sovereignty over the realms; he is in essence a spy, intended to understand the sundered worlds so that Xar may reunite and conquer them.

In lieu of an Innocent Abroad and their associated guide, and in order to avoid infodumps, Weis and Hickman instead opt for using footnotes to enhance their world-building and give the reader needed context, and, in the later books, reminders. It is also in keeping with what we finally discover to be the historical nature of the series. According to Mendlesohn, the "experienced reader is conditioned to see footnotes as dry, as a way of grounding the text in reality. But footnotes are also an intervention, or intrusion into the flow of the text".[35] It can also be argued that footnotes can prevent world-building from being too intrusive in texts. Perhaps the two best known recent examples of footnotes are Terry Pratchett's *Discworld* series (1983–2015) and Susanna Clarke's *Johnathan Strange & Mr Norrell* (2004), which use footnotes for different primary purposes, but both of which have the secondary purpose of ensuring the integrity of the secondary world. Pratchett's footnotes are for the purpose of expanding on a joke:

> She still wasn't sure about Maladict, but Igor had to be a boy, with those stitches around the head and that face that could only be called homely.★
> ★And even then it was the kind of home that has a burned-out vehicle on the lawn.[36]

Pratchett's footnotes function as a jocular wink, an almost Shakespearian aside to the reader, inviting them into a joke, but more importantly they prevent the expanded joke from interfering with the narrative, particularly in the case of this example, where the footnote is more evocative of the Primary World rather than the Discworld. Clarke's footnotes are more focussed on world-building, in two ways. The first is in providing verisimilitude to the text, with the first footnote acting as an academic reference to an in-world text following a quote: "*The History and Practice of English Magic*, by Jonathan Strange, Vol. I, Chap. 2, pub. John Murray, London, 1816".[37] However, Clarke's footnotes also serve an important world-building function, as demonstrated by footnote 6 which follows this line: "Mr Segundus took down *The Instructions* of Jacques Belasis and, despite Mr Norrell's poor opinion of it, instantly hit upon two extraordinary passages".[38] The footnote then proceeds to take up over three quarters of the page, describing the two passages, which also give the reader information about the past of Clarke's world, as well as some details about fairies.[39] While this footnote is interesting, it is too much information to be included without disrupting the narrative. So for Clarke, footnotes are for the information which help construct her secondary creation, but which has no place in the narrative. It is, in fact, a way to present an infodump without boring the reader.

Weis and Hickman's use of footnotes is similar to Clarke's, though they have several variants and make interesting uses of them. The first footnote is in the first chapter of *Dragon Wing* and is used to explain what a tier is. What is unusual about this is that the footnote is not introduced until the fifth use of the word "tier" to explain that the tier is a large, mostly useless bird with powerful legs, used as a beast of burden by humans.[40] This footnote also gives the reader one of their first impressions of the cultural differences in Arianus, as it specifies that elves consider tiers "unclean", with strong implications that this view might extend to humans.[41] Weis and Hickman's use of the footnotes also allows them to give explanations for phenomena like Arianus's water-based currency[42] and floating islands[43] without interrupting the flow of Hugh the Hand's attempted execution.[44] As the Sartan and Patryn who are the intended readers for the series have no way of travelling to the other worlds, these footnotes give them the information they need to understand the text, without the need to refer to other documents.

Weis and Hickman also use their footnotes for more than just pure world-building. In *Dragon Wing*, there are 25 footnotes, with one in the Appendices, and all are dedicated to world-building. However, as the series progresses, footnotes become more referential for the series, as *The Seventh Gate* contains nine footnotes in the main text, with six in the Appendices. Of the nine footnotes in the text, eight engage in world-building, and one refers to the book's Appendix. Of the footnotes in the Appendices, the first is an explanatory note from the "author" of the Appendices, while the rest are references to other books in the series. In addition to providing new information, Weis and Hickman also reinforce their existing world-building. The 35th footnote in *The Hand of Chaos* (1993)[45] revisits the living stone coralite, which is explained in the third footnote of *Dragon Wing*,[46] giving new information and refreshing the reader's memory of what the substance is, particularly as it has not been mentioned for the intervening three books.

Footnotes are also used to refer to the next technique Weis and Hickman use: Appendices, with Chapters 26 and 27 of *The Hand of Chaos* containing three footnotes to refer the reader to the first Appendix of the book, which explains the assassin's society called The Brotherhood of the Hand.[47] This is where Weis and Hickman's ability to balance their world-building techniques is at its height; the encounters with The Brotherhood of the Hand are tense, filled with intrigue, and to interrupt them to explain the assassins' society, even in a footnote, would interrupt the narrative flow. Instead the Appendices are designed to enhance the world-building and engage the reader once the action has finished. The Appendices of *The Death Gate Cycle* are prolific, encompassing 12 distinct Appendices, and eight songs, and ranging from treatises on Sartan and Patryn magic to discussions of the nature of the living islands on Chelestra, to explanations of the workings of the great machine, the Kicksey-winsey, on Arianus. However, like Clarke's first footnote, the Appendices of *The Death Gate Cycle* seek to insert verisimilitude in the text by having different authors, ranging from unknown Sartan and Patryn to reports from Alfred and Haplo, and even a sales brochure for the submersibles of Chelestra, with explanatory footnotes by Alfred.[48] It is the Appendices which serve to demystify Sartan and Patryn magic, with in-depth and highly technical descriptions of the possibility magic which both use. This complements the in-text references to drawing runes with magical effects, as the technical detail has no place in the narrative. In Chapter 54 of *Dragon Wing*, Sartan magic is described as follows:

> Slowly, gently thrusting aside the dog, Alfred rose to his feet. Walking to the center of the room, he lifted his arms into the air and began to move in a solemn and strangely graceful —for his ungainly body— dance. . .
>
> The air around him began to shimmer as his dancing continued. He was tracing the runes in the air with his hands and drawing them on the floor with his feet.[49]

In comparison, the Appendices of *Dragon Wing* has the following description:

> The key to rune (or runic) magic is that the harmonic wave that weaves a possibility into existence must be created with as much simultaneity as possible. This means that the various motions, signs, words, thoughts and elements that go into making up the harmonic wave must be completed as close together as possible.[50]

The difference is stark. The in-text description of magic is almost lyrical at times, whereas the Appendix is scientific. This is easily explained by the nature of the intended Sartan and Patryn audience, who, from a young age, must be educated in possibility magic. The technical details are meant to assist them in understanding their world, using language that they would be immediately familiar with. This reinforces the role of the Appendices as being for further edification and information, and not immediately necessary for the reader to understand the narrative. This is what differentiates Appendices from foot-notes; footnotes are what the authors feel the reader needs to know immediately, while Appendices are meant to be engaged with after the action, with both serving to bolster and enrich the existing textual world-building.

The final world-building technique is that of maps. Mendlesohn describes how in the quest narrative, "the portal is not encoded solely in the travelogue discovery of what lies ahead, but in the insistence that there is past and place *behind*, and that what lies behind must be thoroughly known and unquestioned before the journey begins".[51] However, this sense of history, of people creating and naming places in a map, is thrown over in *The Death Gate Cycle* by the fact that the maps are fairly incomprehensible on their own. The expected roads, rivers, mountains, towns, and oceans the fantasy reader expects are often absent. Arianus is a series of floating islands divided into areas called High Realm, Mid Realm, and Low Realm, all contained within an ovoid shell, with a sun at the top and a maelstrom just above a smaller ovoid labelled "Death Gate". The other two maps of Arianus show Mid Realm in greater detail, and the Volkaran Isles, a small archipelago in Mid Realm, where most of the action of *Dragon Wing* takes place. The second and third maps also include something not normally seen in fantasy maps: orbit lines. However, these maps do not make sense until the reader has begun reading *Dragon Wing*, particularly its footnote on page 14, which explains how the islands float. The maps are more than something for the reader to refer to during the quest journey, but rather something for the reader to interpret and understand in conjunction with the narrative, and a great machine, the Kicksey-winsey, which is meant to bring the islands into alignment and turn the world into a manufacturing base. However, the Kicksey-winsey is not working as it should, and the islands are out of alignment. So not only is the map of Arianus difficult to read without the text, but it is also a map of a failed system; when the islands come into alignment in *Into the Labyrinth* (1993), there is no map of how they were always meant to look. Like the intended Sartan and Patryn audience, the reader is left to imagine what a balanced and functioning Arianus looks like.

In contrast to the complete map of all of Arianus, Pryan, the world of fire, is only a partial map, of the known world of Equilan. This is because Pryan is so large —a fantasy Dyson sphere with four suns in its center and life covering the inside of the sphere— that Weis and Hickman chose not to attempt to show it. And even though Equilan has elements familiar to the reader, such as seas and what appears to be landmasses, the text undermines this: the seas of Equilan are actually on the top of a massive canopy of trees so deep that no one on Pryan has seen the ground. Even more confusing are the maps of the dwarven Kingdoms of Equilan, until the reader learns that this is a map of a quasi-cave system, which, while closer to the ground, is still within the trees. As with Arianus, the reader must engage with the text before understanding truly comes about.

Abarrach, the world of stone, and Chelestra, the world of water, are both slightly more traditionally represented, in that both are shown in whole in the void. Abarrach is the only world of the four which is spherical, but unlike traditional globes, it is the cross section of the immense cave structure which is shown. From the information he had access to before he left the Nexus, Haplo's expectations are that of "a world of tunnels and caves, a world of cool and earthy-smelling darkness", but instead he finds himself on a river of fire.[52] This leads the reader to the realization that "fire sea" on the map is a literal description of the sea. So the reader realizes, along with Haplo, that the rivers and lakes on the map are filled with magma, not water. There is also an historical element to Abarrach's maps which is not seen in the other maps; namely, sections with the words "Here the fire sea once flowed" and "Ancient Home of the Little People".[53] After two other books, the reader is aware that the "Little People" were the dwarves, and it is clear that some ecological catastrophe is underway.

Chelestra is an ovoid which is divided into four sections: Longnight, Good-sea, Barrens, and Newbirth, all of which are meaningless to the reader, as is the term Seasun. Throughout the novel, the reader learns that the sun of Chelestra is within the water, and warms certain areas as it moves. As a result, the four sections of Chelestra, of which Goodsea is the most habitable region, are constantly in flux. At this stage, however, the reader can expect to need guidance from the text to understand the maps.

The final map is found in *The Hand of Chaos* and shows the Nexus at the center of the four elemental worlds, as well as diagrams indicating the movement of materials and energy. The reader will be familiar with these connections, however, as with the technical descriptions of magic, there is more to the map than meets the eye. In Appendix II of *The Hand of Chaos*, a technical report from Haplo on Death's Gate and the conduits reveal that all of the realms do not orbit each other, but actually occupy the same space, "harmonically shifted into several different realities. These harmonic realities manifest themselves into the various partitioned realities that we perceive as fire, water, earth, and sky, as well as special subrealities we know as the Nexus and the Labyrinth".[54] In a single Appendices, Weis and Hickman rewrite everything the reader knows about the subcreation they have been engaging with. As subrealities, the Nexus and the Labyrinth are essentially less real than the elemental worlds, and so the trapping of the Sartan and Patryn within them is essential for the final act of balance in *The Death Gate Cycle*: the sociocultural balance.

As a portal text, it is important to understand how the portal affects the sociocultural makeup of each of the worlds, whether or not the characters are aware of the portal. For Arianus, the portal is unwittingly the center of their world, as it is meant to power the very machine that keeps them alive by providing water. However, as the power is not being drawn from Pryan, the effect of the portal is to create a tiered society of vast injustices, bolstered by the inherent racism of the elves. When *Dragon Wing* begins, the humans have only recently won freedom from their Elvish occupiers, and the dwarves remain in thrall to the elves, who they see as gods. However, in Alfred's final summation of the events of the series in the Appendix to *The Seventh Gate*, the reader learns that this was intentional; the Sartan had given the elves instructions on the proper operation of the Kicksey-winsey, which would unite the floating islands of the elves and humans, and give the dwarves control of the machine, and therefore the water supply.[55] This serves to underscore a recurring theme in the series, which is the Sartans' misunderstanding of the relationships between humans, elves, and dwarves, referred to as "mensch" races, and the effects of their own treatment of them. In *Serpent Mage*, Samah refers to the mensch races as children and is insistent that they needed Sartan guidance, and that the Patryn were trying to corrupt them.[56] And although Alfred, who has spent years among the mensch pretending to be one, tries to defend them, the other Sartan are similarly convinced that the mensch need guidance. Even Haplo's original mission, to sow discord and to find a disciple to help the Patryn control the mensch, makes a presumption that they are lesser beings. Indeed, it is notable that the work of Arianus, particularly of maintaining the Kicksey-winsey, falls to the mensch. Whether they are willing to describe them as such, the Sartan are using the mensch as a form of slave labor, allowing themselves to be worshipped and served. In general, the mensch are not aware of the Sundering, and do not realize that their long-lost gods killed most of their populations simply to maintain their own control. The divisions seen on Arianus can also be seen on Pryan in *Elven Star*, and given the favoritism shown to elves on Arianus,[57] it can be presumed that this was in play on the other worlds.

While there are indications that other areas of Pryan have found peace between the races, the only world where mensch are fully described as living in harmony, despite their differences, is Chelestra, where the Sartan had the least amount of influence on their civilization, as the Sartan banished them from the comfortable Chalice structure once they began to quarrel among themselves. After thousands of years without Sartan interference, and forced to live together in relatively close quarters, the princesses of the humans, elves, and dwarves "became closer than most sisters", with the dwarven princess appreciating her Human friend's hurry as a sign of her mortality, and her Elven friend's leisure as a sign of her long life. The importance of the absence of demi-gods to the mensch relations is best seen when their rulers first encounter Samah and the Sartan Council, a group used to the wonder of the mensch, and to their squabbling.[58] Samah's attempt to show favor by using human language falls flat, as the mensch have long understood each other's languages as a sign of respect and kinship, as does his attempt to impress them by materializing golden chairs.[59] The meeting devolves further as Samah is unable to understand that the squabbling "children" have evolved socially, to the point where they offer to negotiate peace between the Sartan and the Patryn, much as they did for themselves.[60] When the Sartan offer to let them stay on their lands, and that they will govern and educate themselves, the mensch are offended at the presumption of their inability.[61] When the mensch offer to make the Sartan an equal partner in their alliance, Samah becomes outraged, reminding them that they had once worshipped the Sartan, which serves only to confuse the mensch, who now worship one god, the one who controls the Wave, bringing balance.[62] This interaction demonstrates the vast imbalance between the self-declared demi-gods and the mensch. The Sartan could never respect the mensch enough to trust them to govern themselves, to eventually resolve their differences and come together. As such, there could never be balance between the races as long as the Sartan and the Patryn were present to exert a controlling influence.

It is no coincidence that the only group of mensch who interact peacefully worship this power; the Sartan encountered the power before they sundered the world, and learned that they could have lived in peace with the Patryn without the Sundering.[63] However, fear and doubt as to their experience of the higher power did not allow them to try another path. This fear and doubt combined with the violence of the Sundering to create another imbalance, as the "evil that had always existed in the world prior to the Sundering had now gained the power to take on physical shape and form. Evil was manifested in the serpents or dragon-snakes".[64] The Wave attempted to correct this by the creation of the good dragons of Pryan, but this was prevented by Samah's fear of the serpents, as he closed Death's Gate and sent the Seventh Gate away.[65] The Wave corrected itself by Chelestra's sun moving away from the Sartan and the serpents, both of whom were frozen for thousands of years.

It is at this point that it is necessary to presume some higher plan by the Wave in the series, as Chelestra's sun's return to awaken the Sartan and the serpents happens just as the unlikely friendship between a Sartan and a Patryn has sprung up between Alfred and Haplo. Both men are quintessential archetypes of their people, arrogant in their own way, mistrusting each other, each convinced that their own way is the right way. Alfred is convinced of the rightness of the Sartans actions, where Haplo has experienced first-hand just how cruel the results became. It could be surmised that the swapping of consciousness experienced in Death's Gate was more than just the swapping of memories as a temporary, but intentional, sharing of soul and consciousness to bring them together to destroy the Seventh Gate and Death's Gate. When Lord Xar attempts to ensure Haplo's loyalty through emotional and physical torture, the dog, a part of Haplo's soul, disappears.[66] However, it reappears next to Alfred later in the novel, at a point where he defended the mensch's good qualities against their bad, by saying "I found that it all balanced itself out, somehow".[67] The dog's appearance is an indicator of their linked souls, reinforced by Alfred recounting Haplo's experiences in the Labyrinth as if he were Haplo, and becomes the balance between their souls, emblematic of the loyalty they feel toward each other.[68] The dog's existence and link to Alfred later prevents Lord Xar from raising Haplo as a lazar, [69] but disappears once it enters the Seventh Gate, as Haplo's soul is made whole in order to be revived and help Alfred to restore the balance. The disruption to the plan to restore balance is the presence of the serpents, feeding off hate, strife, and chaos, who seek to not only create a war between the Sartan and Patryn in the Nexus and the Labyrinth, but who also try to ensure that Lord Xar would attempt to reform the Earth and fail:

> 'Thank you, Lord of the Nexus, for casting the spell to tear down the worlds,' said the serpent, its head rearing upward. 'It was, I admit, a plan we had not considered. But it will work out well for us. We will feed off the turmoil and chaos for eons to come. And your people, trapped forever in the Labyrinth.'[70]

However, the serpent does not realize that the Seventh Gate is a place of equilibrium, so its attempts to unbalance the world cannot succeed there.[71] Once the green dragons of Pryan enter the Labyrinth, they act as the counter to the serpents they were meant to be, with the battle between the Sartan and Patryn ending with a truce between a necromancer Sartan and a half-Sartan, half-Patryn resident of the Labyrinth. Therefore, by their actions in sealing the Sartan, Patryn, serpents, and dragons into the Nexus and the Labyrinth, Alfred and Haplo not only create the potential for balance between their own peoples, but also give this potential to the mensch. With no demi-gods to claim their right to rule over them, the mensch have the opportunity to find their own balance.

The exploration of the worlds of *The Death Gate Cycle* is ultimately an exploration of hope; the Wave is both a force for good, and a preserver of free will; it gave the Sartan the choice to fight for balance, but the freedom not to, a choice which they themselves denied the mensch. However, the Wave also used both a Sartan and a Patryn to begin the process of restoring balance; the dead would be free to move on, the mensch could solve their own problems, and the Sartan and Patryn found peace at last, by joining each other in their magics. The four elemental worlds remained connected by conduits that would allow them to function, because no one element could survive on its own. As with the peoples and magic of the series, the worlds functioned best when they worked together, even if it took thousands of years to create the balance between them.

Notes

1 Weis, W., and Hickman, T., *The Death Gate Cycle Volume 1: Dragon Wing*, New York: Bantam Spectra, 1990, page 2.
2 Ibid., pages 1–3.
3 Ibid., pages vii–x.
4 *The Death Gate Cycle Volume 1: Dragon Wing* (1990), *The Death Gate Cycle Volume 2: Elven Star* (1990), *The Death Gate Cycle Volume 3: Fire Sea* (1991), *The Death Gate Cycle Volume 4: Serpent Mage* (1992), *The Death Gate Cycle Volume 5: The Hand of Chaos* (1993), *The Death Gate Cycle Volume 6: Into the Labyrinth* (1993), and *The Death Gate Cycle Volume 7: The Seventh Gate* (1994), New York: Bantam Spectra.
5 Weis and Hickman, *The Death Gate Cycle Volume 1: Dragon Wing*, pages 418–419.
6 Ibid., page 419.
7 Weis, W., and Hickman, T., *The Death Gate Cycle Volume 2: Elven Star*, New York: Bantam Spectra, 1990, pages 361–367.
8 Weis , W., and Hickman, T., *The Death Gate Cycle Volume 4: Serpent Mage*, New York: Bantam Spectra, 1992, page 377.
9 Ibid.
10 Weis, W., and Hickman, T., *The Death Gate Cycle Volume 7: The Seventh Gate*, New York: Bantam Spectra, 1994, pages 300–301.
11 Ibid., page 308.
12 Weis and Hickman, *The Death Gate Cycle Volume 1: Dragon Wing*, page 142.
13 "Lost and Found", *Haven*, Season 4, Episode 5, 2013, Syfy channel.

14 Farah Mendlesohn, *Rhetorics of Fantasy*, Middletown, Connecticut: Wesleyan University Press, 2008, page 2.

15 Weis and Hickman, *The Death Gate Cycle Volume 4: Serpent Mage*, page 296.

16 Weis, W., and Hickman, T., *The Death Gate Cycle Volume 5: The Hand of Chaos*, New York: Bantam Spectra, 1993, pages 454–456.

17 Weis and Hickman, *The Death Gate Cycle Volume 7: The Seventh Gate*, pages 325–326.

18 Weis, W., and Hickman, T., *The Death Gate Cycle Volume 3: Fire Sea*, New York: Bantam Spectra, 1991, pages 1–2.

19 Ibid., pages 62–64.

20 Ibid., pages 64–69.

21 Weis and Hickman, *The Death Gate Cycle Volume 4: Serpent Mage*, pages 228–229.

22 Ibid., page 239.

23 Weis and Hickman, *The Death Gate Cycle Volume 7: The Seventh Gate*, page 321.

24 Ibid., page 233.

25 Ibid., page 238.

26 Ibid., page 306.

27 Ibid., page 334.

28 King, Stephen, *The Dark Tower I: The Gunslinger*, Hampton Falls, New Hampshire: Donald M. Grant, 1982.

29 King, Stephen, *The Dark Tower IV: Wizard and Glass*, Hampton Falls, New Hampshire: Donald M. Grant, 1997.

30 Wolf, Mark J. P., *Building Imaginary Worlds: The Theory and History of Subcreation*, New York: Routledge, 2012. page 29.

31 Prucher, J., *Brave New Words: The Oxford Dictionary of Science Fiction*, Oxford, England: Oxford University Press, 2007, page 98.

32 Weis and Hickman, *The Death Gate Cycle Volume 1: Dragon Wing*, pages 1–2.

33 Mendlesohn, *Rhetorics of Fantasy*, page 13.

34 Weis and Hickman, *The Death Gate Cycle Volume 1: Dragon Wing*, page 147.

35 Mendlesohn, *Rhetorics of Fantasy*, page 167.

36 Pratchett, Terry, *Monstrous Regiment: A Discworld Novel*, London, England: Doubleday, 2003, page 181.

37 Clarke, S., *Jonathan Strange & Mr Norrell*, London, England: Bloomsbury Publishing, 2004, page 3.

38 Ibid., page 14.

39 Ibid.

40 Weis and Hickman, *The Death Gate Cycle Volume 1: Dragon Wing*, page 7.

41 Ibid.

42 Ibid., page 8.

43 Ibid., page 14.

44 Ibid., pages 4–17.

45 Weis and Hickman, *The Death Gate Cycle Volume 5: The Hand of Chaos*, page 189.

46 Weis and Hickman, *The Death Gate Cycle Volume 1: Dragon Wing*, page 14.

47 Weis and Hickman, *The Death Gate Cycle Volume 5: The Hand of Chaos*, pages 268–288.

48 Weis and Hickman, *The Death Gate Cycle Volume 4: Serpent Mage*, pages 427–436.

49 Weis and Hickman, *The Death Gate Cycle Volume 1: Dragon Wing*, page 397.

50 Ibid., page 422.

51 Mendlesohn, *Rhetorics of Fantasy*, page 14.

52 Weis and Hickman, *The Death Gate Cycle Volume 3: Fire Sea*. New York: Bantam Spectra. p. 71–72.

53 Ibid. p. vi–vii.

54 Weis and Hickman, *The Death Gate Cycle Volume 5: The Hand of Chaos*, page 453.

55 Weis and Hickman, *The Death Gate Cycle Volume 7: The Seventh Gate*, page 330.
56 Weis and Hickman, *The Death Gate Cycle Volume 4: Serpent Mage*, pages 297–298.
57 Weis and Hickman, *The Death Gate Cycle Volume 7: The Seventh Gate*, page 330.
58 Weis and Hickman, *The Death Gate Cycle Volume 4: Serpent Mage*, pages 338–342.
59 Ibid., pages 338–340.
60 Ibid., page 340.
61 Ibid., page 341.
62 Ibid., pages 341–342.
63 Ibid., page 239.
64 Weis and Hickman, *The Death Gate Cycle Volume 7: The Seventh Gate*, page 326.
65 Ibid., page 326-328
66 Weis and Hickman, *The Death Gate Cycle Volume 4: Serpent Mage*, pages 9–11.
67 Ibid., page 127.
68 Ibid., pages 228–229.
69 Weis and Hickman, *The Death Gate Cycle Volume 7: The Seventh Gate*, page 100.
70 Ibid., pages 274–275.
71 Ibid., page 285.

11

WELCOME TO THE "SECOND-STAGE" LYNCHVERSE

Twin Peaks: *The Return* and the Impossibility of Return Vs. Getting a Return

Matt Hills

Despite being relatively short-lived as an ABC television series in the 1990s (1990–1991), and returning as a one-off film *Twin Peaks: Fire Walk With Me* in 1992, *Twin Peaks* has continued to cast a long cultural shadow. It has been positioned as both "classic" and "cult" television (Garner, 2016), and as Mark J. P. Wolf argues in *Building Imaginary Worlds* (2012), even "smaller-scale series… began franchises; *Twin Peaks*, for example, inspired a feature film, several books, an audio book, and a set of trading cards" (2012, p. 124). More than this, however, the enduring fandom for *Twin Peaks* (Halskov, 2015, p. 214) made it a show that remained ripe for reinvention long after its cancellation (Williams, 2015, p. 178), and fans were duly rewarded when *Twin Peaks: The Return* was formally announced as a Showtime project on October 6, 2014. After a troubled pre-production process, when co-creator and proto-showrunner (Newman and Levine, 2012, pp. 26–27) David Lynch's involvement became unclear (Williams, 2016), *The Return* eventually premiered on May 21, 2017. With Lynch asserting in pre-publicity that he viewed the production as one lengthy "film" that just happened to be divided up into arbitrary "Parts" for transmission (rather than "episodes" of a television serial; see Biderman et al., 2019, p. 179), and with Lynch also directing every one of the 18 "Parts", it was perhaps inevitable that this third season of *Twin Peaks* would be viewed as a strong re-assertion of Lynchian ownership and auteurism.

Martha Nochimson's study of the imaginary worlds realized across Lynch's *oeuvre* characterizes these as sharing specific qualities. Indeed, Nochimson goes so far as to refer to a "Lynchverse" (2013, p. 163), arguing that multiple imaginary worlds can be explored as linked, not diegetically but rather "omnidiegetically" via authorial statements and strategies (Atkinson, 2014, p. 7). With this in mind, Nochimson divides Lynch's works into "first-stage" and "second-stage" phases, suggesting that in "Lynch's first-stage cinema, he creates some fascinating representations of *parallel* worlds, but nothing as disturbing to the traditional worldview as what emerges in his later work" (2013, p. 13). This stage includes the original *Twin Peaks* (Nochimson, 2013, p. 167), whilst the second-stage is identified as running from *Lost Highway* (1997) to *Inland Empire* (2006) (Nochimson, 2013, pp. 1 and 11), and would also presumably include *The Return*. Rather than presenting ontologically multiple but stable parallel worlds, e.g., the town of Twin Peaks interacting with the otherworldly realms of the Black Lodge and Red Room in 1990s *Twin Peaks*, Nochimson argues that "second-stage" Lynch adopts a more quantum-mechanics-indebted perspective, instead representing "the dissolution of the external world" (2013, p. 8) in his films in favor of a poeticized "many worlds" orientation (2013, p. 13). Rather than parallel but intersecting worlds being narratively focused upon, there is a more pluralistic, multiversal set of possibilities, and a more radically destabilized sense of diegetic ontology on show. These are not primary/secondary or even tertiary worlds, but "n+1" worlds where the imaginary is seemingly multiplied into diverse fractions and fragments. Cultural theorist Mark Fisher makes a similar argument in *The Weird and the Eerie* (2016), observing that 1990s *Twin Peaks* was constructed around a "division between worlds. . . often marked by one of Lynch's frequently recurring visual motifs, curtains", whereas by the time of *Mulholland Drive*, "the stability of the opposition which has structured. . . *Twin Peaks* begins to collapse" (2016, p. 53). In place of the "superficial coherence" of a "real" versus a "fantastical" narrative world, this later Lynchian approach instead "proliferates embedded worlds" (ibid).

In this essay, I want to follow Nochimson (2013) and Fisher (2016), considering how *Twin Peaks: The Return* can be explored as part of this "second-stage" Lynchverse. I will begin by analyzing how the show's reinvention suggests that there can be no nostalgic and "fan service" return to the established franchise of 1990s *Twin Peaks* —it is not simply that the past is a different country, but rather that the latest version of the series allegedly refuses to stabilize into a singular narrative ontology, instead offering what, in Mark Fisher's terms, can be identified as a mode of "world-haemorrhaging. . . [resulting in] a terrain subject to ontological subsidence" (Fisher, 2016, p. 58). However, I will then move on to argue that *The Return* cannot simply be characterized as a multiversal evasion of fan service and any stable imaginary world. In fact, it also offers a "return" or pay-off on fans' long-term affective investments by setting out a new "backstory" (Metz, 2017), or even an "origin story" (Hallam, 2018, p. 118), for evil supernatural forces such as BOB which have populated its storyworld. As such, *The Return* may seem to problematize the relative or "superficial" coherence of 1990s *Twin Peaks*, but it also constitutes a new exploration of the franchise, revising and reshaping its prior imaginary world in terms of a renovated (and no less coherent) mythos. This iteration of "second-stage" Lynch, then, very much rewards enduring fans at the same time as frustrating what Lynch imagines and projects throughout the text as a normative type of "fan service" (Hills, 2018, p. 317). But if the brand's reimagining frustrates and fascinates by design, I will begin with its frustration of fan expectations and world-building hopes.

World-Hemorrhaging and the Impossibility of Return: "What Year Is This?"

Where the original *Twin Peaks* had been accompanied by *The Secret Diary of Laura Palmer* (1990) (see Hallam, 2018, p. 103), *The Return* is book-ended by two official tie-in books written by series co-creator Mark Frost; *The Secret History of Twin Peaks* (2016) and *The Final Dossier* (2017). However, these books seem to work in a highly distinctive way. For example, *The Secret History* contains a number of continuity "variations". Given that Mark Frost produced this title, and was both "the co-creator and co-showrunner of *Twin Peaks*, these inaccuracies do not seem to be the result of shoddy research" (2019, p. 171), as Donald McCarthy has observed. Why else might a by-now standard mode of transmedia world-building and narrative expansion present continuity "errors"? McCarthy notes how

> For instance, Norma Jennings' mother is described as having died in 1984 when, in fact, she appeared alive and well in the television series. The novel also has an excerpt that describes how Ed and Nadine (Wendy Robie) became a couple, which involves Ed going to Vietnam, an aspect of their relationship that is never discussed in the television series. The specifics of how Nadine lost her eye are also at odds with a monologue Ed gives in the second season premiere of the program.
>
> *(2019, p. 171)*

Such details are not central to *Twin Peaks*'s established meanings and mythology, perhaps, but they nevertheless challenge the fan cultural capital and knowledge amassed by attentive fans over the years, threatening to undermine the "epistemological economy" (Hastie, 2007, p. 81) of *Twin Peaks*'s fan-created guides and wikis. Rather than reinforcing a sense of one coherent or canonical imaginary world which can be mapped by its fandom, and iterated by its creators, *Twin Peaks* starts to dissolve here into multiple versions. In fact, this "world-haemorrhaging" (Fisher, 2016, p. 58) is even more starkly portrayed in *The Return*, which sent

> Agent Cooper back to February 23, 1989... in Part 17 to ensure that the murder of Laura Palmer (Sheryl Lee) never occurred. This act of unraveling—which placed present-day Dale Cooper in familiar 25-year-old scenes with Laura Palmer and reused footage from the series pilot from which the plastic-sheathed corpse had been removed—epitomizes

the way *The Return* both revives and undermines the original show's established patterns.

(Fallis and King, 2019, pp. 55–56)

Nor does *The Final Dossier* restore any sense of final narrative determinacy after the cliffhanger ending of Part 18. As McCarthy concludes, "in keeping with the spirit of *Twin Peaks*, Frost. . . manages to retain mysteries that audiences were hoping would be solved. Whether Cooper changed the timeline when he went back in time to rescue Laura Palmer or just changed people's memories is still an open question" (2019, p. 180). Insofar as *The Return* and its transmedia tie-in fictions fit together, then, it is through a mode of "ontological subsidence" (Fisher, 2016, p. 58) where reader-viewers apparently cannot be sure of the settled events of *Twin Peaks*'s narrative, and where the ontological status of different timelines or multiversal possibilities also cannot be definitively confirmed. As Daniel Neofetou suggests in *Good Day Today: David Lynch Destabilizes the Spectator* (2012), "Lynch's films. . . could often be said to have syuzhets without fabulas, with their scenes composed in a manner which would appear to elucidate a diegetic reality, but which never does so to a satisfactorily coherent degree" (2012, pp. 11–12). By contrast, in 1990s *Twin Peaks*

> the Black Lodge *is* framed as a supernatural space and thereby. . . while Cooper's traversal of it certainly disorients the spectator. . . it does not necessarily leave the spectator destabilised on a fundamental level. . . Far more profound spectatorial destabilisation is cultivated, however, when the timespace of locales which have hitherto been established as coherent and quotidian in terms of the films' diegeses are problematized.

(Neofetou, 2012: 24)

And yet *The Return* does problematize the "coherent and quotidian" timespaces of Twin Peaks the town, both by suggesting that Laura Palmer was never murdered after all, and by returning an older, adult Laura —known as Carrie Page in what seems to be an alternative reality— to what had been the Palmer's house. In a stunning final cliffhanger, Carrie/Laura hears Sarah Palmer (Grace Zabriskie) calling her and responds with a terrified scream. Elsewhere, *The Return* has implied that Sarah is herself possessed by a dark elemental force, known as Judy, which is opposed to the light and life-force represented by Laura (Lowry, 2019, p. 46; Hallam, 2018, p. 118), all of which contextualizes this enigmatic ending as part of a recurrent supernatural struggle. But this reading remains fragmentary and ambiguous, just as it remains unclear how the different timelines and versions of "quotidian" Twin Peaks relate to one another, given that the events of 1990s *Twin Peaks* seem to be somehow bleeding over into the "Carrie Page" version of this reality. When Agent Cooper/ Richard asks "what year is this?" then he is expressing a level of doubt about the ontology of the timespace he has entered. Pondering *when* he is also raises the associated, unspoken question of just *where* he is, leaving the fabula —or what should be an objectively agreed-upon or derivable sequence of narrative events— opaque at best. Rebecca Williams also notes that Lynch has form in this regard, arguing that "Brand Lynch" (Todd, 2012, p. 108) means that

> Lynch's involvement [in *The Return*] does not necessarily provide the reassurance and security that we may expect; given his authorial status as someone who provides shock and surprise, as a creator of forms of cinematic ontological insecurity, fans cannot necessarily expect anything certain. As [Linda Ruth] Williams notes, Lynch's "marketing catchphrase is Expect the Unexpected" (2005: 40). *Twin Peaks'* predilection for mystery and uncertainty —for representing the uncanny and often attempting to shock and disorient the viewer— is well-known.
>
> *(Williams, 2016, p. 59)*

Rather than guaranteeing an auteurist sense of "ontological security", reinforcing fans' level of basic trust in the coherence and integrity of the imaginary world, Lynch's "trickster" authorial identity (Jenkins, 1995) instead consistently threatens to undermine any such certainty.

At the same time, *The Return* also recurrently undermines any notion of a nostalgic "return" to much-loved, familiar, and franchised fan pleasures. Although Kyle MacLachlan again plays Agent Dale Cooper, the denotative restoration of this character is delayed until Part 16 of 18. In place of fans' expected pleasures, MacLachlan plays Dougie Jones and Mr. C —these are fantastical refractions of Cooper, one an evil doppelgänger and the other an amnesiac, embodied imprisonment of Agent Cooper's true consciousness. As critics have observed, this slow-paced obstruction of Dale Cooper's actual narrative return self-reflexively engages with fans' "[a]nticipation, nostalgia, and the pleasures linked with these. . . [T]he discomfort of waiting produces a conscious viewer aware of the mechanics of storytelling" (Anderson, 2019, p. 190). Ironically, *The Return* is intensely pitched at original series fans, reuniting as many original cast members as possible, centrally involving co-creators Mark Frost and David Lynch, and liberally drawing on the brand "icons" of the original show such as its red curtains and distinctive chevron designs (Ryan, 2017). Yet it also "acknowledges that this is no time for nostalgia" (Lim, 2018, online), and sets out to frustrate fans' expectations. The same thing occurs around the character of Audrey Horne (Sherilyn Fenn), whose much-loved dance sequence (Gillan, 2016) is re-activated, only to terminate in an ontologically uncertain fate for the character, where it is radically unclear how her storyline does (or doesn't) relate to the rest of the third season. Indeed, she almost seems to feature in a different pocket universe or "world" to the rest of the characters (Anderson, 2019, p. 191; Hawkes, 2019, p. 158). Returning to beloved fan favorites seems to only be possible on the basis that fans accept that familiar figures of *Twin Peaks* will be refracted, reflected, and distorted in unexpected ways —the final, jolting appearance of Audrey Horne shows her starkly confronting her puzzled, unmade-up face in a mirror. The imaginary world of the series is not additively accumulated here, instead breaking up into disconnected fragments of narrative non-sense and ambiguity.

David McAvoy argues that with *The Return*, Lynch's investment in a mode of artistic television that's coterminous with his "second-stage" and multiversal films results in the director actively trolling fans:

> [D]esigned to upset the kinds of Peak TV expectations about narrative 'payoff' created by the online fandom of *Twin Peaks*'s original run, *The Return* instead validates the patience it takes to simply sit, marking time's passage as its own fulfilling aesthetic experience... But beyond simply a television auteur setting out to upset our expectations, Lynch is more aggressively trollish in his disdain for what fans want from a Peak TV version of *Twin Peaks*. Lynch has a habit of taking his aggression with the system of television out on the fans who love him most: lest we forget, he opened his theatrical film expansion of this universe in *Twin Peaks: Fire Walk with Me* (1992) with a television set smashed with a sledgehammer.
>
> *(McAvoy, 2019, p. 98)*

If *Fire Walk With Me* represents a world-building continuation of *Twin Peaks* which is also a partial reset in favor of Lynch's vision for the show, then *The Return* represents further revisionism via Lynch's asserted artistic vision — elements from Season Two, disliked by Lynch, are blatantly ignored (Fallis and King, 2019, pp. 55–56). Continuity with *Fire Walk With Me* is instead emphasized in a series of ways, most especially via a focus on Agent Jeffries (David Bowie) and the Blue Rose agents' investigation into the mysterious "Judy" (Hallam, 2018, pp. 107 and 114–115).

But much of *The Return* quite simply refuses to cohere into a familiar revisiting of the show's imaginary world. As McAvoy argues (2019, p. 91), the latest run of episodes offers an internalized image of its attentive fans via the character of Sam (Ben Rosenfield) being instructed to watch an intensely technologically monitored glass box. For long periods of time nothing at all happens, and it is only when Sam is distracted, and not paying proper attention, that a violent supernatural force blinks into existence in the box, promptly escapes its confines, and savages the hapless watcher. Consequently, the figure of Sam has been read as coding "forensic fandom" (Garner, 2017, online), where

> The entire tableau is a warning to fans: be sure to watch the glass box extremely carefully, using all of the tools at your disposal, even when it

appears that nothing is happening... or you will miss the most important, indelible, and unique images that the show has to offer. This premiere episode allegory tells us that not adopting the kind of online forensic fandom that characterized only the most ardent viewers of the original run is the way of narrative death... And yet, that metaphor builds into it the antagonism and tricksterism fans had already come to know and love: watch closely, Lynch seems to say, but also prepare to be bored for long stretches of time.

(McAvoy, 2019, p. 91; see also Hawkes, 2019, p. 153)

However, by stressing a lack of narrative pay-off and ontological coherence, this approach fails to focus on the ways in which *The Return does* reward long-term fans. That is to say, the series does not collapse entirely into boredom, deferral, and world-hemorrhaging or ontological fracture, despite much of it being preoccupied with such frustrations, and hence with the performative cultural capital of sophisticated "art television" (Thompson, 2003; Polan, 2007). In the next section, I want to mount a counter-argument to the almost critical orthodoxy which has replayed David Lynch's auteurist discourses of "trickster" TV, instead considering how long-term fan investments are, in actuality, offered specific "returns" on their accumulated (fan) cultural capital.

World-Reshaping and Getting a Return: "Gotta Light?"

Though it has been tempting for critics and scholars to (re)produce a narrative of *The Return*'s "ontological subsidence" (Fisher, 2016, p. 58) via its dispersal into discontinuity and multiple timelines, or what I've previously called the "fan disservice" of character dislocation and deferral (Hills, 2018, p. 317), it is important to consider how *Twin Peaks*' imaginary world is not simply destabilized or multiplied in the third season. At the very moment that *The Return* most clearly indicates Lynch's bid for cultural distinction via art discourses — namely the black-and-white experimentalism of Part 8, "Gotta Light?"— it is also marked by conventional franchise world-building. This same episode, as Walter Metz has noted, "reveals the hidden backstory of *Twin Peaks*: The murder of Laura Palmer has its roots in the creation of American evil, the development of atomic weapons" (2017, online). The supernatural, demonic force known as BOB, which has constituted *Twin Peaks*'s major antagonist, is shown to enter the diegetic world in relation to America's 1945 "Trinity" testing of the atomic bomb.

Whilst unexpectedly stepping back in narrative time, this Part also shows a young woman going on a date in 1956; we witness her being attacked by a bizarre frog-moth hybrid which crawls into her open mouth while she's asleep. Fans immediately speculated that this woman was Sarah Palmer, who would go on to become Laura's mother (Joyce, 2019, p. 24), and this theory was indeed confirmed in Mark Frost's 2017 *Final Dossier* book (McCarthy, 2019, p. 180). The implication of this cryptic scene is that an otherworldly entity has taken up residence within Sarah Palmer —something that is narratively affirmed by her supernatural, murderous powers in Part 14— implying that she has been commandeered as a vehicle for "Judy", a female counterpart to BOB which *The Return* establishes as a new narrative threat.

Part 8 therefore introduces both BOB and Judy as players in the ontological reality of *Twin Peaks* "ordinary" world, but it also features an entirely new backstory for Laura Palmer. As Lindsay Hallam puts it,

> In Part 8, a truly ground-breaking episode of television that seems to play out a possible origin story for the larger forces that emanate from beyond the world, both positive and negative, there is a moment where a golden orb is formed, and inside it is the image of Laura Palmer from her Homecoming photograph.
>
> *(2018, p. 118)*

This golden orb fits into a pattern established in other moments of *The Return*, where "light signaling love typically turns to gold. . . For instance, when Carl joins the grieving mother at the side of the road he watches her child's spirit, a yellow light, float into the air (Season 3, Ep. 6). The same golden orb is seen when Dido and the Fireman ostensibly send Laura down to earth—a golden orb of light" (Lowry, 2019, p. 46). The representation of BOB and Laura as cast into *Twin Peaks*'s everyday world in this way suggests that they are part of an ongoing epic struggle between elemental forces of light and dark, or good and evil, which long predates the events of *Twin Peaks* Season One, and possibly even predates the atomic bomb's testing (Ewins, 2018, p. 36). As Ashlee Joyce notes, this calls into question any cultural-political reading of Part 8 which sees

> the idea of the bomb as the birth of evil. . . [N]uclear war might not in fact be a starting point for evil but, instead, merely its latest iteration. . . . [T]he idea of BOB/Judy as ancient entities that connect the evil of the bomb to something much older. . . reinforces. . . [an] "apolitical" posture that. . . downplays the specific politics of nuclear armament.
>
> *(Joyce, 2019, p. 25)*

By moving back to 1945 and 1956, and moving far outside the town of Twin Peaks, *The Return* is able to open up a new set of storyworld questions and answers. Joyce argues that, in fact, Part 8's "visuals offer a key to the entire *Twin Peaks* mythology (or at least as close to a key as fans of David Lynch can ever hope to expect). For audiences of Lynch's work, this is what we crave" (2019, p. 13). This is not so different from the narrative maneuvers of *Twin Peaks* Season Two where, as Marc Dolan has pointed out,

> plots. . . moved forward by moving backward, filling in more and more of the enigmatic "backstory" of the series in order to advance from the previously established narrative lines into fresh areas. This "backward, then forward" movement of the plot. . . is. . . [an] inventive solution to the standard continuous-serial problem of how to stimulate interest in the plotlines of future episodes in a way that is consistent with the raw material of previous ones.
>
> *(1995, p. 42)*

And likewise, by opening out its account of BOB and Laura, *The Return* is able to reshape its imaginary world into a seemingly timeless and potentially recurrent battle between elemental forces —with another cycle of struggles between Judy and Laura (in the guise of Carrie Page) apparently beginning at the end of Part 18. Yet this also preserves the series' prior narrative events and fan cultural capital or accumulated knowledge regarding established Lynchian continuity. Adding Judy centrally into the imaginary world, and showing Sarah Palmer as possessed by this entity, supplements the paternal evil of Leland Palmer/BOB with a maternal demonic presence, suggesting a particularly dark, twisted version of gender inclusivity and enhanced female agency. The fact that Sarah Palmer kills a vile, misogynistic male in Part 14 also fuels this reading. In any case, this new "backstory" (Metz, 2017, online) or "origin story" (Hallam, 2018, p. 118) sets out new ontological rules for the imaginary world of *Twin Peaks* rather than merely disrupting its previous incarnation.

Writing in the *Routledge Companion to Imaginary Worlds*, Benjamin J. Robertson rightly observes that any "discussion of backstory requires not only recognition of its importance to what takes place in a given world in the form of narrative, but the underlying conditions of that narrative, the ontology and epistemology of the world itself" (2018, pp. 38–39). To this end, he argues that "backstory" and "origin story" should be run together for imaginary worlds with fantastical aspects, representing "parts of the stories that explain "where they come from" not only in a psychological or sociological sense [as backstory does], but in an ontological one. That is, origin stories make clear that subsequent stories are authorized. . . because the world. . . operates in such a way" (Robertson, 2017, p. 39). It may thus be no accident that scholars have hesitated over describing Part 8 as "backstory" or "origin story", since it offers up both new narrative background and a reshaped ontology for *Twin Peaks* as a whole. Although *The Return* has already established that the Black Lodge can intersect with "ordinary" life, as "Black Lodge residents roam America" (Hawkes, 2019,

p. 156) in a more thorough-going encroachment than that shown across Seasons One and Two, Part 8 goes beyond this by setting out one possible "birth of the Black Lodge" (Ewins, 2018, p. 36), as well as depicting a realm where "the Fireman and Dido reside somewhere in the heavens, above Blue Pine mountain, and are able both to ascend (and pull other people up) to their domain, and to descend (and send others down) to earth" (Lowry, 2019, p. 42). And as the cliffhanger to Part 18 also reveals, via Sarah Palmer's/Judy's distorted cry of "Laura", this battle between forces, apparently overseen by the Fireman and Dido, can bleed between and across alternative realities. Consequently, Lindsay Hallam's analysis of this conclusion argues that "Carrie's scream is her realisation of her true identity, but also the realisation of her role as 'the one' to defeat Judy. . . .The fight will continue" (2018, p. 119). Whether the ending of *The Return* is interpreted as a matter of tragic eternal recurrence, or as an ongoing and open-ended struggle, it nevertheless implies that the imaginary world of *Twin Peaks* has not been entirely dissolved into ambiguity and multiplicity. Rather, a female-centered battle between Judy/Sarah and Laura, or mother-spirit and daughter-energy, has shifted into narrative centrality, with the issue of paternal abuse/BOB's presence seemingly being brought to a halt via the showdown between Freddie Sykes (Jake Wardle) and BOB in Part 17 (Fradley and Riley, 2019, p. 207).

On this account, *Twin Peaks* fandom is neither univocally trolled (McAvoy, 2019, p. 97), targeted for fan disservice (Hills, 2018, p. 317), nor punished (Anderson, 2019, p. 189) by *The Return*. Although elements of the season may feature lengthy detours, fan knowledge and attentive viewing are ultimately rewarded by Lynch and Frost. The show's imaginary world is explored afresh, and by going backwards to go forwards, *The Return* is able to layer in newly identified supernatural forces and new character backstories —that is, a re-shaped world ontology— which nonetheless remain continuous and coherent with established lore. For example, "Diane" moves from being an off-screen, unseen figure implied in the narrative world, to becoming not only a flesh-and-blood character (played by Laura Dern), but also a "tulpa" or un-natural doppelganger of the same ontological order as "Mr. C", Cooper's evil double. *The Return* consistently plays with, and across, a broader canvas than either Seasons One and Two, or even *Fire Walk With Me*, straying far beyond the boundaries of Twin Peaks the town, and placing the Black Lodge and "ordinary" reality into a longer timeframe and a multidimensional (yet policed or overseen) array of timelines.

Lynch's use of film/TV "art" discourses (Thompson, 2003, p. 115) are also intensified by Part 8, which has been described as "by far the weirdest episode of television ever made. . . and unmistakably a work of arthouse storytelling. No one will ever try to make an episode like this ever again, and rightly so. It's a masterpiece" (Heritage, 2019). But rather than viewing "second-stage" Lynch as opposed to franchise world-building via notions of artistic status, I would argue that both franchise-based and "TV art" aspects of *The Return* work together to affirm fans' cultural capital.

Dana Polan has argued that television art and its reception are precisely "a sociological phenomenon" (2007, p. 261). Polan emphasizes how television shows positioned and lauded as "masterpieces" involve tapping "into an audience that has been trained (through, for example, years of high school and college courses in literary study as theme-hunting) to understand cultural work as hermeneutic – as meaning-making" (2007, p. 265). The artistic distinction of shows such as *The Return* is thus simultaneously a marketing strategy aimed at reaching a specific audience/consumer demographic. As a result, a "class of viewers comes to constitute itself as veritable cultural mediators between the show itself and a broader public that, it is felt, need to be instructed about the true –and deeper– meaning within that show" (Polan, 2007, p. 267).

Expanding *Twin Peaks*' imaginary world via an ever more intensive "art" discourse and through reshaping its hyperdiegetic ontology (Hills, 2002, pp. 137–138) means opening that world into "ever more complex bits of background information, . . . [that] turn. . . the narrative space of the series into a game. . . in which there are always new permutations" (Polan, 2007, p. 277). But the game of treating *The Return* as a puzzle to be translated into "philosophical meaning" (Polan, 2007, p. 280) strives to align fan cultural capital (knowledge of the imaginary world's details which has value within fandom) with cultural capital itself (knowledge recognized more widely as having cultural status). As Hadas Weiss has recently argued, the accumulation of such "capital is even more recognizable a component of the middle-class ideology than property in its material incarnation, because it resonates so well with the spirit of investment" (Weiss, 2019, p. 95). The "art" of *The Return*, vividly figured through Part 8, but also keenly and recurrently coded through the figures of Dougie Jones and Audrey Horne, and introduced partly through the glass box of Part 1, thus positions viewers in a powerfully middle-class "ideology" which "describes our proclivity. . . to . . .identify as self-determining investors of work, time, as resources", and where "human capital is its most intimate manifestation" (Weiss, 2019, p. 118). Indeed, only "by continuing to watch, listen, read and learn –that is, by reinvesting– can we hope to nod knowingly at the next cultural reference" (Weiss, 2019, pp. 104–105).

Fan knowledge, on this account, is a form of classed investment in television-as-culture; the knowing fan imagines herself to be a self-determining investor in the imaginary world, which promises a return in terms of (fan-)cultural recognition. As Beverley Skeggs has suggested, "sub-cultural capital could be seen as a form of mis-recognition of a version of middle-class. . . distinction-making" (2004, p. 150), and the same might be said for *Twin Peaks*'s fan cultural capital. If the show languished for nearly three decades as a "dusty" and largely inactive franchise (Johnson, 2013, p. 28), then bringing it back as a "second-stage" Lynchian artwork made the newly expanded imaginary world, retooled via "backstory" and ontological "origin story", a rich source of cultural capital for long-term fans.

Twin Peaks: The Return may well have frustrated certain imagined/projected versions of narrative fan service and franchised nostalgia, but at the level of world-building, it gave fans a clear return on their long-accumulated and perhaps dormant fan cultural capital. This was (re)shaped as the once more industrially/critically recognized cultural capital of a media artwork —that is, David Lynch's latest "film". Here, exploring an imaginary world all over again meant going backwards to go forwards, in Marc Dolan's terms (1995, p. 42), allowing Lynch and Frost to make a performative show of not delivering a standardized, franchised product whilst still respecting fans' (classed) investments in the artistic world of *Twin Peaks*, and hence revising and expanding its ontological scope without wholly displacing prior fan knowledge. Part 8 remains the most visible blending of these protocols, since it is both the apotheosis of Lynchian and aestheticized/experimental *Twin Peaks*, at the same time as coherently expanding the imaginary world in a manner that could be subsequently affirmed by commodity tie-ins such as *The Final Dossier* (Frost, 2017), and which proffered a canonical return on fans' speculations about BOB and the Black Lodge. By seeming not to serve fans, Part 8 could self-reflexively adopt a position as art and hence as a space of "emerging" cultural capital (Savage, 2015, p. 113) rather than target-marketed commerce. Yet by representing a newly epic struggle between hyperdiegetic forces of light and dark, Laura and BOB, it also fused cultural capital with fan cultural capital, recognizing and rewarding fan theorizations which may have run over many years. Parts 17 and 18, taken together, also make visible this interplay between the cultural capital of "TV art" (e.g., Part 18's cliffhanger and multiversal ambiguities) and the fan cultural capital of world-based expectations (e.g., the showdown with BOB in Part 17).

Analyzing the successful return of *Twin Peaks* means highlighting how its imaginary world became acutely twinned, providing enough "backstory" and "origin story" to reassure fans that the storyworld they'd wrestled with over time remained canonically validated, and also providing just enough "trolling" to reassure followers of the Lynchverse that Lynch was pursuing his own artworld vision —with co-creator Mark Frost— rather than commercially reviving a franchise. If it makes sense, therefore, to discuss "Brand Lynch" (Todd, 2012, p. 108) then this is surely an anti-brand brand, overseeing an anti-franchise franchise, and an approach to world-building that fuses subversive world-hemorrhaging with more conventional world-(re)shaping.

References

Anderson, Donald L., (2019), "'There is no return': *Twin Peaks* and the horror of pleasure" in Victoria McCollum, editor, *Make America Hate Again: Trump-Era Horror and the Politics of Fear*, London, England: Routledge, 2019, pp. 177–194.

Atkinson, Sarah, (2014), *Beyond the Screen: Emerging Cinema and Engaging Audiences*, London, England and New York: Bloomsbury Academic.

Biderman, Shai; Gil, Ronen; and Lewit, Ido, (2019), *Life in the Black Lodge: The Twin Challenge of Lanham*, Lexington, Massachusetts: Lexington Books, pp. 177–191.

Dolan, Marc, (1995), "The Peaks and Valleys of Serial Creativity: What Happened to/ on *Twin Peaks*" in David Lavery, editor, *Full of Secrets: Critical Approaches to Twin Peaks*, Detroit, Michigan; Wayne State University Press, pp. 30–50.

Ewins, Michael, (2018), "The Stars Turn and a Time Presents Itself" in *Sight and Sound*, January, Volume 28, Issue 1, 2018, pp. 33–36.

Fallis, Jeffrey; and King, T. Kyle, (2019), "Lucy Finally Understands How Cellphones Work: Ambiguous Digital Technologies in *Twin Peaks: The Return* and Its Fan Communities" in Antonio Sanna, editor, *Critical Essays on Twin Peaks: The Return*, London, England: Palgrave Macmillan, pp. 53–68.

Fisher, Mark, (2016), *The Weird and the Eerie*, London, England: Repeater Books.

Fradley, Martin; and Riley, John A., (2019), "'I don't understand how this keeps happening. . . over and over again': Trumpism, Uncanny Repetition, and *Twin Peaks: The Return*" in Victoria McCollum, editor, *Make America Hate Again: Trump-Era Horror and the Politics of Fear*, London, England: Routledge, pp. 195–210.

Frost, Mark, (2016), *The Secret History of Twin Peaks*, Basingstoke, England: Palgrave Macmillan.

Frost, Mark, (2017), *Twin Peaks: The Final Dossier*, Basingstoke, England: Palgrave Macmillan.

Garner, Ross, (2016), "'The Series That Changed Television'? *Twin Peaks*, 'Classic' Status, and Temporal Capital" in *Cinema Journal*, Volume 55, Issue 3, 2016, pp. 137–142.

Garner, Ross, (2017), "What We Learnt from Sam And Tracey: Does The New *Twin Peaks* Differ To Contemporary 'Quality TV'?", *CST Online*, May 27, 2017, available online at http://cstonline.net/what-we-learnt-from-sam-and-tracey-new-twin-peaks-and-contemporary-quality-tv/.

Gillan, Jennifer, (2016), "Textural Poaching *Twin Peaks*: The Audrey Horne Sweater Girl GIFs", *Series: International Journal of TV Serial Narratives*, Volume 2, Issue 2, 2016, pp. 9–24.

Hallam, Lindsay, (2018), *Devil's Advocates – Twin Peaks: Fire Walk with Me*, Leighton Buzzard, England: Auteur Publishing.

Halskov, Andreas, (2015), *TV Peaks: Twin Peaks and Modern Television Drama*, Odense, Denmark: University Press of Southern Denmark.

Hastie, Amelie, (2007), "The Epistemological Stakes of *Buffy the Vampire Slayer*: Television Criticism and Marketing Demands" in Elana Levine and Lisa Parks, editors, *Undead TV: Essays on Buffy the Vampire Slayer*, Durham, North Carolina: Duke University Press, pp. 74–95.

Hawkes, Joel, (2019), "Movement in the Box: The Production of Surreal Social Space and the Alienated Body" in Antonio Sanna, editor, *Critical Essays on Twin Peaks: The Return*, London, England: Palgrave Macmillan, pp. 149–168.

Heritage, Stuart, (2019), "'No one will ever try this again': The most daring hours of TV ever", *The Guardian*, November 5, 2019, available at https://www.theguardian.com/tv-and-radio/2019/nov/05/no-one-will-ever-try-this-again-the-most-daring-hours-of-tv-ever-twin-peaks-mr-robot.

Hills, Matt, (2002), *Fan Cultures*, London, England: Routledge.

Hills, Matt, (2018), "Cult TV Revival: Generational Seriality, Recap Culture, and the 'Brand Gap' of *Twin Peaks: The Return*", *Television & New Media*, Volume 19, Issue 4, 2018, pp. 310–327.

Jenkins, Henry, (1995), "'Do You Enjoy Making the Rest of Us Feel Stupid?': alt.tv.twinpeaks, the Trickster Author, and Viewer Mastery" in David Lavery, editor, *Full of Secrets: Critical Approaches to Twin Peaks*, Detroit, Michigan: Wayne State University Press, pp. 51–69.

Johnson, Derek, (2013), *Media Franchising: Creative License and Collaboration in the Culture Industries*, New York and London, England: New York University Press.

Joyce, Ashlee, (2019), "The Nuclear Anxiety of *Twin Peaks: The Return*" in Amanda Di-Paolo and Jamie Gillies, editors, *The Politics of Twin Peaks*, Lanham, Massachusetts: Lexington Books, pp. 13–34.

Lim, Dennis, (2018), "Donald Trump's America and the Visions of David Lynch", *The New Yorker*, June 29, 2018, available at https://www.newyorker.com/culture/culture-desk/donald-trumps-america-and-the-visions-of-david-lynch.

Lowry, Elizabeth, (2019), "Extraterrestrial Intelligences in the Atomic Age: Exploring the Rhetorical Function of Aliens and the 'Alien' in the *Twin Peaks* Universe" in Antonio Sanna, editor, *Critical Essays on Twin Peaks: The Return*, London, England: Palgrave Macmillan, pp. 37–51.

McAvoy, David, (2019), "'Is It About the Bunny? No, It's Not About the Bunny!': David Lynch's Fandom and Trolling of Peak TV Audiences" in Antonio Sanna, editor, *Critical Essays on Twin Peaks: The Return*, London, England: Palgrave Macmillan, pp. 85–103.

McCarthy, Donald, (2019), "How Mark Frost's *Twin Peaks* Books Clarify and Confound the Nature of Reality" in Antonio Sanna, editor, *Critical Essays on Twin Peaks: The Return*, London, England: Palgrave Macmillan, pp. 169–181.

Metz, Walter, (2017), "The Atomic Gambit of Twin Peaks: The Return", *Film Criticism*, Volume 41, Issue 3, 2017, available at https://quod.lib.umich.edu/f/fc/13761232.0041.324/--atomic-gambit-of-twin-peaks-the-return?rgn=main;view=fulltext.

Neofetou, Daniel, (2012), *Good Day Today: David Lynch Destabilizes the Spectator*, Alresford, England: Zero Books.

Newman, Michael Z.; and Levine, Elana, (2012), *Legitimating Television: Media Convergence and Cultural Status*, New York and London, England: Routledge.

Nochimson, Martha P., (2013), *David Lynch Swerves: Uncertainty from Lost Highway to Inland Empire*, Austin, Texas: University of Texas Press.

Polan, Dana, (2007), "Cable Watching: HBO, *The Sopranos*, and Discourses of Distinction" in Sarah Banet-Weiser, Cynthia Chris, and Anthony Freitas, editors, *Cable Visions: Television Beyond Broadcasting*, New York: New York University Press, pp. 261–283.

Robertson, Benjamin J., (2017), "Backstory" in Mark J.P. Wolf, editor, *The Routledge Companion to Imaginary Worlds* Routledge, New York: Routledge, pp. 37–44.

Ryan, Scott, (2017), "Credit to the Credits", *The Blue Rose Magazine*, Volume 1, Issue 2, 2017, p. 3.

Savage, Mike, (2015), *Social Class in the 21st Century*, London, England: Pelican.

Skeggs, Beverley, (2004), *Class, Self, Culture*, London, England: Routledge.

Thompson, Kristin, (2003), *Storytelling in Film and Television*, Cambridge, Massachusetts: Harvard University Press.

Todd, Antony, (2012), *Authorship and the Films of David Lynch*, London, England and New York: I.B. Tauris.

Weiss, Hadas, (2019), *We Have Never Been Middle Class: How Social Mobility Misleads Us*, London, England: Verso.

Williams, Rebecca, (2015), *Post-Object Fandom: Television, Identity and Self-narrative*, London, England and New York: Bloomsbury Academic.

Williams, Rebecca, (2016), "'No Lynch, No Peaks!': Auteurism, Fan/Actor Campaigns and the Challenges Of *Twin Peaks*' Return(s)", *Series: International Journal Of TV Serial Narratives*, Volume II, No 2, 2016, pp. 55–65.

Wolf, Mark J. P., (2012), *Building Imaginary Worlds: The Theory and History of Subcreation*, New York and London, England: Routledge.

12

THE FAULT IN OUR *STAR TREK*

(Dis)Continuity Mapping, Textual Conservationism, and the Perils of Prequelization

William Proctor

> You want to explore this universe because it's remarkably coherent. Fans are always going on about canon, but when you really look at it, it's pretty amazing that in hundreds and hundreds of episodes, this universe is so coherent and well-plotted out.
>
> —Manny Coto (showrunner on *Enterprise* Season Four)

> What I have absolutely no respect for however, is their complete lack of effort to ensure that the story and every other detail remained canon.
>
> —Stephen Willets (*Star Trek* fan and blogger)

As an imaginary world, the *Star Trek* universe is a vast narrative system "more internally complex than that of any other American television show".[1] Yet *Star Trek* is also much more than the sum of its televisual parts; rather, as of 2020, it is an expansive transmedia empire, 7 comprising 7 TV series, including an animated series (with more in the pipeline), 13 feature films, countless video games, hundreds of novels and comics, and a library of reference books and encyclopedias that have each augmented the world's fictional architecture considerably over the past five decades. That being said, it is certainly the various television series that form the core, canonical "mothership" of the Star Trek "hyperdiegesis",[2] the narrative station from which other textual shuttles have been launched across the transmedia frontier. With so much content scaffolding the imaginary world, however, it becomes more difficult for writers to fulfill narrative logics of continuity in order to ensure that coherence between texts is successfully achieved and maintained by editorial oversight. As Mark J. P. Wolf argues, "[t]he likelihood of inconsistencies occurring increases as a world grows in size and complexity".[3] As a consequence, "inconsistencies in the storyline distract and disrupt the audiences' mental image of the story as they follow it, especially if they occur in the main storyline driving the work".[4]

Although meticulous devotion to continuity seeks to furnish the imaginary world with narrative coherence, to make the image of the world appear to function as if "real", continuity also imposes creative limitations on writers who are required to stay within the borderlines established by official canon policy, and not "depict events that would conflict with established [*Star Trek*] history".[5] In other words, the concepts of continuity and canon effectively dictate which stories count as "fact", and which are to be understood as "fiction". As a general rule of thumb, the official *Star Trek* canon is comprised of the live-action television and film series, which essentially contracts the imaginary world by indicating that hundreds of tie-in novels and comics "never really happened". Although "the dominant attitude in STAR TREK fandom is that spin-off material does not truly "count" as canon at all; the film and television series are always primary", [6] the ultimate arbiter of what constitutes "official" canon is usually "some agent of the intellectual property holder".[7] It is true that some fans construct their own versions of canon —often defined as "fanon" or "head canon"— through individual processes of selection, acceptance, and rejection. The fact remains, however, that the term emphasizes that canonicity is strictly determined by corporate authorities rather than fan audiences; by creators and "deliverers", not consumers and "receivers".

In 2001, following the conclusion of fourth series, *Star Trek: Voyager* (1994–2001) the next televisual incarnation would go where no *Star Trek* series had gone before: into the future history's past. Yet the decision to create a prequel to *Star Trek: The Original Series* (*TOS*) (1966–1969) with *Star Trek: Enterprise* (2001–2005) would lead to all sorts of issues with established continuity, leading fans to confront producers Brannon Braga and Rick Berman on a nascent Internet. As *Enterprise* became the first Star Trek series to be cancelled since *TOS* in 1969, and the first not to reach the seven-year milestone achieved by *Star Trek: The Next Generation* (*TNG*) (1987–1994), *Star Trek: Deep Space Nine* (*DS9*) (1993–1999), and *Voyager*, the series signified the dying gasp of a franchise that had commanded the science fiction genre on television for 18 consecutive years, accumulating an impressive 25 seasons totaling 624 episodes. It would be 12 years between the cancellation of *Enterprise* and the launch of *Star Trek: Discovery* in 2017 on the new streaming service, CBS All Access.

In the meantime, *Star Trek*'s next regeneration would occur not on television, but in cinema. As if recognizing the challenges of navigating *Trek*'s dense and baroque narrative continuity, director J. J. Abrams, and co-writers Alex Kurtzman and Robert Orci, orchestrated a new narrative direction for the franchise with 2009's *Star Trek* (*Trek '09*). Rather than risk contradicting and contaminating extant continuity, the events depicted in the opening of *Trek '09* installs the film not within the "Prime" universe —the universe inhabited by *TOS*, *TNG*, *DS9*, *Voyager*, *Enterprise*, and the canon films from *Star Trek:*

The Motion Picture (1979) through to *Star Trek: Nemesis* (2002)— but in a new parallel universe, one inaugurated by events within the story itself. In essence, *Trek '09* mobilizes metafictional devices in order to create a new branch of the imaginary world that ostensibly does not interfere with established continuity, effectively bracketing off the "Prime" universe from what has since become known as "the Kelvin Timeline", resulting in a new branch of *Star Trek* continuity, or what Matt Hills terms "neo-canon".[8] In doing so, Abrams and company orchestrated a narrative space whereby canonical "facts" could be either revised or cast aside entirely, a prophylactic strategy that addressed the concerns of continuity acolytes. While also targeting a new audience for whom the franchise had become far too complex to jump into without the need for expertise. In essence, Abrams's ploy suggests "the extent to which the runners of the STAR TREK franchise both fear and revile the core *Star Trek* fandom",[9] many of whom possess "an often-intimidating grasp of the source material".[10] Although this narrative sleight-of-hand did not necessarily satisfy older fans, many of whom saw the Kelvin films as "Trek in Name Only", box-office revenues generated by Abrams's *Trek '09* and sequel, *Star Trek: Into Darkness* (2013), demonstrated that regenerating the franchise had been successful, at least commercially. However, the third (and final at the time of writing) Kelvin film, *Star Trek: Beyond* (2016), struggled at the box office, failing to recoup its combined production and marketing budget despite receiving many positive reviews.

With the release of *Star Trek: Discovery* in 2017, the first Trek TV series since 2005 and the first series released on subscription-only streaming channels, the decision to situate the narrative prior to *TOS* risked tampering with canonical continuity like *Enterprise* before it. Despite *Discovery's* showrunners insisting that the series is set in the "Prime universe", and not The Kelvin Universe or another parallel rift, ardent Trekkers began flooding discussion boards on the Internet to scrutinize whether or not the imaginary world has become burdened and undermined by "snarls" in continuity. Additionally, numerous entertainment articles focused on potential breaches in canon caused by *Discovery's* close proximity to *TOS* —the show is set a decade prior to Kirk and Spock's tenure on the Enterprise— indicating that the imaginary world is not only managed by writers, producers, and showrunners, but is also expertly policed by "textual conservationists", fan audiences for whom adherence to established imaginary history functions to accumulate subcultural capital via displays of expertise, as well as being a key resource for pleasure, play, and critique, each of which support the construction of fannish social identities.

In this essay, I explore both *Enterprise* and *Discovery* to demonstrate the perils associated with prequelization, considering the way in which textual conservationists respond to and criticize producers for introducing new story elements that are not supported by the official history of the *Star Trek* hyperdiegesis. As textual conservationists "expect adherence to established tenets, characterisations, and narrative "back stories," which production teams thus *revise at their peril*, disrupting the trust which is placed in the continuity of a detailed narrative world",[11] producers who fail to understand the importance of canonical governance and coherence thus run the risk of instigating new discursive conflicts, just as they threaten to destabilize *Star Trek*'s "ontological realm", that which "determines the parameters of a world's existence".[12] From such a vantage point, textual conservationists may see producers less as world-*builders* than as world-*destroyers*. In an age where fans are increasingly courted, exploited, and harnessed by corporate entities as "attention-attractor[s], buzz-generator[s], as brand-enricher[s], as community-builder[s]",[13] it is equally as likely that fans behave in ways that work *against* corporate logics, not as attractors, generators, and enrichers, but as *buzz-killers* and *brand-assassins*. Such a slipshod approach to established canonical continuity not only sabotages hyperdiegetic coherence, but also endangers the critical and economic health of the property if fan audiences cry havoc and let slips the dogs of war. For textual conservationists, *de*-coherence and *dis*-continuity are viewed as problems to be fixed, rationalized, or for the purposes of this essay, exposed, catalogued, and critiqued. Although there are a number of academic studies that have provided important, substantive work on sequels, especially in film, [14] there has been much less focus on prequels, especially concerning the creative difficulties that go along with ensuring that new stories do not conflict with "later" ones. Just as writers of tie-in fiction find themselves constrained by the "creatively crippling strictures"[15] of official canon, the same constraints are certainly at work with prequels. As we shall see, the principles of canonical continuity function to guide authors and producers to ensure, at least theoretically, that the good ship *Star Trek* should not always boldly go where no one has gone before.

Methodologically, I draw from discourses related to continuity and canon articulated within and across on-line territories: in discussion threads located on websites like Quora and Reddit; in fan-oriented entertainment journalism; and on fan wikis such as Memory Alpha —which is dedicated to cataloguing the *Trek* canon— and Memory Beta, the non-canon apocryphon. Although at times I directly quote from fannish "canon discourses", I anonymize both author and platform for ethical reasons. I begin with *Enterprise* before turning to the re-emergence of *Star Trek* on television with *Discovery*.

"It was Always Going to be Hard Doing a Prequel when Considering Continuity"

From the late-1990s to the early 2000s, fan cultures became newly invigorated and emboldened by the affordances of cyberspace, leading to a steady increase in fan-producer conflicts across the on-line frontier. Yet this heightened activity, this "mainstreaming" of fan practices, behaviors, and discourses, did not first emerge with *Enterprise*, but four years or so earlier with Joel Schumacher's *Batman and Robin* (1997), "perhaps the first film to fully incur the wrath of the digitally connected fan-base".[16] By the time *Enterprise* was launched in 2001, however, the on-line population continued to rise significantly in numbers due to the introduction of broadband technology, a massive (300x) increase in bandwidth that stimulated the development of social media platforms, fan wikis, and other participatory portals. As Sam Ford argues, "the ability a much wider portion of society now has to share, discuss, debate, and critique texts with various communities constitutes the greatest shift in the media ecology in a digital age",[17] a shift that has led to producer/fan —and fan-on-fan— conflicts becoming common place.

As showrunner and "torchbearer" on *Enterprise*, Brannon Braga fueled the flames of "fantagonism"[18] by not heeding nor taking seriously criticisms regarding several issues, including what was viewed as a reactionary flouting of Gene Roddenberry's liberal-humanist ethos;[19] a lack of "visual fidelity" with *TOS* as the "next" series in the timeline; a retrograde shift in gender and sexual politics,[20] and breaches in canonical continuity. As such, "*Enterprise* was. . . at odds with Star Trek's narrative universe" from the start, as "the executive producers didn't seem to care about the show, its fans, or the legacy it drew upon, despite their prior involvement in the franchise".[21] Rather than placating fans, however, Braga ended up courting "producer/fan wrangling over accurate continuity" by vilifying seasoned textual conservationists as "continuity pornographers".[22] Prior to the first episode's broadcast, the two-part pilot "Broken Bow", Braga and Rick Berman emphasized that "changes had to be made to the historical canon", which immediately set in motion "a growing tension between producers and fans over what is considered important in the Star Trek canon".[23] This is not to suggest that Star Trek was canonically "pure" before *Enterprise* wrecked it. As Canavan emphasizes, "there is simply too much material produced across too many decades by too many production teams in too many divergent media environments for it to truly cohere in a single, unitary "whole"" (2017, 167). *Star Trek* has been "famously riddled with inconsistencies"[24] since inception, mainly due to the fact that "none of the writers could have anticipated that they were laying the foundations for an entertainment franchise that would come to span decades and grow to encompass hundreds of episodes and [over] a dozen films".[25] As George Kovacs states, "[w]riters were only loosely concerned with standards of continuity and consistency of detail — *the obsessive examination of the series' fans had not yet manifested*".[26]

In many ways, Braga and Berman's frustration is understandable: prequels always-already run the risk of contaminating pre-established narrative facts unless editorially managed with either a modicum of expertise at the helm, or the creative will to do so. On the one hand, it is entirely possible for prequels to follow, obey, and ultimately shore up, extant chronologies, whereas on the other, it becomes difficult to innovate when canonical governance imposes "a limited degree of creative license",[27] to create new worlds and new civilizations that are not supported by future events; or as the case may be, by actively contradicting what has already been established. As prequels are defined by a "narrative sequence element that comes before an already-existing narrative sequence",[28] production teams may feel creatively constrained by canonicity, and as a result, end up in a situation whereby generic and narrative innovation might lead to established facts, histories, and back-stories being contradicted, suggesting that there are perils associated with prequelization. Indeed, prequels like *Enterprise* may operate to provide backstory and augment the imaginary world, but situating texts before an already-existing narrative sequence suggests that care should be taken by producers to align with what we might describe as a variation on backstory, which in the case of prequels becomes the "frontstory", that is, narrative data that occurs in *Enterprise's* future —in this case, *TOS, TNG, DS9, Voyager,* and the feature film series.

This is not solely the turf of *Star Trek*, however. George Lucas received a lion's share of scorn for the Star Wars prequels for a number of reasons,[29] one being the introduction of elements not supported by the original trilogy. Likewise, Ridley Scott's Alien prequels, *Prometheus* (2011) and *Alien: Covenant* (2016) have become grist for the fannish mill, most notably regarding the evolution of the xenomorph, and the way in which the films struggle to build "transfictional bridges" between franchise installments.[30] Among other criticisms, J. K. Rowling has come under fire for the Fantastic Beasts films, especially second installment, *The Crimes of Grindelwald* (2018), for revising elements first articulated in the Harry Potter novels and film series. Fans understand these kinds of revisions as forms of "retroactive continuity" (or "retcon"), a concept derived from superhero comic books, which refers to

> a narrative process wherein the creator(s) and/ or producer(s) of a fictional narrative/ world… deliberately alter the history of that narrative/ world such that, going forward, future stories reflect this new history, completely ignoring the old as if it never happened.[31]

Unlike rebooting, which wipes the slate clean of continuity in order to "begin again" with a new narrative sequence,[32] ret-conning occurs "in continuity". Whether or not fans accept revisionism of this type depends in large on the narrative rationale explained within the imaginary world itself. For instance, J. R. R. Tolkien seemed to be

> well aware of this kind of reaction when he retconned *The Hobbit* to bring it in line with *The Lord of the Rings*, doing so quietly, and even finding a way to cleverly make both versions canonical; the older version is said to be the story Bilbo told, but a distortion of the truth, while the "newer" corrected version tells the story as it really was.[33]

Conversely, should retconning occur because of editorial mismanagement, whereby extant continuity is ignored or viewed as a constraint to be circumnavigated, then fan audiences have been shown to respond unkindly, and at times vehemently. After almost two decades of broadband speeds and band-widths, and with the introduction of even speedier systems like fiber-optic technologies, fan discourses related to what I have termed elsewhere as "canonical fidelity"[34] have become quotidian. Besides the participatory affordances of social media platforms, where producer/fan conflicts are played out publicly, other fans, usually continuity acolytes, mobilize textual conservationist discourses by cataloguing, archiving, essaying, and ultimately policing, the ontological health of the imaginary world. As with debates about canon —and by extension, other fannish discourses— on-line "narractivity"[35] indicates that displays of expertise are also bids for "subcultural capital", bids that seek to develop and shore up one's status as connoisseur and cognoscenti, as the "good" fan in possession of knowledge as a form of symbolic-currency. Policing violations in continuity not by correcting them through transformative works like fan fiction, but through indexical labor that doesn't seek to repair, but rather, to expose and criticize such violations becomes one of the ways that fans deploy their expertise.

Consider Trek fan Bernd Schneider's website, *Ex Astris Scientia*, which frequently publishes forensic indexes of the *Star Trek* universe: from the "Treknology" Encyclopedia to Starship Databases; from episode synopses and analyses to extensive commentaries centered on matters of canon and continuity (and more besides).[36] In a page titled "Enterprise Continuity Problems", Luther Root exposes significant issues with the first *Star Trek* prequel TV series, focusing on two episodes that introduce elements not supported by the imaginary world's ontological index.[37] In "Acquisition", for example, the Ferengi are introduced, an alien race that Starfleet did not encounter until over two centuries later, according to *TNG*. "This is a major problem", complains Root, "regardless of the lame trick not to mention the word "Ferengi" in the whole episode".[38] In the article, Root mobilizes evidence gleaned from other canonical Trek series and films, most notably *TNG*, *DS9*, and the film *Generations* (1995), to emphasize the temporal anomaly set in motion by the episode. By expertly mounting a scholarly rejection of the episode as a "continuity blunder", much in the same way that academics draw upon textual evidence to support their critical exegesis, Root deploys his expertise by performing indexical labor, by patrolling the hyperdiegesis as textual conservationist and continuity cop, thus bidding for subcultural wages to deposit into his symbolic "bank". What Root does not do, however, is offer resolutions and hypotheses as to why and how the Ferengi could have logically appeared at this point in the timeline. Instead, Root argues that this is more about roughshod storytelling, which actively works against the fannish tendency to proffer ontological repairs through fan fiction, etc.:

Of course, we may always make up chains of coincidences and oddities to explain inconsistencies, but not mentioning "Ferengi" to the TV viewer does anything but help. Aside from their name, Earth Starfleet and the Vulcan High Command should have at least some basic knowledge about the Ferengi about this incident [depicted in "Acquisition"].

At the heart of Root's argument is the idea that "Acquisition" fails to meet narrative criteria pertaining to continuity and canon, and consequently, the episode's status is queried and criticized, regardless of whether or not *Enterprise* as a whole is considered fully canonical according to standard rules of qualification.

Textual conservationists, like Root, shine a light on continuity snarls through close narrative analysis and archiving without seeking to provide rationale explanations for "continuity blunders"; whereas the latter can be understood as authors of transformative works that offer solutions articulated in fan fiction, fan films, etc. in order to rationalize and repair ontological fractures in continuity and canon. For continuity acolytes such as Root, however, "conserving" the *Star Trek* canon arguably means identifying temporal ruptures not as a problem to be fixed, but as a criticism levelled at producers for lacking the necessary expertise to protect canonical continuity from contamination. Fans might very well "do more than merely reproduce official textual material, but instead reorder narrative information to produce expert chronologies, continuities, and encyclopedic fan wikis",[39] but others perform their subcultural expertise by spotlighting continuity glitches, and by critiquing and shaming showrunners for editorial mishaps and/or mismanagement. Fan practices of this kind do not seem to align with either "transformational" or "affirmational" fandom, both of which are essentially celebratory,[40] but an associated, parallel mode of engagement and participation. Naturally, fans tend to occupy multiple performative and discursive identities, but textual conservationists of the type I am interested in here tend to focus less on unabashedly celebrating the fan-object than they are in exposing errors in continuity to indicate that their expertise is more advanced than the people making the series; and in many cases, *this may in fact be accurate.*

Perhaps one way of understanding fans of this "expose-and-criticize" bent is to recognize that the binary "fan/anti-fan" is not explicitly an either/or situation, but implies a complex mode of *affective shifting* vacillating between different poles, a performative spectrum that exhibits the complexities of love *and* hate, passion *and* indifference, without negating the middle ground between such polarities. Fans can occupy multiple affective positions simultaneously, such as displaying and possessing characteristics of anti-fandom while also maintaining a positive relationship with the fan-object in general terms, what Vivi Theodoropoulou describes as "the anti-fan within the fan" (2007, 316).[41] Ultimately, "fandom is a precondition of anti-fandom".[42] As Henry Jenkins reminds us, fandom "is born of fascination and frustration", not fascination *or* frustration.[43] For instance, anti-fans of *Enterprise* are often already dedicated Trek fans, and their fascination with the core principles of the fan-object can provoke frustration with the way that the franchise is handled by corporate showrunners. In this light, textual conservationists might also be transformational and affirmational fans at one and the same time, but those who deploy their expertise to expose fault-lines in canonical continuity *without proffering resolutions*, can be viewed as, for want of a better term, a specific type of *derogative fandom*, meaning that they discursively hold producers to account for what they see as negligent storytelling. By defaming and shaming producers, showrunners, and writers, fans that bid for subcultural capital through displays and discourses of expertise and connoisseurship implies a conflict whereby textual conservationists jockey for authority by demonstrating that producers' knowledge is eclipsed by "fandom's epistemological economy".[44]

One might be tempted to blame this apparent lackadaisical approach to canon for *Enterprise's* cancellation. While it certainly didn't help endear the series to veteran Trekkers, it is more likely that a confluence of forces and factors led to its demise. Executive Producer Rick Berman blamed "franchise fatigue" for *Enterprise's* ratings decline, suggesting that audiences had had enough of *Star Trek* after 18 consecutive years on network TV and in syndication.[45] However, such a stance seems to react against claims that the series was simply not good enough. Many fans opined that Berman and Braga were to blame for "the sharp decline in the quality of *Trek* television",[46] for "urinating on Roddenberry's grave and fornicating with his corpse".[47] Roberta Pearson and Marie-Messenger Davies argue that *Enterprise* "failed artistically, just as it failed commercially".[48] Braga himself has more recently articulated his repentance about the fact that early episodes fell short of the quality expected by audiences for whom *TNG*, *DS9*, and *Voyager* are exemplars of "Golden Age" Trek (with the caveat that each series performed less well in ratings compared to their antecedents, suggesting that the series' popularity also declined respectively with each iteration).

By the time that Braga was replaced as showrunner by Trek aficionado Manny Coto for Season Four, the writing was on the wall. Although Coto was praised for at least aiming to connect the series with *TOS* by establishing transfictional bridges between the two programs (and by extension, the rest of the imaginary world), he admitted that "we were mostly gearing episodes towards people who knew the "Star Trek" universe. *We were not worried about people who didn't. They were gone anyway*".[49] What is striking about Coto's remarks here is that *Enterprise's* declining ratings could not reasonably have been about continuity issues in the main; continuity is hardly the dominion of casual viewers, but of ardent Trekkers ("people who knew the "Star Trek" universe"). Ultimately, then, *Enterprise* failed to capture the imaginations of "floating voters", indicating that fans are a minor cluster within the broader "coalition audience", and as a result, do not generate enough of a viewership to capture healthy enough ratings that would ensure survival in the brutal TV marketplace. It would be four years before the Enterprise would fly again in J. J. Abrams's *Trek '09*, but televisual *Star Trek* languished in the cultural wilderness for 12 years.

Yet as Michael Burnham of the *USS Discovery* sparked war with the Klingons in a new prequel series, fans once again turned to the affordances of cyberspace to make their frustrations known.

"It's all the Changes to the Existing Timeline that have a lot of People Mad"

Over the past decade or so, continuity has increasingly become part and parcel of corporate logic, one that can be largely accredited to the critical and commercial success of the Marvel Cinematic Universe. Yet the fact remains that producer/fan quarrels over canonical alignment have continued to accelerate, indicating that corporate logics often fall short of the fannish demand for canonical consistency, especially where prequels are concerned. As Aaron Taylor argues, contemporary transmedia franchises are symptomatic of a shift in corporate logic, one being "*the appropriation of the economics of continuity*".[50] Although continuity is essentially a narrative conceit, one that directly services textual conservationist/cultish tendencies, it is also dialectically intertwined with commercial impulses, a type of "commodity braiding"[51] that establishes signposts, or "entertainment stepping stones", that lead toward other texts within the hyperdiegesis. In a sense, fan investment and corporate logics become intrinsically aligned insofar as the principle of continuity is concerned.[52] Given the array of "user-generated discontent"[53] that circulated *Enterprise*, the lessons imparted at the time to Berman and Braga, and the "new" corporate logics that place a high emphasis on continuity, one would imagine that any new *Star Trek* series would involve producers learning from historic producer/fan conflicts in order to defend against similar criticisms in the future. When writing *Trek '09*, it is plausible that Abrams, Orci, and Kurtzman were intimately aware that tampering with established continuity could potentially spark new confrontations from textual conservationists; hence the quantum trickery that narrativized an alternative (Kelvin) timeline within the film itself as a way to strategically protect the Prime universe from contamination, permitting a heightened degree of creative license. Yet this temporal panacea did not necessarily convince fans of its canonical legitimacy, nor did it resolve fannish queries regarding hyperdiegetic "fact".

In November 2015, CBS announced that a new *Star Trek* TV series, titled *Discovery*, would be entering production. Guided at first by veteran Trek writer Bryan Fuller, it later emerged that *Discovery* would not be set in the Kelvin Timeline, but would return to the Prime Universe for the first time since the cancellation of *Enterprise*, insofar as live-action Trek is concerned. Although *Discovery*'s producers were initially secretive about *when* the series would be set, fans began marshalling theories based on early promotional images of the *USS Discovery* that were shown at a San Diego Comic-Con panel in 2016. Most notably, fans forensically analyzed the images, theorizing that the series would be yet another prequel because of the ship's registry number —NCC-1031— which as one fan argued, "would suggest it is set after *Enterprise* but before *The Original Series*". As *Discovery's* status as prequel was confirmed, some fans turned to social media to discuss, debate, and defame the decision, often by invoking *Enterprise* as short-hand for canon/prequel contamination:

> The show will have many of the same problems Enterprise had —trying to create a show for modern sensibilities that can act as a plausible predecessor to something made in the 60s. This affects everything from aesthetics to storylines to characterization [. . .] But this show, fitting into the prime universe just ten years before Shatner-Kirk turns up, is going to be a real head-scratcher if it doesn't align neatly with the blinking lights and space Nazis of the original series. Am I the only one who thinks this is a mistake?

For some fans, the notion that a new Trek series would again function retroactively —looking backwards rather than into the future— became cause for concern.

> I'm not a fan of the decision to go pre TOS either and I just want them to move forward. Many people including myself wanted the series to pick up 50–100 years post Nemesis and go from there, but we all know that's not happening now. I'm a lot less excited now that pre TOS is official, but I'm still happy for a new show. We'll see what happens. . .

It is worth noting that the emergence of textual conservationist discourses centered on *Discovery's* status as prequel occurred well in advance of the series premiere. "The writers will definitely have to be even more careful than the folks on ENT [*Enterprise*] to avoid causing major backstory problems", explained one fan.

These anxieties would eventually be realized as additional information came to light, in particular the news that series' protagonist Michael Burnham, played by Sonequa Martin-Green, would in fact be Spock's adopted sister, a new "fact" that isn't supported by the universe's "frontstory". From a textual conservationist stance, this newly established familial relationship is little more than a cheap, hackneyed retcon, a transparent attempt to address older Trekkers' nostalgia by attempting to shoehorn transfictional bridges between *TOS* and *Discovery*, regardless of whether or not such a maneuver is narratively and canonically warranted. Some textual conservationists drew from established canon to criticize the Spock/Burnham dyad, especially concerning Spock's half-brother, Sybok, who features in *Star Trek V: The Final Frontier*, but has yet to be mentioned in *Discovery* even though they were "raised as brothers".

(A discussion thread on Quora titled "Where is Sybok in Star Trek Discovery?" captures the debate well.)[54]

As the series premiered in November 2017, textual conservationist discourses continued apace, not only on social media platforms, but also across fannish entertainment journalism websites that were not yet active during *Enterprise's* original broadcast. Although the inception of broadband/fiber optic speeds and bandwidths certainly led to fan practices and behaviors becoming publicly visible, the participatory affordances of so-called Web 2.0 also created space for an armada of websites dedicated to fan journalism to emerge, such as *Den of Geek*, *i09*, and *The Mary Sue*, etc. It is within this discursive universe that producers have also sought to paratextually respond to the complaints of textual conservationists. For example, Aaron Haberts, one of two showrunners on the first season, claimed that: "[t]he aim is not to violate things that are very important to people [and] I think that so far we've found a way to balance it. If we sat there and worried about it and studied it every single hour, it's easy to choke. You have to push through".[55] Much to the consternation of *Trek '09* anti-fans, Alex Kurtzman took over as showrunner for season two (although he has been involved as executive producer and co-creator with Fuller from the start). Like Haberts and Goldsman, Kurtzman has attempted to paratextually rehabilitate the series regarding canon complaints by asking fans to "be patient with us", implying that the series will eventually align with the rest of the Trek hyperdiegesis.[56] Said Kurtzman: "[t]he show has been made by people who are trying to protect that [canonical] legacy. . . so it's a constant debate about where the line is in terms of canon violation, there's a supreme court of debate that allows us to stay true to canon and also stretches the boundaries of it".[57] In the Supreme Court of on-line fan opinion, however, *Discovery* has not only stretched the boundaries of canon, but snapped it irreparably. The criticisms have been varied and multiple: from the design of the Klingons to the lack of visual, costumal, and technological fidelity with *TOS* onwards; from Sarek's newfound ability to converse with Burnham across great distances; to the implications of sporedrive technology; from Burnham's status as mutineer to Spock's comment in *TOS* episode "The Tholian Web", that there has never been a mutiny in Starfleet ("absolutely no record of such an occurrence"); from advanced hologram and holodeck technology to the temporal coordinates of the Klingon War.

That being said, however, I reject the notion that continuity blunders are part of a nefarious scheme to upset the Trek faithful. In fact, *Discovery's* relationship to canonical continuity is more ambivalent than the majority of textual conservationist discourses have allowed. Rather, it seems that 21-century *Star Trek*— or at least *Star Trek* that followed in the wake of *Enterprise's* cancellation— has been hitherto reluctant to explore new regions of future history in a post-TNG/DS9/*Voyager* temporal locale. Hence, *Discovery's* status as prequel —or as the case may be, an "interquel"[58]— could be perhaps recognized as "safe harbor" for the producers. Despite seeming to violate the principles of canonical continuity, *Discovery* has also invoked multiple linkages with the imaginary world's "frontstory", by establishing connections with canonical events, locations, and characters. From this perspective, the idea that Burnham is Spock's adopted sister may be strategic for the producers as it immediately pulls one of Trek's formative and famous characters into the orbit of the new series, perhaps in an attempt to justify *Discovery*'s existence as an authentic branch of the hyperdiegesis. Likewise, the inclusion and insertion of Harry "Harcourt Fenton" Mudd—from *TOS* episodes "Mudd's Women" (1966) and "I, Mudd" (1967)—establishes a canonical relationship between *TOS* and *Discovery*, just as the "Mirror Universe" arc midway through *Discovery*'s first season ricochets across *TOS*, *Enterprise*, and *DS9*, each of which include episodes that feature trips to the alternative universe. Moreover, the appearance of Captain Pike's *Enterprise* at the close of Season One aims to further weave interconnective tissue between various canonical threads. By the same token, the introduction of Spock himself in Season Two —played by Ethan Peck, the third actor to play the character after Leonard Nimoy and Zachary Quinto— as well as Pike taking command of the *Discovery*, there is an argument to be made that the producers have been anxious to cultivate a canonical "aura" by consistently threading "narrative braids"[59] onto *Star Trek*'s frontstory, especially *TOS*. Arguably, there doesn't seem to be a solid rationale for situating *Discovery* before *TOS* rather than after the final TNG film, *Nemesis*. In fact, some fans have expressed that they'd be more than satisfied with *Discovery* if it was located in post-*TNG* narrative space. I would argue that the series' close proximity to *TOS*, and to Kirk and Spock, implies that the producers were not yet confident that *Star Trek*'s televisual renaissance could successfully launch without at least some support from canonical characters and events. Yet instead of servicing fans, *Discovery* seems to promote ""fan disservice," where continuity is pointedly ignored, revised, or discarded".[60]

On the one hand, perhaps one could extrapolate that *Discovery*'s showrunners have not yet learned from textual conservationist discourses that surrounded *Enterprise*. On the other hand, however, it seems that the producers' various attempts to construct canonical linkages between *Discovery* and *TOS* are viewed as arbitrary by some fans, and lacking the necessary textual support to bulk up the world's infrastructure, mainly based on the use of retroactive continuity principles that *disassemble* the imaginary world rather than support its augmentation and extension. Writing for *Screen Rant*, John Orquiloa explained that "many fans just couldn't reconcile how Star Trek: Discovery could come before the hokier-looking The Original Series";[61] or as one fan put it, "c'mon can't anybody here be bothered to research and keep true to history?"

It is possible to infer that *Discovery*'s producers might well be observing the concerns of textual conservationists, at least to some extent, by seeking to further develop substantive bridges between series. The introduction of Pike, the *USS Enterprise*, and Spock in Season Two aims to promote such bridge-building, regardless of a lack of visual, narrative and/or generic fidelity with frontstory, with the episode "If Memory Serves" (2019) proffering a continuation of the original *Star Trek* pilot, "The Cage" (1965, but unaired until 1988), which did not yet feature William Shatner as Captain Kirk, but Jeremy Hunt as Pike). Although "The Cage" was Gene Roddenberry's first but unsuccessful attempt at launching a *Star Trek* TV series —critics thought the episode was "too cerebral" for 1960s audiences— it was canonized in *TOS* episode "The Menagerie" (1966), an episode that depicted Pike sharing his memories of the episode with Kirk and Spock before his death. Furthermore, "If Memory Serves" opens with a "Previously on *Star Trek*" lead-in, which summarizes "The Cage" by reusing footage from the original pilot, and by extension, "The Menagerie". In the episode itself, Pike and the *Discovery* return to Talos IV, the planet from "The Cage", where Pike experiences a vision of the future and learns of his ultimate fate. In essence, "If Memory Serves" operates as a direct sequel to "The Cage", although visual fidelity between the episodes is sorely lacking, as summed up by one fan's criticisms:

> That "previously on Star Trek" with clips from "The Cage" (1965) and the MTV-like transitions, then the cut to Pike's face — like, WHUHHH? How are we meant to process the different film quality, costumes, Talosian makeup, and the actors? I mean, audiences are already complaining that we're supposed to take the aesthetic change on faith, and now it's rubbed in our collective faces. It would've been more consistent (additional cost, but cheap relative to DSC's movie-quality expenses) to re-shoot with new-Pike, new-Spock and new-Number One in new-quarry.

This commenter's critical perspective rehearses the perils associated with prequelization related to visual congruence, which we can understand conceptually as being in concert with technological and narrative consistency as sub-elements of canonical fidelity. It seems as if some textual conservationists expect *Discovery* to channel *TOS*'s dated aesthetic, or in this case, to "remake" elements of "The Cage" with "new-Pike, new-Spock", etc., as a way to avoid juxtaposing radically different televisual contexts.

Based on production discourses for Season One, the introduction of Spock did not seem to be planned for the series' future. Akiva Goldsman explained that "we are trying to be very gentle about any kind of direct intersection with what we would consider hero components of "TOS" [. . .] It's certainly mentioned, but it's not explored".[62] When asked if audiences would eventually find out what Spock thinks of Burnham's mutiny, Goldsman stated simply: "Nope". Although Goldsman departed the series as executive producer once the first season ended, there is nothing "gentle" about Season Two's "intersections" with *TOS*'s "hero components", with the arrival of the *Enterprise*, Captain Pike, Number One, and Spock being front-and-center. It may be that the inclusion of so many elements pulled from *TOS* and into *Discovery*'s ambit is a direct response to textual conservationist discourses pertaining to the series' ambivalent relationship to canonical continuity.

As Kurtzman took over as showrunner for Season Two, several changes were made based on fan responses, the largest being the kerfuffle over the design of the Klingons (signified by the Twitter hashtag #NotMyKlingon). But perhaps the most interesting shift comes in the two-part season finale, which ends with the *Discovery* hurtled from the 23rd century and into the 29th. Spock seems to speak directly (and metafictionally) to *Discovery*'s textual conservationist critics, stating that "the very existence of *Discovery* is a problem". Spock also explains to Starfleet Command that the *Discovery* and its spore-drive technology should be strictly "classified", and not to be discussed "under penalty of treason". In doing so, the Season Two finale arguably conducts a kind of *continuity patching* that works to redress narrative "blunders" in one fell swoop: first, by demonstrating that *Discovery*'s "very existence" is not necessarily contradicted by pre-existing "frontstory" should it be henceforth contained within the classified vaults; and second, that the series' temporal leap into the 29th century frees the narrative from the constraints of canon; although it would still need to comply with what will now be backstory (as opposed to frontstory).

For some fans, however, this was nothing less than "a kind of sweeping-under-the-carpet move", "a cheap move", and "lazy writing to fix lazy writing":

> This "solution" is not credible. It also doesn't fix lots of stuff, like the wrong insignia, holographic communications, beyond-weird Klingons, non-pregnant tribbles, and an unrecognizable NCC-1701 [the *USS Enterprise*]. Glad they're outa' here though. Here's hoping they've traveled into the future just a minute before the sun goes supernova.

For many textual conservationists, *Discovery* simply does not meet the criteria as far as world-building goes, not only related to continuity as a mode of logical and structured storytelling, but also regarding canonical fidelity in its various forms and guises: from the series' aesthetic, technological, and visual designs (uniforms, Starships, spore-drive) to generic and narrative incongruities ("beyond-weird Klingons", ship-to-ship transporting, no "blinking lights and space Nazis").

Conversely, some fans believe that *Discovery* is "obsessed with canon", as one fan put it. "Discovery is trying to tie in as much old Trek stuff as possible, e.g., Mirror Universe, Spock's family, the Enterprise and Pike and Number One, Talos IV, Section 31, the Borg (probably) and time travel. Too much!" We could also include the way that *Discovery*'s opening theme music begins and ends with samples lifted from the *TOS* theme, as well as the mobilization of other audio cues and sound effects from *TOS*. We could describe such audio linkages as examples of *sonic fidelity*, a faithfulness that has been tested with the use of audio signifiers from both *TNG* and the Kelvin films (*TNG* is set over a century after *Discovery*, the Kelvin films are located in a parallel universe). "There's absolutely no continuity in this dang show", complained one fan, "and they're just using sonic iconography without any care".

From both positions, then, *Discovery's* relationship to canonical continuity is troublesome. Although this essay has focused on textual conservationists' response to canonical continuity, many fans appear to be satisfied with the series, and embrace it is a welcome addition to the fifty-plus year franchise, illustrating that *Star Trek* fandom, as with other media fan cultures, is neither a "coherent culture or community", but "a network of networks, or a loose affiliation of sub-subcultures, all specializing in different modes of fan activity", activities that bring different modes of engagement and affective nodes and nuances.[63]

Final Thoughts: Prequel Rights?

Unlike *Enterprise*, *Discovery* seems to be in rude health for the time being, with a third season in production as of this writing. Despite mixed reviews, many of which praised the series' "cinematic" production values while criticizing the quality of writing, *Discovery's* maiden voyage captured over 9 million viewers in November 2017.[64] Although these figures did not generate the same quantity as *Enterprise's* premiere, which garnered over 12 million before steadily declining, in this era of narrowcasting and streaming, 9 million is a respectful number indeed. More than this, the first two episodes of *Discovery* "drove a significant number of single-day sign-ups"[65] for the subscription-only service, CBS All Access (although the fact that the series was not first aired on network TV or in syndication was also heavily criticized by Trekkers). Perhaps the most profound indicator of CBS's newfound faith in the *Star Trek* television branch and brand lies with the news that Kurtzman had signed a five-year deal with the studio in 2018 to spearhead the creation of several new series, and expand the franchise considerably. At the Las Vegas *Star Trek* convention, it was announced that Patrick Stewart would be reprising his role as Captain Jean Luc Picard for the first time in almost two decades, legitimating those fans who complained that the franchise should be trekking into uncharted future territories rather than looking backwards like *Enterprise*, the Kelvin films, and *Discovery* before it. Other projects include two animated series, a comedy titled *Lower Decks* — created, written, and co-produced by Mike McMahan, the head writer on the popular animated series *Rick and Morty* (2013-present)— and an animated series for children to be aired on Nickelodeon.

This does not mean, however, that prequels are no longer on the production roster. Kurtzman has since green-lit a new series focused on "Section 31",

Starfleet's "Black Ops" branch, which is set to feature Michelle Yeoh as the alternative Phillipa Georgia from the Mirror Universe; as well as a potential trilogy of TV films featuring classic villain Khan, which may be helmed by Trek alumni Nicolas Meyer, who directed *Star Trek II: The Wrath of Khan* (1983), a film that many fans consider to be Trek at its finest. (Meyer also served on the production team for *Discovery's* first season.) In a surprise twist in *Star Trek* prequel discourse, fans petitioned CBS in 2019 to produce a series based on the adventures of Christopher Pike's *Enterprise*, with Anson Mount from *Discovery* in the Captain's Chair, indicating that prequels are not necessarily out-of-bounds for the Trek fan-base *per se*, but that prequels should be approached with caution and diligence, especially where canon and continuity are concerned. "The fans have been heard", stated Kurtzman, "Anything is possible in the world of Trek [and] I would love to bring back that crew more than anything".[66]

Notes

1 Roberta Pearson and Máire Messenger Davies, *Star Trek and American Television*, Berkeley, California: California University Press, 2014, page 5.

2 Matt Hills, *Fan Cultures*, London, England: Routledge, 2002.

3 Mark J. P. Wolf, *Building Imaginary Worlds: The Theory and History of Subcreation*, New York and London, England: Routledge, 2012, page 43.

4 Ibid.

5 Mark Clark, *Star Trek FAQ 2.0*, Milwaukee, Wisconsin: Applause Theatre and Cinema Books, 2013, page 375.

6 Gerry Canavan, "Hokey Religions: Star Wars and Star Trek in the Age of Reboots", *Extrapolation*,58(2–3), 2017, page 167.

7 Adam Kotsko, "The Inertia of Tradition in Star Trek: Case Studies in Neglected Corners of the 'Canon'", *Science Fiction and Television*, 9(3), 2016, page 347.

8 Matt Hills, "From 'Multiverse' to 'Abramsverse': Blade Runner, Star Trek, Multiplicity, and the Authorizing of Cult//SF Worlds" in J. P. Telotte and Gerard Duchovnay, editors, *Science Fiction Double-Feature: The Science Fiction Film as Cult Text*, Liverpool, England: Liverpool University Press, 2017, page 32.

9 Canavan, "Hokey Religions: Star Wars and Star Trek in the Age of Reboots", page 167.

10 Kotsko, "The Inertia of Tradition in Star Trek: Case Studies in Neglected Corners of the 'Canon'", page 349.

11 Hills, *Fan Cultures*, page 28.

12 Wolf, *Building Imaginary Worlds: The Theory and History of Subcreation*, page 36.

13 Jack Braitch, "User-Generated Discontent", *Cultural Studies*, 25(4–5), 2011, page 624.

14 For example, see Carolyn Jess-Cooke, *Film Sequels: Theory and Practice from Hollywood to Bollywood*, Edinburgh, Scotland: Edinburgh University Press, 2009; Stuart Henderson, *The Hollywood Sequel: History and Form, 1911-2010*, London, England: BFI/ Palgrave, 2010.

15 M. J. Clarke, "The Strict Maze of Media Tie-In Novels", *Communication, Culture and Critique*, 2, 2009, page 435.

16 Liam Burke, *The Comic Book Film Adaptation: Exploring Modern Hollywood's Leading Genre*, Jackson, Mississippi: University of Mississippi Press, page 163.

17 Sam Ford, "Fan Studies: Grappling with an Undisciplined' Discipline", *Journal of Fandom Studies*, 2(1), 2014, page 65.

18 Derek Johnson, "Fan-tagonisms: Factions, Institutions, and Constitutive Hegemonies of Fandom" in Jonathan Gray, Cornell Sandvoss, and C. Lee Harrington, editors, *Fandom: Identities and Communities in a Mediated World*, New York, New York: New York University Press.

19 David Greven, "The Twilight of Identity: Enterprise, Neoconservatism, and the Death of *Star Trek*", *Jump Cut: A Review of Contemporary Media*, No. 50, available at https://www.ejumpcut.org/archive/jc50.2008/StarTrekEnt/.

20 Duncan Barrett and Michèlle Barrett, *Star Trek: The Human Frontier*, London, England: Routledge, 2016, page 261.

21 Sue Short, *Cult Telefantasy Series*, Jefferson, North Carolina: McFarlane & Company, page 181.

22 Hills, "From 'Multiverse' to 'Abramsverse': Blade Runner, Star Trek, Multiplicity, and the Authorizing of Cult//SF Worlds", page 30.

23 Lincoln Geraghty, *Living with Star Trek: American Culture and the Star Trek Universe*, London, England: I. B. Taurus, 2007, page 37.

24 Kotsko, "The Inertia of Tradition in Star Trek: Case Studies in Neglected Corners of the 'Canon'", page 348.

25 Ibid., page 352.

26 George Kovacs, "Moral and Mortal in Star Trek: The Original Series" in B. M. Rogers and B. E. Stevens, editors, *Classical Traditions in Science Fiction*, New York and Oxford: Oxford University Press, 2015, page 202 (my italics).

27 Sue Short, *Cult Telefantasy Series*, page 181.

28 Wolf, *Building Imaginary Worlds: The Theory and History of Subcreation*, page 380.

29 Will Brooker, *Using the Force: Creativity, Community, and Star Wars Fans*, London, England: Continuum, 2002.

30 William Proctor, "Trans-Worldbuilding in the Stephen King Universe" in Matthew Freeman and William Proctor, editors, *Global Convergence Cultures: Transmedia Earth*, 2018, London, England: Routledge.

31 Andrew Friedenthal, *Retcon Game: Retroactive Continuity and the Hyperlinking of America*, Jackson, Mississippi: University of Mississippi Press, 2017, Kindle Edition.

32 William Proctor, *Reboot Culture: Comics, Film, Transmedia*, London, England: Palgrave, forthcoming.

33 Wolf, *Building Imaginary Worlds: The Theory and History of Subcreation*, page 273.

34 William Proctor, "'I've seen a lot of talk about the #blackstormtrooper outrage, but not a single example of anyone complaining': The Force Awakens, Canonical Fidelity, and Non-Toxic Fan Practices", *Participations: International Journal of Audience and Reception Studies*, 15(1), 2018, available at https://www.participations.org/Volume%2015/Issue%201/10.pdf

35 Paul Booth, *Digital Fandom: New Media Studies*, New York: Peter Lang, 2010, pages 103–127.

36 See http://www.ex-astris-scientia.org/.

37 See http://www.ex-astris-scientia.org/inconsistencies/enterprise_continuity.htm.

38 Ibid.

39 Matt Hills, "The expertise of a digital fandom as a 'community of practice': Exploring the narrative universe of Doctor Who", *Convergence: The International Journal of Research into New Media Technologies*, 21(3), page 361.

40 See https://obsession-inc.dreamwidth.org/82589.html.

41 Vivi Theodoropoulou, "The Anti-Fan Within the Fan: Awe and Envy in Sport Fandom" in Jonathan Gray, Cornell Sandvoss, and C. Lee Harrington, editors, *Fandom: Identities and Communities in a Mediated World*, New York: New York University Press, pages 316–328.

42 Ibid., 316.

43 Henry Jenkins, *Convergence Culture*, New York, New York: New York University Press, 2008, page 258.

44 Matt Hills, "The expertise of a digital fandom as a 'community of practice'", pages 360–374.

45 See https://www.syfy.com/syfywire/star_trek_producer_reveal.

46 Ina Rae Hark, "Franchise Fatigue?: The Marginalization of the Television Series After The Next Generation" in Lincoln Geraghty, editor, *The Influence of Star Trek on Television, Film and Culture*, Jefferson, North Carolina: McFarlane & Company, 2007, page 31.

47 Karen Anijar, "A Very Trek Christmas: Goodbye" in Lincoln Geraghty, editor, *The Influence of Star Trek on Television, Film and Culture*, Jefferson, North Carolina: McFarlane & Company, 2007, page 231.

48 Pearson and Davies, *Star Trek and American Television*, page 81.

49 See http://www.nytimes.com/2005/05/01/arts/television/01itzk.html?_r=0.

50 Aaron Taylor, "Avengers disassemble! Transmedia superhero franchises and cultic management", *Journal of Adaptation in Film and Performance*, 7:2, 2014, page 182, author's italics.

51 Matthew Freeman, "The Wonderful Game of Oz and Tarzan Jigsaws: Commodifying Transmedia in Early Twentieth Century Culture", *Intensities: The Journal of Cult Media*, 7, 2014, page 44–54.

52 Kotsko, "The Inertia of *Star Trek*", page 347.

53 Briatch, "User Generated Discontent".

54 See https://www.quora.com/Where-is-Sybok-in-Star-Trek-Discovery.

55 See https://screencrush.com/star-trek-discovery-canon-movies-books/.

56 See https://www.inverse.com/article/37357-star-trek-discovery-canon-changes-tos-tng.

57 See https://uk.ign.com/articles/2017/08/02/whats-canon-and-whats-not-in-star-trek-discovery.

58 According to Wolf, an 'interquel' is a "narrative sequence element that fits chronologically in between two already-existing narrative elements in the same sequence." Wolf, *Building Imaginary Worlds: The Theory and History of Subcreation*, page 377.

59 Ibid.

60 Hills, "From 'Multiverse' to 'Abramsverse'", page 32.

61 See https://screenrant.com/star-trek-discovery-franchise-future-no-prequels/.

62 See https://variety.com/2017/tv/news/star-trek-discovery-akiva-goldsman-1202569789/.

63 Matt Hills, "From Fan Culture/ Community to the Fan World: Possible Pathways and Ways of Having Done Fandom", *Palabra Clave*, 20 (4), 2017, page 860.

64 See https://deadline.com/2017/09/star-trek-discovery-draws-9-6-million-viewers-sunday-premiere-1202176478/.

65 See https://deadline.com/2017/09/star-trek-discovery-cbs-all-access-record-sign-ups-1202176110/.

66 See https://comicbook.com/startrek/2019/04/21/star-trek-discovery-captain-pike-spinoff-alex-kurtzman/.

APPENDIX

ON MEASURING AND COMPARING IMAGINARY WORLDS

Mark J. P. Wolf

Looking at the collection of essays in this volume, each exploring a single, particular imaginary world, it is natural to consider to what degree it is possible to compare worlds, and, in order to do so, to measure them in some useful way, so that worlds, described by their measurements, can then be quantitatively compared. These measurements should allow one to compare and contrast examples, perhaps even to locate them along a spectrum or within a phase space (which is really a multidimensional spectrum), where one can plot the points representing a collection of entities for comparison, and immediately see how similar or different they are, and what kinds of distributions occur.[1] Such tools are helpful even in areas which are more typically studied qualitatively; for example, in Film Studies, one can compare the lengths of films, the number of shots per film, film budgets, cast sizes, number of lines of dialogue, and so on. Similarly, a study of literature could compare short stories, novellas, and novels, looking at the number of words used, the number of characters, story events, and so on. Conceiving of entities as sets of interrelated parts is the basis of structuralism, and mythemes, narremes, and lexemes are examples of attempts to reduce something to individual units (in mythology, narratology, and lexical meaning, respectively). The term "narreme", defined as the basic unit of narrative, was first coined by Eugene Dorfman in 1969, and was further refined as a concept by Henri Wittman in 1974. Roland Barthes attempted to examine the codes and units of narrative in *S/Z* (1970), and others since then have tried to precisely define what constitutes an individual unit of narrative. So far, however, no proposed unit has succeeded to the point of being widely accepted, apart from larger divisions like chapters, episodes, or scenes. Imaginary worlds, then, are even more difficult to divide into basic units (*mundemes?*), due to all the possible types of world data that can be used in the construction of a world.

Imaginary worlds are notoriously hard to quantify precisely, making measurements and comparisons difficult. First, there is the problem of form; the transmedial nature of many worlds means that they can be made up of words, images, sounds, moving images, and so on, and such elements are difficult, if not impossible, to translate from one form to the other. Too often, no amount of *ekphrasis* is sufficient to convey an image in verbal form (a picture is often worth *more* than a 1000 words), and likewise, verbal descriptions can be written that are impossible to concretely visualize. Second, there is the problem of content; even within a particular medium, world elements can be depicted with varying degrees of narrative density and resolution. A decades-long world war with millions of participants can be summarized in a page of text, while two characters conversing during a single dinner involving could take dozens of pages to describe fully. Finally, there are the related questions of cohesion and coherence. Cohesion is how well world data sticks together or works well together, whereas coherence is the ability of a collection of world data to form a coherent whole, a world that makes sense and seems feasible or plausible. *Coherence*, which has to do with meaning, differs from *consistency* insofar as it underlies the potential for consistency; without coherence, there is no way to consider whether or not a set of world data is consistent or inconsistent. The worlds of Tolkien's Arda and Wright's Islandia are both very coherent, and thus we can judge how consistent they are, whereas the collection of world data found in the *Codex Seraphinianus* (1981) has some aesthetic or stylistic cohesion, but there is little or no coherence binding everything into meaningful infrastructures, much less a coherent whole, and without such relationships, notions of consistency and inconsistency cannot be meaningfully applied.

At first glance, it may seem like there are some good places to start an attempt at measuring and comparing worlds, such as spatiotemporal size, the number of world data present, or the amount of time needed for a user to experience the whole world. So let us examine each approach, and the resulting promises, perils, and pitfalls they contain.

Spatiotemporal Size

The most common way to compare locations in the empirical, Primary World is by size; the geographic sizes of countries, in square miles or kilometers; the surface areas and circumferences of planets, population numbers, and so on. Imaginary worlds, however, cannot be compared as easily, however, because they are often not described statistically by their authors; for example, Tolkien never specified the population nor the exact square mileage of Gondor (though cartographer Karen Wynn Fonstad has estimated it at 716,426 square miles).[2] Beyond that, there is also the question of how much of a world is actually used, with story events occurring in it. A world can have vast deserts and seas, but few or no inhabitants, and likewise little or no narrative activity; or, on the other hand, one could have a very small area (like Barsetshire or Lake Wobegon) which has a rich geography and history, and events covered by multiple works. The world of Georges Perec's *Life: A User's Manual* (1978) is only an apartment block in Paris at 11 rue Simon-Crubellier, but it is described in hundreds of page of exhaustive detail; and although the descriptions all occur frozen in time on June 23, 1975, shortly before 8:00 pm, the events discussed in flashbacks span over a 100 years, with around 100 interwoven subplots based on the apartment building's many residents. Likewise, Richard McGuire's graphic novel *Here* (2014) takes place all in one location, a small plot of land on which a room of a house is built, but covers the events happening there from millions of years before humans appeared on earth to thousands of years after the present day, with all of its hundreds of individual moments presented out of order and often visually overlapping each other. Both Perec and McGuire present worlds which are very small spatially, but which contain a great degree of detail and history, whereas other worlds might be vast, stretching across galaxies, but still only be the settings for short stories of science fiction.

And then, in the medium of video games, there are procedurally generated worlds, like those of *Minecraft* (2009) and *No Man's Sky* (2016), which are so large that a player could not even hope to explore them within multiple human lifetimes. It has been claimed that a Minecraft world can be made of up to "Two hundred sixty-two quadrillion, one hundred and forty-four trillion blocks"[3] and that if each block is said to be a cubic meter, that the surface area of a Minecraft world is around four billion square kilometers (compared to the Earth's approximately 510 million square-kilometer surface).[4] *No Man's Sky* is even bigger, with 18,446,744,073,709,551,616 procedurally generated planets that you can actually fly to, land on, and explore (meaning that if you visited one per second, it would take you 585 billion years to see them all). If we were to measure the land area of all these worlds, we would have to conclude that *No Man's Sky* has the largest world, at least geographically; but the vast majority of these worlds also have no history or narrative associated with them, either. *Dwarf Fortress* (2006), on the other hand, procedurally generates landscapes along with characters who live there, generating histories for each of them which include such things as who they battled and where they traveled.

Compared to hand-crafted worlds, procedurally generated worlds are often criticized for being too repetitive, with world elements that are oversimplified, and little more than recombinations of the same elements. They reveal the value of hand-crafted worlds, where a human author makes things that have meaning and are interrelated with other objects and events. Authors write histories that are driven by causality, as opposed to being merely lists of disconnected events. While procedural-generation methods are ever-improving, it is still difficult even for human beings to create interesting stories and characters consistently over time; so it seems unlikely that such things will ever be automated well. And there is only so much that a given author can create within a given timeframe. That brings us to our next method of comparison, that of counting world data.

Number of World Data

Procedurally generated worlds demonstrate that mere numbers of world data usually reveal little or nothing about a world. In a few kilobytes of memory, one could write a short program to generate random character names, and leave it running for weeks, generating a long list of a world's inhabitants, but even with billions of names, there is really no world created as a result. Limiting our discussion to world data hand-crafted by humans does not help much, since humans can also employ mindless methods of procedural generation.

And what exactly is a world datum? A name, an object, a design, a location, a character, an event; world elements can be as varied as we like, and of course, any given imaginary world will have to have a finite number of them, however we define them. Sometimes it is obvious which worlds have more data, without making a count; we can all agree that the worlds of *Star Wars* or *Star Trek* are larger and more detailed than the world of Stanisław Lem's novel *Solaris* (1961), or that the worlds of *Myst* (1993) and *Grand Theft Auto V* (2013) are larger than the worlds of *Asteroids* (1979) or *PONG* (1972), but not all comparisons are so obvious (for example, which is bigger, the world of *Star Wars* or *Star Trek*?).

No matter how we even try to define a world datum, or divide a world into individual data, we will run into problems; it would seem world data cannot be completely quantized. How many world data are there in an image of a dense cityscape? Or a multi-layered soundtrack of a location's ambience? Where do we draw the line when considering what counts as world data? John Williams's musical scores are an integral part of experience Star Wars films, but while some of the music is diegetic (like the Cantina Band music), much of it is not, so should we not include anything that the characters of a world could not see or hear, even if the audience is aware of it? Trying to actually count the world data of a world of any size or complexity quickly reveals the shortcomings, if not the impossibility, of applying such a method. But questions regarding the experiences of the audience who is vicariously exploring the world brings us to the next method of measuring user experience time.

User Experience Time

The amount of time needed to experience an entire world seems like a good place to start, particularly when you consider media usage. We can compare the numbers of hours of TV shows and movies which depict a world, or the numbers of pages of novels, or hours needed to complete the narratives found in video games, and all of these figures are usually used when describing various media experiences of worlds. Of course, reading speeds vary, and not all players will advance through a game at the same rate. Audiovisual media like movies, radio, and television may seem to provide the most similar and standardized experience for all audience members, as they have a set running time, so counting the hours and minutes would seem to be a good way to compare them. But all these media, especially the visual ones, can be more or less dense with detail; soundtracks can be more layered, and images more intricate, and packed with enough detail to require multiple screenings in order for all the detail to be noticed. Home viewing media also allows freeze-framing and re-viewing so that audiences can spend greatly varying amounts of time with the same movies or television show episodes.

User experience time also can vary based on the conditions surrounding the experience; watching something in a darkened movie theater is of course different than watching something on a cell phone screen in a noisy, busy public environment in daylight (can any horror movie be as effective in the latter environment as in the former?). Watching with distractions means interruptions, and possibly more re-playings, changing viewing time, as well as the whole experience itself. Also, a user's experience of a world will depend much on the amount of time allotted for the completion of world gestalten, which may require some contemplation of the world data, allowing connections between them to be recognized by the user. Some presentations of world data, and the media in which they appear, promote reflection time, while others do not.

In any event, user experience time is still too variable and even more difficult to measure when it comes to transmedia worlds appearing across a variety of media.

So What Comparisons Can Be Made?

Can worlds be compared in any useful way, or is the point of this essay merely to abandon any hope of finding a way to discuss worlds in relation to each other in some systematized way?

To some degree, we can still compare various *aspects* of imaginary worlds, such as invention (the degree to which a secondary world relies on Primary World defaults), completeness (how fully imagined a world is), consistency (the degree to which the parts of a world are in agreement), cohesion (how well the parts of a world are connected together), coherence (how well the parts of a world form a coherent whole), and the various amounts of media (words, images, moving images, sounds, etc.) that are used to convey all the world's data to an audience. But can we compare the entire worlds themselves with each other? Or derive some statistical measures of them for the purpose of comparison?

Maybe… if we carefully build our conceptions of the worlds being measured from several different sources. Instead of trying to consider whole worlds all at once, we can first look at the individual infrastructures that make them up, but in an abstracted way.[5] For example, starting with maps and locations, rather than thinking in terms of square mileage, we could consider what we might refer to as "salient locations", regardless of their size, each of these being a place, treated as a single location, where some narrative event occurs, and the number of narrative events occurring at each location. To use an example familiar to a wide audience, consider the planet Hoth in *The Empire Strikes Back* (1980). While Hoth is an entire planet, the number of salient locations on it is rather small; there is Echo Base (which is made up mainly of the control room, the hallway, and the garage where the *Millennium Falcon* is parked), the Wampa's cave where Luke is held prisoner, the generator (seen at a distance), the trenches where the rebels await the Empire's troops, and the open, featureless land where much action occurs (the ATAT attack, the shooting of the probe droid, Han Solo opening the dead Tauntaun with a lightsaber, and so on). From an extradiegetic standpoint, this is like making a list of the sets needed for the Hoth sequence of the film. While the entire planet of Hoth has a relatively small number of salient locations, other places might have a large number of them, even in a much smaller geographic area, such as the towns of Twin Peaks or Wayward Pines found on the eponymous television shows. Thus, a small town may have more salient locations than an entire planet, and perhaps even seem more expansive, at least narratively speaking. The concept of salience applied to locations also allows one to deemphasize places which are only seen on a map but never used, or merely referred to but never visited; and likewise, salience itself could be seen as a spectrum, since some locations may contain a majority of a story's action while others are only visited momentarily (thus, one still has to set a bound as to what will count as "salient").

The notion of salience can be applied to other infrastructures as well, usually using narrative importance to determine their salience (admittedly, non-narrative worlds may not work as well, though they may have other ways of indicating salience). Once the salient elements are identified, we can determine the overall shape of each infrastructure, and the connections between them. This, of course, still becomes more difficult the larger a world is, but we could compensate by simplifying our scales, by selecting only those elements with a higher degree of salience, or by chunking elements together into larger groups (for example, considering Hoth's Echo Base as a single location, rather than dividing it into control room, hallway, and garage, or even, at a still broader scale, considering Hoth as one location among many other planets). Naturally, changing the scope and scale used to measure a world means parsing a world at different resolutions, some more coarse than others, but we may want a lower-resolution conception for the purpose of a comparison, especially for larger or more complex worlds.

There are, however, two main problems with the method of comparing interconnected infrastructures; the subjective process of dividing infrastructures into elements, and the reliance on narrative for the determination of salience.

The first problem is one that is encountered in any kind of structuralist venture; defining boundaries between individual elements and precisely defining what constitutes an element. For example, in regard to spatial locations: one might have a chase which passes through an ever-changing landscape on a planet's surface. The chase scene, which could be done in a single take with moving camera, could pass seamlessly through a variety of different environments, giving us two possibilities: we could try to determine some criteria for deciding where one location ends and the chase crosses over into another one (for example, using bridges or changes in terrain as boundaries), or we could consider the entire chase route as a single location, since the action is continuous and no part of the route seems more salient than the rest of it (if that is the case). No matter how you slice it, it is a subjective decision, and one which will likely depend on the scale of the world and the purpose of the comparison. Although it is subjective, a useful comparison can still result as long as the same method of division is applied to all the worlds involved in the comparison.

The other problem, the reliance on narrative for salience, becomes a problem when the worlds being compared differ in regard to their own reliance on narrative. Some worlds contain a straightforward narrative, others a branching or multi-threaded narrative, some (like video game worlds) may even rely on user input for narrative to emerge. Some may contain little or no narrative at all. Even if we consider only worlds with a single, linear narrative line in them, there can still be a varying relationship between story and world; in some cases, there is just enough world to support the story, while in others there may be much world data and material beyond what is needed for the story.[6] In worlds with multiple storylines, something that is salient in one storyline may not be salient in another, although some things may be salient in multiple storylines. Storylines themselves can also vary in salience in regard to the world in which they appear (to use another *Star Wars* example, Anakin Skywalker's storyline is far more salient than that of Greedo or Tion Medon). Overall salience, then, may depend on a combination of things, though it should not be difficult to determine what the main storyline is, and how important something is in relation to it; especially when narrative fabric is itself one of the infrastructures being considered.

I am aware that the preceding suggestions do not solve all the problems involved in measuring and comparing worlds, nor do they completely remove the subjective element that seems an inevitable part of such an activity. Worlds may take on many shapes and forms, and may even differ as to which infrastructures they rely upon, but these infrastructures, and even their presence and absence, do give some starting ground upon which measurement and comparison can be built. Still, comparisons of worlds will mostly likely be made using criteria specific to each comparison, on a case-by-case basis, while an objective standard of measurement applicable to any secondary world seems unlikely to be found. But the more worlds we examine, and the greater the variety of those worlds, the more we may able to discern what is essential to all imaginary worlds, and more firmly ground the basis by which we are able to measure and compare them. If anything, this essay was intended to at least raise some of the issues involved in the measurement and comparison of worlds as entities, and suggest directions for further work in his area. In the same way that David Hilbert's famous list of unsolved problems in Mathematics inspired attempts to find their solutions, perhaps the difficult nature of these problems will attract more interest in them; but for now, an objective standard for the measurement of imaginary worlds remains one of the great unsolved problems in Subcreation Studies.

Notes

1 Websites like Gapminder.org are particularly good at visualizing data in this manner.
2 See Karen Wynn Fonstad, *The Atlas of Middle-earth, Revised Edition*, Boston, Massachusetts: Houghton Mifflin Company, 1991, page 191.
3 See Jeremy Peel, "Just how big is a Minecraft world? Big, as it turns out", *PC-GamesN.com*, February 3, 2013, available at https://www.pcgamesn.com/minecraft/just-how-big-minecraft-world-big-it-turns-out.
4 See Sarah Fallon, "How Big is Minecraft? Really, Really, Really Big", *WIRED.com*, May 27, 2015, available at https://www.wired.com/2015/05/data-effect-minecraft/.
5 For a list of world infrastructures and their descriptions, see chapter three of Mark J. P. Wolf, *Building Imaginary Worlds: The Theory and History of Subcreation*, New York, Routledge, 2012.
6 This would itself be an interesting thing to try to measure along a spectrum, though it is beyond the scope of this essay.

INDEX